HOW TO WIN THE PEACE

HOW
TO WIN
THE PEACE

by

C. J. HAMBRO

J. B. LIPPINCOTT COMPANY

Philadelphia
New York
1792—1942

To my two jurist sons, Dr. Edvard Hambro and cand. jur. Johan Hambro, without whose critical assistance this book, such as it is, could not have been completed.

Preface

No book can make us win the peace. And the peace can never be won in one single battle, in one single decision, in one single conference. It can only be won day by day, laboriously and painfully, through a change in national mentality and conceptions of international responsibility. But the peace can easily be forfeited before it is in sight. The longer the war lasts the graver the danger of losing the peace. Individuals and nations are growing more and more impatient, more and more embittered, the temptation is getting ever stronger to give up the principles of right and fight evil by employing the strategy and the tactics of evil. The directed propaganda for a maximum of war-effort has a tendency to accentuate all those forces of heroic, but primitive, nationalism which it will be essential to curb in our peace efforts. The fight against one type of imperialism may easily build up another type of imperialism, exceedingly dangerous to the future of the world. Any number of contrasting and contradictory ideas and forces are let loose and there is a sentiment abroad that it is the privilege and duty of every individual, who never before studied or had any experience of international relations, to decide the fate and future of every country except his own. This new-found interest for world politics is encouraging and has in it elements of hope for the post-war period. But only if it can be canalized.

This epoch of world disaster and of individual misery and tragedy beyond the imagination of man is also a period of colossal dimensions and of vast promise, if only the minds be opened not only for the needs of the day and the immediate future, but also for the broad vistas of an organized international existence.

The military battle we are fighting in this fatal hour is only one aspect of a tremendous conflict, and unless we realize that the peace-effort is as essential to our nations as is the war-effort, unless we understand that the intellectual, the mental, the moral fight will decide the outcome of the battles of tomorrow, unless we recognize that the spiritual preparedness for war and for peace must be the supreme concern of the leaders of nations, every sacrifice of blood, sweat and tears will have been made in vain.

Every one of us has his responsibility for the day and for the morrow. To some of us it may be a responsibility of experience. Our participation in international work and our public duties may have given us some insight that might be of use, certain ideas which may not be entirely without value. As a result of our endeavors, our attempts and our failures in the field of world coöperation, we should at least know where and what are the real difficulties and the real problems of international peace-making and peace-living; we should know where a peace-offensive has a prospect of success and where it is most likely to fail. We should know the danger of raising international expectations to stratospheric altitudes without the assurance of tangible results. We should know what patience is needed, and more patience and still more patience.

Our contribution, modest as it may be, is of the character of a leaven. It is for us to try to make our friends think constructively in the international field and not only react instinctively; to try to direct their imagination toward practical concrete efforts of international coöperation, to interpret the lessons of our decades of activity in such a way that they can be of aid to the next generation.

Any book intended to be such a contribution must of necessity be incomplete. Some problems may be given an

undue prominence, others be left too much in a chiaroscuro. But to some of us it seems of importance to realize
that only a small number of problems can be solved.
Organic growth in itself can never be made to conform
to any blue-prints; it creates constantly new problems. A
universal solution of every problem means cessation of life.
We can never define clearly the final objectives of our
efforts, we can only indicate a direction and point to the
roads by which our objectives may or may not be reached.

In this book it is attempted to show that it may be
easier to find a way out of political difficulties than to find
a road to any social or economic millennium. And it is
emphasized that any highway to a better future must be
paved with open speech and honest dealing. If persons
named or unnamed should feel hurt, if any national sentiment should be shocked, the author can only say that more
than a quarter-century in active international work has
convinced him deeply of the truth of Edmund Burke's
words:

"Refined policy has ever been the parent of confusion and will be so as long as the world endures."

C. J. Hambro

NOTE: The term "Versailles Treaty" as used in the book is meant to
include the whole complex of peace treaties after the last war, also the
subsequent minority treaties and declarations.

Contents

Part One

Part Two

PART ONE

I: Prelude to Peace Aims

The old and venerable London *Punch* which has so often given an adequate expression to common sense and popular sentiment in England, in its last issue for 1941 printed a poem called "Soldier, Young Soldier." Two stanzas of this poem were a popular prelude to peace aims. The young soldier, on being asked what would be his pleasure when fighting is passed, gives the following answer:

> "I'd like me to feel when the job has been done
> We'll all have a hand in the peace we have won;
> That all of us strong by the pattern of war
> May build for the future as never before.
>
> "I'd like me to know that all over the world
> A just flag of freedom was flying unfurled.
> That none of the nightmare was really in vain,
> That none of the nightmare need happen again."

It is very simple and very matter-of-course, and just because of its simplicity it is of importance. During the last war peace aims and post-war problems were under debate between the learned and the leading. This time they are discussed by the lowly and unsophisticated.

It is good and it is right that it should be so, for the peace to come is not primarily a concern of the big and mighty; it is the concern of every toiling man and woman in every country, whether in the war or not. And woe unto the nation where this deadly serious fact is permitted to be obscured by any wave of public propaganda intended for interior consumption.

And in most countries on earth simple and humble men and women with troubled minds want to be told about the peace aims. Letters from soldiers in training camps and in the field are full of questions. They realize that if they or their governments do not win the war, the unbelievable sufferings of millions of men and women, the tortured death of hundreds of thousands of innocent victims and martyrs, will have been in vain. Dimly they feel that there may never come another opportunity of discussing peace aims or war aims or hopes and visions for the future, the inarticulate constructive dreams and longings in the subconscious minds of men in the street.

We are fortunate in having a natural starting point for the discussion of peace aims. Not only have international statesmen made their contribution, church bodies sent out pamphlets and questionnaires, the Quakers stated their convictions, the Pope said his word, the American National Peace Conference, writers and philosophers expressed their opinions, but the two great leaders of the greatest democracies have made their statement and summed up in eight points what all the known and unknown men in their countries and in all the allied and affiliated countries agree to.

This document, internationally known as the "Atlantic Charter," on January 2, 1942, was officially endorsed in Washington, D. C., by the governments of twenty-six nations and will be of fundamental importance at the Peace Conference to come.

The text runs as follows:

"The President of the United States of America and the Prime Minister, Mr. Churchill, representing His Majesty's Government in the United Kingdom, being met together, deem it right to make known certain common principles in the national policies of their respective countries on which they base their hopes for a better future for the world.

"FIRST, Their countries seek no aggrandizement, territorial or other;

"SECOND, They desire to see no territorial changes that do not accord with the freely expressed wishes of the peoples concerned;

"THIRD, They respect the right of all peoples to choose the form of government under which they will live; and they wish to see sovereign rights and self-government restored to those who have been forcibly deprived of them;

"FOURTH, They will endeavor, with due respect for their existing obligations, to further the enjoyment by all States, great or small, victor or vanquished, of access, on equal terms, to the trade and to the raw materials of the world which are needed for their economic prosperity;

"FIFTH, They desire to bring about the fullest collaboration between all nations in the economic field with the object of securing, for all, improved labor standards, economic adjustment and social security;

"SIXTH, After the final destruction of the Nazi tyranny, they hope to see established a peace which will afford to all nations the means of dwelling in safety within their own boundaries, and which will afford assurance that all the men in all the lands may live out their lives in freedom from fear and want;

"SEVENTH, Such a peace should enable all men to traverse the high seas and oceans without hindrance;

"EIGHTH, They believe that all of the nations of the world, for realistic as well as spiritual reasons, must come to the abandonment of the use of force. Since no future peace can be maintained if land, sea or air armaments continue to be employed by nations which threaten, or may threaten, aggression outside of their frontiers, they believe, pending the establishment of a wider and permanent system of general security, that the disarmament of such nations is essential. They will likewise aid and encourage all other practicable measures which will lighten for peace-loving peoples the crushing burden of armaments."

After the formal acceptance of the Atlantic Charter by twenty-six governments, the President of the United States, in his radio address of February 23, 1942, condensed his peace program in the following sentences:

"We of the United Nations are agreed on certain broad principles in the kind of peace we seek. The Atlantic Charter applies not only to the parts of the world that border the Atlantic but to the whole world; disarmament of aggressors, self-determination of nations and peoples, and the four freedoms—freedom of speech, freedom of religion, freedom from want and freedom from fear."

But even after this plain and clear statement the ever inquisitive spirit of mankind is not entirely set at rest. Ordinary men and women wholeheartedly embrace the broad principles. But they feel that broad principles alone do not give a full answer to the questions in their minds. They desire to know how the principles shall be worked out, under what system they shall be applied.

Even if they do not fully understand the oneness of the war of today and the peace of tomorrow, the complete fusion of war aims and peace aims, they have a disquieting and disturbing suspicion that the peace may be lost, even if the last battle is won, and instinctively they feel that if this should happen, there will be no hope of preventing another cataclysm.

Without articulate reflection they sense that something may go amiss. Nothing is more easily forgotten than the sufferings of others, nothing is more bitterly resented than being reminded on the day of triumph of broad principles outlined in the hour of need and never given a clear interpretation.

Ordinary men and women, who do not write letters to the editors, and do not advertise their names, are sometimes worried at heart. They vaguely fear that the longer the war is going to last, the more difficult will it be to raise the voice of calm reason and of farsighted fairmindedness on the day of reckoning. They sense the danger that the public mind may become more and more brutalized by the war, that people will grow more obtuse and callous. And on the other hand, they have a very troublesome presentiment that the grossly vulgar, invincibly ignorant isolationism in various countries will lift its unkempt head as soon as the war is over, and try to make nations shirk their responsibility for the peace and for intelligent international solidarity and coöperation.

This spirit in all its dangerous and illogical sullenness was demonstrated in a letter to the editor of the *New York Times* for January 20, 1941.

The correspondent, grateful to Mr. Herbert Hoover for his book "America's First Crusade," writes as follows:

"It shows up our Allies in that crusade for what they are worth: contemptible underhand double dealers. . . . I am for fighting this war to a finish and grabbing everything we can get our hands on."

Ordinary men and women are not convinced that this will be the best approach to the discussion of peace problems; in their simple way they think that distrust, jealousy, hatred and greed will not help us in the future.

When they listen and look they are troubled by the feeling that among the allied nations there seems to be a growing fault-finding and recrimination; even within the national borders of the individual democratic state there is political tension, upbraiding, an exchange of bitter reproaches and expostulations, in many quarters a hoping for the day when the individual and national self-restraint imposed upon countries by the war, shall come to an end.

Ordinary men and women can't help thinking that if the war and the conduct of the war are the only things that bind together all these nations, there can be but a very obscure hope for the future. Only if we realize that there must be a continuous effort, that the united nations will have to march in step, even after the war, can we believe that "we'll all have a hand in the peace we have won." To win the war is the supreme duty of all; but winning the war is only the first stage. And it may prove more difficult to discipline the allied nations under a united command after the war than during the war.

Nations have a longer memory than most statesmen suspect. It is not clear, it is not always articulate, but still it is there, vaguely groping for light. They may have forgotten the last war, but they have not entirely forgotten the last peace.

One of the things dimly remembered in every country is the declaration of the fourteen points made by President Wilson in his address to Congress, January 8, 1918. They read as follows:

1. Open covenants of peace without private international understanding.
2. Absolute freedom of the seas in peace or war except as they may be closed by international action.
3. Removal of all economic barriers and establishment of equality of trade conditions among nations consenting to peace and associating themselves for its maintenance.
4. Guarantees for the reduction of national armaments to the lowest point consistent with domestic safety.
5. Impartial adjustment of all Colonial claims based upon the principle that the peoples concerned have equal weight with the interest of the Government.
6. Evacuation of all Russian territory and opportunity for Russia's political development.
7. Evacuation of Belgium without any attempt to limit her sovereignty.
8. All French territory to be freed and restored, and reparation for the taking of Alsace-Lorraine.
9. Readjustment of Italy's frontiers along clearly recognizable lines of nationality.
10. Freest opportunity for autonomous development for the peoples of Austria-Hungary.
11. Evacuation of Roumania, Serbia and Montenegro, with access to the sea for Serbia, and international guarantees of economic and political independence and territorial integrity of the Balkan States.
12. Secure sovereignty for Turkey's portion of the Ottoman Empire, but with other nationalities under Turkish rule

assured security of life and opportunity for autonomous development, with the Dardanelles permanently opened to all nations.

13. Establishment of an independent Polish State, including territories inhabited by indisputably Polish populations, with free access to the sea and political and economic independence and territorial integrity guaranteed by international covenant.

14. General association of nations under specific covenants for mutual guarantes of political independence and territorial integrity to large and small States alike.

It has become a tradition to deride the fourteen points, which is easy enough. To mention them is to invite sneers and abuse. German sympathizers in many countries made them a byword of ridicule. A malicious member of the Swedish Academy suggested that to Woodrow Wilson should be given the Nobel Prize in mathematics; for he had been the first to prove that fourteen equals zero.

And yet, in the long perspective, the fourteen points were not made in vain. President Wilson's address was a history-making document, even if he did not succeed at Versailles. And looking back one is tempted to apply on Wilson and his fourteen points G. K. Chesterton's words about the Crusaders: "They were renounced by their children and refuted by their biographers, they were exposed, they were exploded, they were ridiculed and they were right."

It is also fair to remember that before President Wilson left Washington to go to Paris, he had condensed and to a certain extent modified the fourteen points.

On July 4, 1918, he stated in his noble Mount Vernon Speech:

"The Past and the Present are in deadly grapple and the peoples of the World are being done to death between them.

"There can be but one issue. The settlement must be final. There can be no compromise. No halfway decision would be tolerable. No halfway decision is conceivable. These are the ends for which the associated peoples of the world are fighting and which must be conceded them before there can be a peace."

And then he made his four points, which are not less emphatic or less clear than the eight points of August 14, 1941:

"I. The destruction of every arbitrary power anywhere that can separately, secretly and of its single choice disturb the peace of the world; or if it cannot be presently destroyed, at least its reduction to virtual impotence.

"II. The settlement of every question, whether of territory, of sovereignty, of economic arrangement, or of political relationship, upon the basis of the free acceptance of that settlement by the people immediately concerned, and not upon the basis of the material interest or advantage of any other nation or people which may desire a different settlement for the sake of its own exterior influence or mastery.

"III. The consent of all nations to be governed in their conduct towards each other by the same principles of honor and of respect for the common law of civilized society that govern the individual citizens of all modern states in their relations with one another; to the end that all promises and covenants may be sacredly observed, no private plots or conspiracies hatched, no selfish injuries wrought with impunity, and a mutual trust established upon the handsome foundation of a mutual respect for right.

"IV. The establishment of an organization of peace which shall make it certain that the combined power of free nations will check every invasion of right and serve to make peace and justice to the more secure by affording a definite tribunal of opinion to which all must submit and by which every international readjustment that can not be amicably agreed upon by the peoples directly concerned shall be sanctioned."

There is no doubt that the Mount Vernon Speech was a wiser document than the address of the fourteen points. If any statesman in a responsible position in the midst of war tries to outline more than the broad principles of a peace to come, he invites trouble and dissension, and very likely an ungrateful posterity will forget what he accomplished and stress any promise or alleged promise that was not fulfilled.

It will be seen that in character the four points from Mount Vernon are very like the Atlantic Charter and far more guarded in their terms than the Address to Congress. But, unfortunately, the fourteen points had been given a more worldwide publicity than ever before given to any political document. And a critical analysis will show that only Point 14 was fully realized after the letter, not at Versailles where the defeated countries were barred from membership in the League, the "General Association of Nations," but gradually and slowly at Geneva. Belgium, France, Italy, the resurrected Poland were given wider frontiers than supposed by President Wilson. Montenegro was not given back her independence. Colonial claims were not impartially adjusted; Russia was not given any opportunity to develop. But the most important thing about the fourteen points was not that they were not fully realized, but that they had been stated. And how much better for the world if they had been accepted as the formal basis for the peace treaties!

There is one principle outlined in the Mount Vernon Speech which was not embodied in the fourteen points— and which is not mentioned in the Atlantic Charter: "The consent of all nations to be governed in their conduct towards each other by the same principles of honor and of respect for the common law of civilized society that govern the individual citizens of all modern states in their relations with one another."

It was a sentence that contrasted with the old-time diplomatic school of thinking and with imperialistic traditions, and the principle passed out in the atmosphere of Versailles.

The words of the Mount Vernon speech are not remembered, but the impression was left on the public mind that something of this kind went wrong at Versailles. And it will be a touchstone for the peace to come whether Point III in the Mount Vernon speech will be honored or not.

The catchwords had been coined twenty-one years ago that this was the war to end wars and to make the world safe for democracy. The words turned bitter on the lips of men; in no other epoch have democracy and the very spirit of liberalism been threatened as during these last decades; the world has been living in a state of permanent latent war, and few statesmen in the countries primarily responsible for the maintenance of peace have given their action to make democracy safe for the world.

These thoughts, even if not clearly formulated, are very active in the minds of ordinary men, making them fearful for the days when the war shall be over if no real program has been outlined for the years to follow. Nations are no longer willing to accept at their face value vague and general phrases. They want something clear, definite and outspoken. No sweeping statements or declarations of basic principles are enough. People distrust them; and more especially in the United States. There is also a strong undercurrent of reserve based on the knowledge that the prospect of a secure and peaceful future held out before the Expeditionary Force that sailed out in 1917 did not come true. There were not only monetary but also moral war debts which were never honored.

And so singleminded, honest people want to know what next. They want an open discussion of peace-problems and post-war conditions; they want to see general ideas made tangible and concrete.

In an article in the *New York Times* on the first anniversary of the Atlantic Charter the excellent columnist Miss Anne O'Hare McCormick discusses the principles of the Atlantic Charter and states:

"These principles are generalizations, the platitudes of international life. They are going to be variously construed when the time comes to put them into effect. They will be very hard to reconcile with the ambitions of the winners and the ideas of the governments in exile. But man has discovered in travail that the platitudes are his articles of faith."

Maybe she underestimates the critical sense of common men. Most of us do at times. Mr. Emery Reves, the well-known international journalist of *Cooperation* remarks in "A Democratic Manifesto" (August, 1942, p. 13):

"The complete lack of any reaction to the Atlantic Charter, the complete lack of enthusiasm with which it has been received in the democratic countries, prove that the peoples have an unconscious feeling of the unreality of this past order."

There may be an element of truth in both statements. But ordinary men do not care much for dialectic philosophy. They feel instinctively. They grope for truth, for principles simplified.

Mr. Ernest Bevin, the British Minister of Labour and National Service, in his speech of welcome to the Emergency Committee of the Governing Body of the International Labour Office on April 20, 1942, made the following statement:

"This is a people's war—it is not a rich man's war . . . What really has to be determined is whether we are to be allowed to evolve and work out our destiny, carried forward by the great spiritual urge that is within us for higher achievement and higher civilisation, or whether we are to be dominated and made mental and spiritual slaves for generations to come by a few people who have command of the weapons of destruction."

The dictators have announced that they will establish "a new order." And no sane man can doubt what that order would be like. It was aptly indicated in the title of a book published by one of the leading lights of the new

Germany as long ago as in 1923: "Slavery. Its Biological
Foundation and Moral Justification." *

It is a very, very old order. It is the order of the Roman
Empire, with countries disciplined and garrisoned, with
men and women enslaved and without any legal rights
whatsoever, not even the rights of cattle; with "good" nations allowed to chop wood and draw water for the "master
nation"—"Das Herrenvolk"—and graciously permitted to
be slaughtered when there was any war to wage. But combined with the military system of the old Romans there
will be all the vices of the Oriental despots, their cruelty,
their torture, their secret police; there will be the tribunals
of the Inquisition to eradicate any attempted heresy.
There will be the rack and the wheel for men of free
will and of free minds, and there will be the oubliettes
for those who might spread liberal contagion in the concentration camps.

Bulgaria, Hungary, Roumania have been told with
how many legions they will have to feed the war-machine
—lost legions who will be sacrificed to save the priceless
lives of German soldiers. The helots of Belgium, of
France and Holland are put under lock and key in the
munition factories to manufacture the means for their
own permanent enslavement. The teachers and professors of Norway are sent to do forced labour behind the
front of the aggressor.

But still, some people will claim, there is order! There
will be no war in "the third world." There will seem to be
security for all those willing to abstain from thinking and
acting except under orders from the powers that be.

What kind of order will be instituted in the world of
the Atlantic Charter? It is a question that has to be answered. The broad outlines given in the eight points of the
two democratic leaders are essential, and they are neces-

* *"Die Sklaverei. Ihre Biologische Begründung und Sittliche Rechtfer-
tigung"* by Franz Haiser.

sary. Moreover, to the keen observer, used to weigh words critically, they are cautious and statesmanlike. Their authors are not committed to any details of execution. But the eight points do not answer any practical questions. No men are more aware of this than the two men of destiny who sent out their declaration. Not for one moment was it intended to be a panacea for the restlessness of the alert mind and the troubled conscience. And it would be a sad misinterpretation of the desire of the leaders if their collaborators—and in a democracy we are all the trusted collaborators of our leaders—should not make their contribution to the elucidation of the all important questions of peace aims and post-war organization. We have been given the framework. Our duty is to clear the ground and prepare the soil so that the eight points can be given an organic life. The public mind must be prepared, and we must be on our guard lest we be suddenly faced with some surprising *fait accompli.*

Within our gates there are many enemies of democracy; and they have powerful allies in the inertia and fatigue of men's minds, in the distrusts and jealousies of their hearts. Anxious men and women are not blind to the fact that a humanity having suffered for long years under lack of order and dead tired under the prolonged and increasingly unbearable strain of every variety of insecurity will be under a terrible temptation to accept political and moral indifference rather than more mental worry, lethargy rather than continued effort.

Miss I. A. R. Wylie, who lived for years in Germany and loved Germany, tells in "My Life with George" an incident which popularly explains the acceptance of Hitlerism in Germany and points to the danger of such resigned acceptance on an international scale:

"I remember an illuminating conversation I had with a young Nazi after Hitler's rise to power. He expressed himself as ecstatically happy because he said he was at last free. 'Free from what?' I asked in astonishment. 'Free from freedom,' he retorted exultantly."

It is a very peculiar kind of freedom for which millions of men and women are secretly longing. They want to know exactly where they stand; they do not want to face the qualm of a choice or a new decision every day; they have no deep desire for responsibility; they do not want to be disturbed. They want security. They want to be mounted on rails and taken along to their unquestioned destination.

And it is only reasonable to expect a certain reaction after the war. Especially in the countries which have not suffered very much, there may be a longing to forget all about it, to get back to something called normalcy, to have done with making every day due allowance for allied and united nations, of showing due consideration to exiles and refugees. There will be a natural desire to exclaim: "At last we are at home and ourselves once more." Among many nations there may be this instinctive feeling that it will be good once again to be rid of foreign influence and peoples who after all are strangers. Narrowminded, ignorant and opinionated "practical" men in more than one country will classify all foreigners in the terms of the ardent admirer of Mr. Herbert Hoover.

Much spade-work has to be done to build up a reasonably united peace front and make certain "that none of the nightmare need happen again."

In every country men and women who do not live for the moment only have the feeling that if it was a disaster to many nations that they were unprepared for war, it might become an even greater tragedy if they were unprepared for peace.

II: The Strategy of Peace

In order to prepare for peace it is necessary to articulate our ideas and desires; and if we accept the term most widely used, "a just and durable peace," we shall have to find out both what will be just and what shall be needed to make the international settlement a lasting one. We shall have to make clear to ourselves and others exactly what kind of world order should be the practical outcome of our striving for this kind of peace. And, as we are living in a world of realities, and it is our will that the structure we intend to erect shall be both tangible and enduring, we have got to work in the world of the concrete and not only in the realm of philosophical abstractions. In the world of realities we have to build on what is, and to recognize that we have to march to our future through the gate of the past. In other words, it is not sufficient to sail forth in stratospheric altitudes of pure political speculation, but necessary to have both feet planted on the good earth. Mankind, in the year of grace 1942, does not start from scratch. And only by carefully studying recent history and examining with an open mind the experience of the last twenty-five years of international history can we qualify ourselves to be of assistance in mapping out the future and trying to chart the approaches to a new world order.

And as nations when they prepare for war need some kind of an intelligence service, want to be informed concerning the state of preparedness, the mobilization plans, the military equipment, supplies, the whole state of armaments in other countries, so nations preparing for peace need another kind of intelligence service; they must know what peace means to the other party, on what ground to meet him. They must study the strategy of peace to be able to resist any dangerous peace offensive of the enemy, they must be ready to turn it off, to make it a rout and a disaster and proceed toward peace along their own lines.

If we want to study the tactics and the strategy of peace, we must first know in as clear terms as possible what we mean by peace.

In any American dictionary peace is defined as "freedom from war and hostilities, also freedom from strife and dissension, also an agreement between contending parties to abstain from further hostilities."

The first two explanations try to describe the substance of peace; the next simply states that the word "peace" is used sometimes as synonymous with peace-treaty.

To this barren and negative definition of peace is added, in the new edition of the Century Dictionary, a new and very interesting conception. Peace is defined as meaning "also freedom from mental disturbance."

If we then turn to the definition of peace given on behalf of the United Nations by President Roosevelt in his address of February 23, 1942, we find that the peace we seek shall mean not only the three "freedoms" mentioned in the dictionary, but also four more, "freedom of speech, freedom of religion, freedom from want and freedom from fear." And this fourth freedom the President, in his message to Congress on January 6, 1941, "translated into world terms" as meaning:

"a worldwide reduction of armaments to such a point and in such a way that no nation will be in a position to commit an act of physical aggression anywhere in the world."

If, for the present, we accept the definitions of the dictionary and of the President as giving us an intelligible idea of what is meant by peace in the democratic countries, let us look for one moment at the totalitarian definition. For this purpose it is sufficient to turn to authoritative statements made in Germany.

There is no systematic fascist theory of war and peace. For years Mussolini extolled peace and was a candidate for the Peace Prize. (See p. 89.) Then for the benefit of the Ethiopian campaign he glorified war and today he probably is most desirous to extol peace again. In Japan, as far as a modern social philosophy exists at all, it is only an adapted imitation of the pattern made in Germany. The German conception of peace is clear.

In 1915 Professor Max Schuler wrote:

"War means the State in its most actual growth and rise—it means politics." *

Twenty years later the gospel was the same: "War is the secret master of our century; peace has merely the function of a simple armistice between two wars." † And, as this simple armistice is looked upon in Germany rather as a strange than as a healthy interlude in the history of man, a *durable* peace can never be one of the war aims of Nazism.

The sympathetic but terrible and tragic mistake of the Western World has been to act on the assumption that German mentality was not too fundamentally different from Scandinavian mentality, from English and French mentality, from American mentality, that the same words corresponded to the same ideas in their several languages. Even now comparatively few people seem to realize that in order to understand German mentality an American or

* *"Der Genius des Krieges und der deutsche Krieg"* ("The Genius of War and the German War").
† *"Deutsche Wehr"* ("German Defense"), official organ of the German military organization (December issue, 1935).

a Norwegian has to divest himself of his entire conception of humanity and assume a totally different set of ideas and superstitions very strange to his nature. Few things are more illuminating in this respect than the German outlook upon peace and war, upon the social ideal as a whole.

The leading German authority on International Law, Professor Erich Kaufmann, wrote in his book,* "The Essence of International Law"—and this was in 1911:

> "Not a community of men of free will but victorious war is the social ideal . . . it is in war that the State displays its true nature."

On the strength of this book, which was used at practically all the universities in Germany, Professor Kaufmann was called to the University of Berlin, and after the First World War he was made legal adviser to the Foreign Office in Wilhelmstrasse.

The German attitude of condescending contempt towards all peace effort is well expressed by Ewald Banse, the great professor of Wehrwissenschaft (Military Science), and, since Hitler came to power, the official leader in education for war. In his book published in 1932,† "Room and Nation in World War" (American edition under the title "Germany Prepares for War," 1940), he explains (p. 347) that Germany "on the threshold of a national renaissance" is "rejecting the poison of internationalism and pacifism." He extols the warlike man, "the man who does not fight to live but lives to fight. For him battle is the everlasting yea, the fulfilment and justification of existence." Next ranks "the passively warlike man," to whom war is a sacred business, a moral duty towards house and home." But Herr Banse has no use for those who believe in and toil for a just and durable peace.

> "How utterly different is the peaceloving man, the pacifist! Peace is the only state for which he is fitted; and he will do

* *"Das Wesen des Völkerrechts."*
† *"Raum und Volk im Weltkriege."*

everything to preserve it; he will endure any humiliation, including loss of liberty and even the most severe damage to his pocket, in order to avoid war. His dim, lustreless eye betokens servility (which does not rule out impertinence), his clumsy body is obviously built for toiling and stooping, his movements are slow and deliberate. This type is the born stay-at-home, smallminded, completely flummoxed by the smallest interruption of the normal course of events, looking at the whole world from the standpoint of his little ego and judging it accordingly."

Any American, any Norwegian reading these lines would take them to be a picturesque description of the philosophy of the lusty robber barons, the knights errant of the dark centuries of the Middle Ages. That Banse's words give a serious and sober picture of German mentality just before the middle of the twentieth century would seem unbelievable to him—because he had not had the benefit of any peace intelligence system.

Even the words of Mr. Banse are comparatively moderate. The climactic praise of war as against peace is given in a book by another Nazi writer: Fritz Lenz, "Race as Principle of Value" (2nd edition, Munich, 1933).* Having regretted that the greater part of humanity was against Germany in the last war and against the aggressive spirit of his "race"—he comes to his somberly triumphant conclusion:

"Far be it that humanity should, in our minds, refute war, nay, it is war that refutes humanity."

To any non-German these words seem like a dark dictum by an old medicine man in an antipodal tribe of man-eaters; he cannot grasp the conception that war is the supreme principle, that mankind is taken on probation by war and may be rejected, and that it is a presumptuous usurpation of human beings to discuss questions of war and peace. But this is German mentality.

* *"Die Rasse als Wertprinzip."*

Compared to the colorful words of Mr. Banse, and Mr.
Lenz beating the tom-tom in the tropical jungle of prehistoric instincts in the subconscious, the democratic conception of peace appears somewhat anemic and a little
stale. With all the "freedoms" mentioned the definition
still rests negative. And if we shall succeed in making
peace something more than a sweet sound in the mouths
of orators and a pious wish in passive minds; if we shall
make it a working program; if we shall make it alive with
aspirations in such a way that soldiers at the fronts and
sailors on their rafts and aviators between heaven and
earth can have reason to think "that none of the nightmare was really in vain," then we must give to our definition of peace an *active* substance.

This fact is fully realized by every group in the United
States working in a realistic, informed and practical way
to prepare the peace to come.

In the preliminary report of the Commission to Study
the Organization of Peace, published by the Carnegie
Endowment for International Peace, the "Nature of
Peace" is described in these terms:

"Peace under modern conditions cannot be a static condition of life achieved by the renunciation of war, nor a mere
pious desire to live at peace. Peace must be a dynamic and
continuous process for the achievement of freedom, justice,
progress, and security on a worldwide scale. Many problems
can never be finally solved. They recur in different forms as
eternally as life itself. The processes of peace, however, should
make possible ways of meeting these emerging problems on
a plane higher than mass physical combat.

"Peace requires the substitution for war, which becomes
ever more destructive, of international processes which while
protecting national ways of life against external violence, will
facilitate adaptation to new conditions and will promote creative changes in the general interest. Peace involves whatever
international organization is necessary under conditions of the
times to protect the interests and promote the progress of
mankind. The world has so shrunk that the loose political

organization of the past which rested on balance of power, on neutrality and isolation, is no longer adequate."

In a very similar way the American Friends Service Committee has tried to define peace in their declaration of June 1941:

"Peace is not a static condition to be attained after the defeat of those who disturb it. On the contrary, peace is a dynamic method by which to remove injustices, to accomplish necessary readjustments and to remedy instead of aggravating the evils that have been inflicted on the world by military aggression."

And most important, Mr. Sumner Welles, Assistant Secretary of State, in the speeches in which he has discussed the peace to come, has also used the words "dynamic peace" and emphasized that under the conditions of this century peace cannot be static.

It may safely be said today that when peace has not succeeded in the past, when it has not been durable, it is to a large extent because politicians and diplomats have lulled themselves to believe that peace was a static condition, and have failed to accomplish the necessary readjustments at the right moment.

The men who were the authors of the Versailles Treaty were not blind to this necessity. They included in the covenant of the League of Nations the ill-fated Article 19:

"The Assembly may from time to time advise the reconsideration by Members of the League of treaties which have become inapplicable and the consideration of international conditions whose continuance might endanger the peace of the whole world."

But their successors at the Council of the Great Powers and the representatives of some of the states created by the war, or enriched in territories by the war, relegated that article to the dead-letter office and tried to make it a criminal offense for any other state to mention Article 19 in the Assembly of the League of Nations. It was never applied.

In 1929, before the Manchurian question had become intensely acute, China tried to make Article 19 a living reality and attempted to persuade the Assembly of the League to establish the procedure by which action could be taken under this article. But China was rebuked by the Great Powers, the efforts were unsuccessful and Article 19 remained a dead letter.

In the Washington Agreement, the joint declaration by the twenty-six United Nations in which they announce their adhesion to the Atlantic Charter, the scope is broadened and vistas opened to a future rule of justice, of a more sharply defined character than indicated by any previous declaration.

The twenty-six governments declare that "complete victory over their enemies is essential to *defend life, liberty, independence and religious freedom, and to preserve human rights and justice in their own lands as well as in other lands.*"

These words constitute the political translation of the popular phrase that the world can not remain half slave and half free. The twenty-six nations are not content to guarantee liberty and religious freedom in their own countries; their statesmen have realized (at least we may hope that they have) that for the preservation of peace it is of vital importance that religious or national persecution should not be tolerated in any country. There is an evil infection in such things; and if human rights are trampled under foot with impunity in one country, freedom, as indicated by the twenty-six nations, is threatened in every land on earth.

In the various statements and declarations here quoted we have some of the elements necessary to lay the foundations for a dynamic peace: freedom from hostilities, freedom from fear, freedom from want—which transcribed into positive terms will mean political security, spiritual security, social and financial security, and something more than that: the rule of justice and of equity, nationally and internationally, between classes and individuals; liberty for every single nation to develop its own civilization and the form of government it desires, under the terms of international law; and freedom for the individual men and women to follow the voice of their own consciences and convictions.

It is perfectly obvious that the realization of this program will require some sort of international machinery; and that the worldwide reduction of armaments, emphasized by the President of the United States and indicated in the eight points, can be reached only by way of intimate international coöperation. It is also clear that the practical solution of the economic, the social, the humanitarian problems mentioned in the Atlantic Charter, will render necessary some kind of universal organization. In the world of today isolation is an optical and mental illusion; and no more possible in the political field than in the financial field, in trade relations, in the domains of science and research. The spread of physical, economic and moral epidemics can be prevented only by concerted action. No words more eloquent and at the same time more matter-of-fact can be used to describe the need for international coöperation than those in the so-called Bruce report: *

"The experience of the last twenty years has shown the growing extent to which the progress of civilization is dependent upon economic and human values. State politics are determined in increasing measure by such social and economic aims as the prevention of unemployment, the prevention of

* The Council of the League of Nations on May 29, 1939, invited the Right Honorable Stanley Bruce, High Commissioner for Australia in London and Chairman of the League Committee for the Coördination of Economic and Financial Questions, to preside over a special committee "to study appropriate measures . . . to promote the active participation of all nations in the efforts made to solve the technical problems dealt with by the League of Nations machinery."

wild fluctuations in economic activity, the provision of better housing, the suppression and cure of disease. These matters, which affect the daily life of every man, woman and child, are among the principal preoccupations of statesmen and politicians in all countries, whatever their political structure.

"Modern experience has also shown with increasing clearness that none of these problems can be entirely solved by purely national action. The need for interchange of experience and the coördination of action between national authorities has been proved useful and necessary time after time in every section of the economic and social fields. . . .

"The world, for all its political severance, is growing daily closer knit; its means of communications daily more rapid; its instruments for the spread of knowledge daily more efficient. At the same time the constituent parts of the world, for all their diversity of political outlook, are growing in many respects more similar; agricultural states are becoming rapidly industrialized, industrial states are stimulating their agriculture. Nothing is more striking in this connection, or more characteristic, than the swift industrial development of the great Asiatic countries.

"These changes inevitably give rise to new problems that can only be solved by joint effort. Thus trade and personal contacts are facilitated, but simultaneously economic depressions become more widespread; and were there any relaxation of control, human and animal diseases would spread more widely and more rapidly. Neither the economic nor the physical contagion—nor, indeed, the moral—can be checked by national action alone, except by recourse to almost complete isolation.

"Indeed, to attempt such isolation is one of the first natural reactions to the more frequent and intenser impact of these world forces. But it reflects rather a blind instinct to ward off these impacts than a desire of the constituent parts of a changing world to adapt themselves to what in the long run must prove the irresistible dynamism of these changes; and there can be no development without adaptation. . . ."

The outline of work just mentioned will be sufficient to illustrate the importance for the peace to come of a trained staff of international workers, the value of those funds of experience collected by existing agencies of in-

ternational administration and coöperation. But the words
of the Washington Agreement call for something more; a
supervision of justice for the protection of human rights
in every country, an intelligence service warning of any
danger to peace caused by suppression of personal liberty
and religious freedom in *any* country. For the first time
since the Reformation the spiritual factor is emphasized
in an international state document.

III: The Peace Patrol

In his recent book, "The Lost Peace" * Mr. Harold Butler, the Deputy Director of the International Labour Organization since its inception, and after the death of Albert Thomas its Director, ranks as "the first and most obvious reason why the peace was lost," the "passionate devotion to peace of the rest of the world" which was the greatest asset of the aggressor nations in their drive for world power.

Now, in itself, a passionate devotion to peace can never be a primary reason for losing the peace. But if the statesmen, victims to this passionate devotion to peace, fail to have a spiritual intelligence service, if for lack of such a service quite naïvely they believe that their devotion is universal, that people in every other country think and feel as they do themselves, if they forget to establish a peace patrol, ready to keep them on the alert, warning them of any danger to the peace mentality, most probably they will invite war.

The first and most obvious reason why the peace was lost was the unwillingness of statesmen and displomats to study the nature of peace and the nature of war, the psychology of peace and the psychology of war, the dangers of aggression and the dangers of complacency.

In any great modern industry, it is considered essential to engage the most prominent research workers; in any leading hospital it is felt to be of vital importance to have

* "The Lost Peace, A Personal Impression," Faber and Faber, Ltd., London, 1941.

40

the best experimental laboratory. But no government had any research institute for the development of peace, for the preventive study of diseases that might infect or undermine and kill peace.

It might be tempting to say that the first and most obvious reason why the peace was lost was that there never was any peace. There was no peace in the sense that we have tried to define. Some nations and a number of statesmen blissfully believed that there was a state of peace. Other nations, or their leaders, knew that this was not the case. And those who were "passionately devoted to peace" did not understand the language of the nations who were not devoted to peace, did not understand the language of their thoughts, their aspirations, their passions. And it is obvious that any agreement to end an armed conflict between contending parties, or bind them to abstain from future hostilities, must be concluded in terms meaning the same thing to all signatories. If the interpretation given to the expressions and clauses by one party is entirely different from the interpretation given by the other party, the agreement will be worth nothing, but remain a constant source of danger to the party accepting the terms as being of a positive and binding nature.

When a treaty is concluded between two nations not speaking the same language, it is written in both their languages, also, as a rule, with an official French translation, but the danger of differing interpretations is felt so strongly that usually it is stipulated in the treaty itself, or in the diplomatic note accompanying the treaty, which text shall be binding in case of litigation; for not even the most conscientious translation can make texts in different languages so identical that no lawyer could be found willing to make a case of a possible discrepancy. And it is a peculiar thing that this strong feeling for the need of textual congruence has not gone hand in hand with a presentiment that it was still more important that there should be an identity of conceptions, that an agreement, a concluded peace, was possible only if its terms were laid down in a moral language accepted by both parties.

If non-aggression means armed invasion to one party and open friendliness to the other party; if a promise means to one party a binding obligation, and to the other party a dope given an opponent; if a solemn declaration means to one party a sacred statement of facts or of a serious policy and no more than a bid in poker to the other party—no treaty in any known language is of any value to the old-fashioned party still fondly thinking that a word is a word and a man a man, conceptions non-existent in the moral language of the other party. Any agreement signed by him will lay him open to assault, aggression, invasion, unspeakable oppression, tyranny and cruelty.

This is what the world has been witnessing since the arrival of Nazism. And it should be one of the outstanding facts to be borne in mind at a future peace conference.

After the last war Governments of Great Powers continued to have a secret military service and sometimes a secret foreign office intelligence service, although not so good, perhaps, as it had once been, because responsible democratic statesmen were blind to their own spiritual ignorance and simplicity. Governments had military attachés and naval attachés at their embassies and legations, they had councillors for commerce and fisheries and agriculture and what not; but there was not a single Great Power that had on the staff of the embassies a councillor or an attaché for education, for the study of those mental phenomena which decide the attitude of nations towards peace and war, an expert qualified to teach them the gap between their own moral language and that understood in the country of their mission.

If any government had had any kind of peace patrol on duty, it would never had been unprepared for war.

But until the twenty-six governments signed the Washington Agreement it had not been officially recognized that the suppression of religious freedom in one country was of particular interest to every country and constituted a potential danger to the peace of the world. It had never been officially admitted that the preservation of human rights and justice in one country was a matter of vital interest to the Governments of all other countries. But under our conception of peace this becomes an integral part of the new world order; which again means that an international peace patrol will be on duty and report any national "mental disturbance" likely to become a danger to peace.

The unpreparedness of many nations, the unpreparedness of the United States when the treacherous blow was struck at Pearl Harbor, was a most striking illustration of a truth which Mr. J. Edgar Hoover, the Director of the Federal Bureau of Investigation, has tried, in vain, to impress upon the public mind for years: the necessity of understanding the criminal mind if you want to protect your life and property. He writes in his illuminating book, "Persons in Hiding":

"One of the difficulties which law enforcement men encounter in attempting to make crime understandable to the honest person is that of correctly revealing the criminal brain. It is so hard to persuade the average person that its working is different from that of our minds, that it reasons by different standards. The average sob-sister, for instance, believes that a hardened recidivist should be free from prison because this man protests his "desire to resume an honest life." Thereupon every effort is put forth in his behalf and a dangerous and mad dog often is turned loose on the community." *

Mr. Hoover, of course, only discusses the individual criminal within the individual state. But we are bound to accept the fact that in the world of today there exists such a thing as nations gone criminal. And his wise words ap-

* Quoted by permission of the author and publishers, Little, Brown and Company, Boston.

ply to such nations fully as much as they apply to the gangsters of Chicago. Nothing would endanger the future of any civilized commonwealth of nations more than letting the average sob-sisters of all nations determine peace conditions under the illusion that criminal nations, unreformed, unsentenced and unpunished, desire to resume an honest life, thus "letting hardened recidivists loose" upon the world again.

The parallel is not a paradox. Any German capable of clear thinking has long been aware of the gangster-character of Nazism. Some are proud of it. Franz Haiser, that pre-Hitler apostle of the "master nation," moral wrote in his book, *"Die Judenfrage vom Standpunkt der Herrenmoral"* ("The Jewish Question from the Standpoint of the Master-Moral"), Leipsic, 1926, that the man of the future in Germany must be a man of action; he must have something in common with "adventurers" and "captains of brigands." When Hitler sent one of the most respected administrators of Germany, Herr Regierungsrath Delbrugge, to Norway after the invasion to negotiate with the leaders of the Storting (Parliament) and get them to accept a compromise with Germany, this emissary went back on his word from one meeting to another, and when he was accused of double-crossing and confronted with his declaration of a day before he exclaimed at a full meeting: "Wir sind eine internationale Bande." ("We are an international gang.") *

It will then more easily be comprehended how it can be that Mr. J. Edgar Hoover has given one of the most adequate descriptions of totalitarian mentality—possibly because his mind was entirely free from any idea of discussing Nazism. He has given us a key to a fuller understanding of the leading teachers of the German nation from Treitschke to Goebbels when he writes:

* Professor Jacob S. Worm-Müller: "Norway Revolts Against Nazism," London, 1941, p. 9.

"A criminal does not look upon himself as such. You must accept this as an axiom if you are ever to learn the slightest rules about protecting yourself, your home and your family. His viewpoint is this: He wants something. That ends the matter. Wanting it he feels he should have it. No ideas of justice enter his mind; if they do, they are quickly swamped by selfishness.

". . . if you want to understand the criminal brain, you must become a momentary actor. For the time dispel all your thoughts of responsibility. You owe nothing to anyone but yourself. You must have no sense of loyalty, even to your best friends, but be willing to throw them to the wolves the moment their interests interfere with yours. Become selfish to the degree that anyone who wants to block you in your desires is an enemy to be dealt with as foully as you feel he is dealing with you. Remember that what you want, you must have, no matter how you get it.

"Adopt the attitude that it is smart to delude others into helping you by deceiving them. Tell yourself that if you have a gun in your hand and the man at whom you point it is unarmed, then you are a brave man and he is a coward. . . . Look upon all law enforcement agents as inherent crooks who would be stealing, as you are doing, if they only 'had the nerve.' . . . View any and all means, whether they be stealth, lies, forgery, perjury, the bribery of witnesses, intimidation, pleading of reform, evidences of remorse, eagerness for rehabilitation, or the feigning of illness or even the death of your own mother as right and proper if used by you to escape a sentence for your deeds, or to persuade guileless persons to aid you in leaving a prison cell. Consider any part of the world which runs contrariwise to your narrow, cheap, selfish, egotistic nature as 'being against you.' . . . Be maudlin concerning yourself and cynical about the feelings of others. Believe yourself fine and noble if you indulge in cheap sentimentalities about sweethearts, parents, babies, animals, thus building a psychology by which you can condone murder if you 'have always been a good boy to your mother.' However, should these components become impedimental, have no compunction whatever about deserting your sweetheart, using your mother's home as a hideout, shooting down a baby or choking your dog, all to the purpose that you hate to do it, but after all, you have got to live. To believe all these things implicitly is to have the true criminal point of view. And no person who cannot understand that this is the law-breaker's mind should have any part whatever in dealing with the persons who constitute our army of more than four million enemies of society." *

Nobody can fail to see how the whole system of German philosophy and propaganda has been built up on this pattern.

Hitler, Goebbels and all the minor lights have explained over and over again how the Germans "have been hounded into it," that everybody "is against them," that they are entitled "to make their own luck." From line to line we recognize the familiar German phrases. And Mr. Hoover had probably never read *"Mein Kampf,"* that great manual of crime, when he wrote his book. But, no doubt, the Japanese leaders had studied it, and modeled their minds upon it.

No peace conference will be competent to deal with the problems of the future unless the leaders realize that they are confronted by the problem so adequately described by Mr. Hoover, and have to deal with millions of enemies of mankind, and that no peace can be negotiated between the law and the criminal, even in international matters.

Of course, Hitler did not look upon himself as a criminal, nor did the German nation. There was something they wanted; so they felt they should have it. And other countries were so passionately devoted to peace that they let Hitler have it. Democracies were so busy with having a good time and trying to make people believe that the ultimate aim of democracy was to perpetuate having a good time that they hated to be disturbed. The bigger the country, the greater the public irritation against any disturbance.

Did not Hitler make beautiful speeches? And were they not constantly quoted by leading men in a good many

* Quoted by permission of the author and the publisher.

countries, men who succeeded in convincing themselves, and sometimes others, that they found these speeches a source of international inspiration? In his address delivered in the Reichstag on May 21, 1935, Hitler made this announcement:

"What then could I wish more than peace and tranquility?

"But if it is said that this is merely the desire of the leaders, I can reply that if only the leaders and rulers desire peace, the nations themselves will never wish for war. . . .

"Without taking the past into account, Germany has concluded a non-aggression pact with Poland. There is more than a valuable contribution to European peace, and we shall adhere to it unconditionally. . . .

"The German Reich—and in particular the present German Government—have no other wish than to live on friendly and peaceful terms with all neighbouring states. . . ."

English and French statesmen, and American industrialists and flyers, believed Hitler. In Germany people had their doubts. But they knew that it was all done for their benefit, and they smiled when they told the small anecdotes so popular in Germany before this war, and sometimes of illustrative value. As for instance this little story told when the Lutherans in 1934 celebrated the fourth centennial of the full edition of Luther's translation of the Bible:

"Can you tell the difference between Dr. Martin Luther, Dr. Adolf Hitler, Dr. Goebbels and Dr. Schacht? . . . Dr. Martin Luther said what he believed, Dr. Adolf Hitler believes what he says. Dr. Goebbels does not believe what he says; and Dr. Schacht does not say what he believes."

But it may be doubted how often Hitler believed what he said.

Rauschning in his book "Hitler Speaks" reports a conversation with Hitler in 1934:

"He told me that morning what was his view of treaties . . . any one who was so fussy that he had to consult his conscience about whether he could keep a pact, whatever the pact, and whatever the situation, was a fool. Why not please other people and ease one's own position by signing pacts if the other people thought that got them anywhere or settled anything?"

In the quasi-theological language of the Nazi teachers this philosophy is expressed by Wilhelm Stapel in his supreme ethical conclusion:

"The God of Our Force (*unserer Kraft*) and Our Pride, far from being a guarantor of objective morality, even has the function of easing Our Path *wherever it suits us to wrong others* or those among Us who are less genuinely We." *

Those who were reluctant to accept Mr. Rauschning's unsubstantiated word as valid evidence have been convinced by Hitler's deeds that if Rauschning did not speak his words, he certainly spoke his mind.

Only a few scholars and worried observers in small countries perceived the deadly impact of Nazi philosophy. And the two great democratic leaders who are at the helm today saw the German danger. But in spite of the overwhelming mass of documentary evidence of political actions, of aggressions, of crimes and of murders, good and honest men and women in many countries persisted in their passionate unwillingness to admit open facts, in their ardent desire to shut their eyes and minds to any moral issues, in stubborn loyalty to professions of a good faith that did not exist, in their constant condonation of murder because "those people have always been good boys to their mothers."

The Nazi appeal to brutality, to racial prejudice, to every dark and sinister instinct of man was not so dangerous in democratic countries as the appeal to fairminded-

* The Nazi philosophy of Rosenberg and other official leaders has classified mankind into a superior "I" and an inferior "they," a divine "We" and a contemptible "non-we," a duality of "Our" master race and "their" slave race.

ness, to sentimentality, to a sensitive craving for justice for everybody. What has been called "appeasement" took its strength from many sources, but most of all from the difficulty indicated by J. Edgar Hoover—of persuading the average person that the totalitarian nations reason by standards different from those of the democratic nations.

The German infiltration in America has been tremendous and tremendously successful. Pearl Harbor silenced appeasement for the time being. But still great numbers of good men and women are not fully convinced.

Prime Minister Smuts, in an address to the Legion of Truth in South Africa, said (January 15, 1941):

"Propaganda is becoming a more dangerous method of attack than rifles and guns, and the only means of defence is for us to spread truth as against lies."

If there had been any organized Peace Patrol activity, it should not have been necessary to organize legions of truth. And such a thing as the Japanese stab in the dark should make it easier to lead people to examine how it has become possible that such a thing could happen and what is the moral background for this state of international affairs.

Any such examination will make it clear to the average person that these things did not start in 1939, nor with the Italian attack on Ethiopia, nor even with the Japanese aggression in Manchuria. For years a school of totalitarian philosophers and men of action have preached the gospel that everything is permitted, that there exists no moral code, that the end will justify the means, that lying, perjury, arson, murder are not only legitimate means of obtaining certain results, but that these things far from being despicable, are heroic, the patriotic duty of every citizen.

All human experience has proved that as the means are so will the end be. Violence breeds violence. Even the purest idealist resorting to means which his conscience rejects, will be tainted and lose not only his conceptions of right and wrong, but his spiritual balance. He will be mentally disturbed.

One of the most impressive pictures of such a state of disturbance is that of Oliver Cromwell, demanding that his preacher come to his deathbed and asking in his agony: "Tell me, is it possible to fall from Grace?" "No, it is not possible," said the minister. "Then," said the dying Cromwell, "I am safe, for I know that I was once in Grace."

So perhaps some modern dictator might ask; and he would receive a similar answer; for the ministers of the Gospel have been sent to concentration camps or put on the rack, and only the ministers of his might are around him.

Schiller in his "Piccolomini" has given the classical German expression to this moral law (perhaps that is the reason for his no longer being *poeta grata* in Germany):

> *"Das eben ist der Fluch der bösen Tat,*
> *dass sie fortzeugend immer Böses muss gebären."*

> "That is the very curse of every misdeed,
> that always it goes on to breed new evil actions."

In a still more classical book of wisdom the same truth is spoken in words living in every tongue except the totalitarian: "He who toucheth pitch shall be defiled therewith."

Gradually and slowly nations which would have preferred to stay out of the war have been forced to realize the spiritual character of the conflict. In the second report with annexed papers presented by the Commission to Study the Organization of Peace it is stated (p. 162) that worse than the material losses in this war "is the moral and intellectual havoc wrought by the ideological nature of the present conflict and by the new methods of propaganda, fifth column penetration and terrorism. Principles of civilization which have endured for centuries have been brutally attacked."

With this realization comes the conviction to which so many good and honest people have been unwilling to be led, that there can be no negotiated peace between parties which do not recognize the same principles of civilization, and that this war is not a fight between two groups of empires for more power and prestige, but a deadly struggle between two opposite conceptions of honor and honesty and decency between man and man, and nation and nation. It is the tremendous clash between peoples with a deep-rooted and, in times of crisis, passionate belief in certain moral laws and principles, and peoples who have discarded every moral principle and every fundamental law, except the law of individual egotism and national megalomania. It is a fight between a group of allied countries still believing in equity and justice and freedom, convinced of the right of men to self-government in a world where they are "created equal and endowed by their Creator with certain inalienable rights, among these Life, Liberty and the pursuit of Happiness"; and on the other hand a group of states denying every such idea and trying to enslave all the nations of earth under their crude conceptions of racial mysticism and mythology, more akin to the barbaric rites of blood-offerings in prehistoric ages than to any philosophy known in the Christian era.

It is typical of the new German spirit that the philosophical forerunner of Hitler, Franz Haiser, wrote: "A genuine Deity wants man to be sacrificed to it." So when Helen Hill and Herbert Agar, in their excellent little book, "Beyond German Victory," state: "The ideal community of the Nazis is not an inclusive brotherhood of

men; it is an exclusive community of blood"—the words
are true in a double sense. And only by grasping the sense
of this blood-community and studying its origin and background can we establish that kind of supervision which is
needed to make a peace just and durable.

IV: Heine's Prediction

Owing to the lack of any efficient peace intelligence system, diplomats and statesmen were without reliable information about, and without any understanding of, what took place in the sphere of moral and intellectual development in the countries of Europe. They clung to the old belief that wars are brought about only by questions of trade and traffic, of money and markets, of commerce and colonies. And a few men of outstanding intelligence were misled by their literary brilliancy to believe that wars can be stopped by paper, that any difficulty can be solved if an elegant formula could be invented and embodied in an international resolution.

Señor de Maderiaga in a speech at the League of Nations Assembly in 1933 expressed this opinion as follows:

"Why are there wars? Because there are disputes. Why are there disputes? Because problems become aggravated. Why do problems become aggravated? Because they are not studied at the stage when they are no more than questions."

That was a decade after the first German edition of "Mein Kampf." But four years later Señor de Maderiaga in his book "Anarchy or Hierarchy" pointed out that the solution of problems was not so easy as all that, and that suddenly mankind was back in the sixteenth century, in the period of sanguinary religious wars.

But even the civil war in Spain could not wake up the statesmen of Europe and the senators of America to the true issues.

Hitler had written in his book:

"The question of how to win back German power is not: How can we manufacture arms? Rather it is: How can we create that spirit which renders a people capable of bearing arms? When this spirit dominates a people, willpower finds a thousand ways, each of which leads to a weapon."

But Hitler was not taken seriously—again because no peace patrol had given information concerning his strength and his operations. And leaders of nations were still unwilling to admit that the spirit means more than armaments. The military unpreparedness in the democratic countries was the logical outcome of a mental unpreparedness which was almost incredible. Read the pitiful story, as told in Ambassador Dodd's diary, of Sir Nevile Henderson, the British Ambassador to Berlin; or rather read Sir Nevile Henderson's own book: "Failure of a Mission" (1940): surely one of the most remarkable testimonies of spiritual and political impotence ever published, the memoirs of a gentleman of culture, living entirely outside the world of political ideas and political realities, as innocent and helpless as any baby and of about as much use to Europe. In the face of every open fact this gentleman could give Mr. J. Edgar Hoover a theme for one more chapter on the hopeless task of making complacent people understand their own danger. "Nevertheless, the contrary had first to be proved" is the leit-motiv of Sir Nevile Henderson's book. But he did more than passive harm. By accepting as gospel truth every German distortion and twisting of historical facts, he misled the historically underinformed members of the British cabinet and made an important contribution to that complete misunderstanding of German mentality and German aims so fatally prevalent in influential circles in England.

In his pamphlet "Ourselves and Germany" (1938) the Marquess of Londonderry, with an impressive lack of elementary intellectual and moral knowledge of Germany, discussed Nazism with kind tenderness. As late as in the winter of 1939 men like Lord Lloyd spoke with shoulder-patting benevolence of Mussolini as the man who had restored order in Italy. Mr. Chamberlain's flight to Godesberg will remain the spectacular illustration of this materialistic lack of vision, this spiritual ignorance and intellectual inefficiency; there was something pathetic and heroic in this strange hybrid of a child's crusade and "Innocents Abroad," this simple-minded attempt to stave off a new deluge with an umbrella.

Of course, the men quoted were not exceptions, they were just exponents of a popular creed, and before passing judgment on their wisdom we should remember that they were not alone. The Official Report of the Debate on the Address in the House of Commons a few years back quotes Mr. Winston Churchill as describing Mussolini in the following terms:

"I could not help being charmed as so many others have been by his simple, gentle bearing, his calm, detached poise, despite his many burdens and dangers; and secondly could see that he thought of nothing but the lasting good, as he understood it, of the Italian people and that all else was of secondary interest to him."

On the same occasion Hitler was called in Parliament "a highly competent, cool, well-informed functionary with an agreeable manner and a disarming smile." And in 1937 the old labour leader, Mr. George Lansbury, campaigning for a new peace movement, after an interview with the Führer declared:

"I have looked into that man's eyes and I know that he means peace."

It was pitifully like a famous cartoon by Sir Bernard Partridge in *Punch* when the first Assembly of the League of Nations met in 1920. A huge cobra (bearing the inscription "International Strife") is coiled up ready to attack a shivering little rabbit, decorated with a white ribbon inscribed: "The League of Nations." The cobra is looking greedily at the rabbit who modestly remarks: "As I have no means of attacking him the only thing I can try is to fascinate him by the power of my eye." But the Lansbury eye had no more binding force than the rabbit's eye.

If all the men quoted and other men and women had known more of totalitarian philosophy they would hardly have been misled by the masks the leaders put on for the occasion. And most surely the noble lords mentioned above would have been painfully shocked and greatly surprised if it had been explained to them that they failed so utterly to see the danger and realize what was happening under their eyes, because they were unwittingly the victims of Marxism and strongly imbued with the Marxist conception that the ultimate causes of war are always economic.

It seems very difficult for old social democrats to admit that there are forces stronger than the economic laws laid down by their prophets, and confess openly that the catchwords *labour* and *capital* have no longer any fixed and fast meaning but are at best vague and liquid, that the term "economic laws" is entirely unscientific, and that these laws only express what may be called the astrology of political economy.

It is interesting to follow the development of a writer like Harold J. Laski. He still asserts that the last world war was an economic war on the orthodox pattern: "It was in essence a struggle for markets between the rising power of Germany and allied empires threatened by German economic ambitions." * It was emphatically not. And if those responsible for European and American politics after 1914 had not been told so often and so convincingly by Mr. Laski and his confrères that wars were economic

---

* "Where do We Go from Here?"—1st Ed., New York, 1941, p. 24.

struggles, they might have started thinking on their own; and the history of the world since 1930 might have been an entirely different one. Where economic interests are at stake, there is always a possibility and even a probability for a compromise. From the purely economic point of view, war is waste more than anything else, a sinful waste of money and men, and between states under modern conditions hardly ever a paying proposition. Economic interests will usually try to strike a bargain.

But when the dark racial and religious passions are evoked from the dangerous depths under all veneers of civilization, there is hardly room for any compromise.

Recently, and, we may hope, not too late, Mr. Laski and others have, reluctantly, come to see the sinister and sad truth: "We have moved to an age of new creed-wars as real and not less ferocious than those of the Reformation." *

Still more important: The Rt. Hon. Ernest Bevin, who is so actively connected with the war efforts, and who will also have an important influence on the peace to come, now seems to have fully realized this fact: "We know that we are not merely fighting a state, we are fighting a philosophy." ("The Balance Sheet of the Future," New York, 1941, p. 34.) The German teachers of the Nazis had proclaimed this long ago. So Friedrich Hielscher in *"Krieg und Krieger,"* ("War and Warriors," 1930): "The War against the West will assume the aspect of wars both religious and imperial."

And unless this is fully realized by those who shall discuss peace-terms, their efforts will prove in vain and the same thing will happen over again on a still more tremendous scale and under still more cruel forms.

Mr. Bevin has grasped this fact. He writes in his book (p. 144):

* *Ibid.,* pp. 40-41.

"Whatever may have been the motives of those who tried appeasement, it can be truly said that the policy was bound to fail because these two great principles, one of force and the other of liberty, are irreconcilable; and if Europe, at the close of what is virtually a civil struggle, is to take her part again as the great center of culture, economic knowledge and even finance in rebuilding the world, then we in this country have to see to it that we are not influenced only by questions of geography or what has been described as vital interests . . ."

It is tempting to say that rather it will be necessary to find out in a deeper and more far-reaching sense what *are* the vital interests of states and of nations—and of mankind.

People still talk, and even people in highly responsible positions, of the "good" Germans and the "evil" Hitler. The words are utterly inadequate and do not convey any meaning, because they belong to a language unknown in the third Reich. The removal of Hitler alone would solve no problem; for he is not a cause, he is a result. His Germany is not the product of one man's genius and effort; it is the work of a nation. His government in Germany, until the outbreak of the war, was probably more representative of his country than any other government was representative of its nation.

For any fruitful discussion of peace terms it is essential to understand how that could be.

It is a fundamental mistake to believe that the present German system originated with Hitler. It has been perfected under Hitler; it has been made supreme by his lieutenants. But their action was possible only because the way had been paved for them, and what they taught was not a new lesson.

This evolution in Germany did not even start with Bismarck. He came as the natural product of the German educational and philosophical system. But he belonged to an age when Christianity had not lost its firm grip on the German mind. He was educated before Nietzsche. And the aberrations of German mentality are much older than Bismarck. They date back to the period of the German romantic school in the age of Napoleon and in the years after the battle of Leipsic. "Nationalism" as known to the nineteenth and twentieth centuries is a product of the same period in Germany and in many ways has made the last hundred years less international than any other century since the early Middle Ages.

It is of peculiar interest today to recall how clearly the dangers to come were forecast by Heinrich Heine, the great poet and writer, whose name today is taboo in Germany because he was not of purely "Aryan" race. His monuments in Hamburg and elsewhere have disappeared; his name has been erased from squares and streets called after him; and when "Lorelei" is still found in the German readers for schoolchildren, it is called "old folksong, writer unknown."

In 1834 Heine wrote a series of articles in the leading French magazine *"Revue des deux Mondes"*; they were called "Germany after Luther." In these articles Heine also discusses the futility of the German revolutionary attempt in 1830. He offers consolation to his disappointed revolutionary friends. Their hopes of a German revolution need only be postponed; they are not defeated:

"The revolution will come, and it will be no milk and water affair. The various schools of German philosophy will have seen to that—the followers of Kant, the followers of Fichte and the 'Nature philosophers.' . . . These doctrines have developed revolutionary forces which only await the day to break forth and fill the world with terror and astonishment. The followers of Kant with their lack of reverence for everything, the followers of Fichte with their fanaticism of the will are bound to make a thorough job of it. . . .

"Christianity—and this is its fairest merit—subdued to a certain extent the brutal warrior ardor of the Germans, but it could not entirely quench it; and when the Cross, that restraining talisman, falls to pieces, there will break forth again the ferocity of the old combatants, the frantic Berserker rage of which Northern poets have said and sung. The talisman has become rotten, and the day will come when it will pitifully crumble to dust. The old stone gods will then arise from the forgotten ruins and wipe from their eyes the dust of centuries, and Thor with his giant hammer will arise again, and he will crush the Gothic cathedrals. . . . When ye hear the trampling of feet and the clashing of arms, ye neighbors' children, be on your guard . . . it might fare ill with you. . . . Smile not at the fantasy of one who foresees in the region of reality the same outburst of revolution that has taken place in the region of the intellect. The thought precedes the deed as the lightning with thunder. German thunder is of a true German character; it is not very nimble, but rumbles along somewhat slowly. But come it will; and when ye hear a crushing such as never before has been heard in the history of the world, then know that at last the German thunderbolt has fallen. At this commotion the eagles will drop dead from the skies and the lions in the farthest wastes of Africa will bite their tails and creep into their royal lairs. There will be played in Germany a drama compared to which the French Revolution will seem but an innocent idyll. At present everything is quiet; and though here and there some few men create a little stir, do not imagine these are to be the real actors in the piece. They are only the little curs chasing one another round the arena . . . till the appointed hour when the troop of gladiators appear to fight for life and death. And *the hour will come.*"

The hour *has* come, and Heine's predictions have come true in a way which would hardly have surprised himself, but which seems astounding to all those who are without the historical background of German philosophy and mentality. To any man who has been brought up to or who has accepted the cheap and convenient idea that war is a function of certain economic processes, it has come as a tremendous shock, not yet fully realized, that great wars may be the logical and inevitable outcome of a spiritual process. It is not Versailles and it is no question of "Lebensraum" that is responsible for this war, which was bound to come if all the world would not accept slavery under the German "master-race."

The old Chinese tradition is said to have been that when a man had committed a crime his schoolmaster was punished. So deep-rooted was the belief that the boy is father to the man, the conviction that what is sown in the minds of children will bear fruit in their manhood. It is of some importance that those who will be responsible for the peace negotiations should understand the wisdom of the old Chinese custom. Even a man like the Rt. Hon. Ernest Bevin who often looks far ahead writes in "The Balance Sheet of the Future":

"No peace can be built, nothing can be done until Prussianism is disarmed and the military caste broken. It is impossible for any nation to go to the conference table and attempt to make peace with that type of mentality."

Superficially, this seems quite obvious, and nevertheless, as an explanation of the state of Germany, it gives a false picture. In more ways than one the military caste in Prussia represented what was best in Prussian manhood. The officers were well educated and brought up to certain standards of honor, which explains the friction between the army and the Nazi party. Like the rest of Germans they were brought up under the iron rod of discipline and they were the products of German education. It is the schoolmasters of Germany that must be disarmed; they are the parents of spiritual Prussianism.

V: The German Creed

Those ultimately responsible for the crimes of modern Germany are the philosophers: Kant, Fichte, Hegel and Nietzsche, the great instructors of the German nation, and the ten thousands of teachers and professors who have instilled their theories in the minds of millions of educated Germans until they have permeated the whole nation. Should any delegate, without a sound knowledge of German language, history and thinking be sent to the Peace Conference, it should be requested that he understand that, when German matters are discussed, his role is only that of an intelligent onlooker who does not know the rules of the game.

Kant's skepticism in which all knowledge of reality was denied us and his transcendental agnosticism, as Heine says, led to a lack of reverence for anything, but it was his categorical imperative that made him the prophet and even a founder of the new German religion.

The categorical imperative, the unmistakable voice of conscience, originally the command of God, became through Kant the law of irresponsible self-assertion, ambition and egotism. And his minor followers taught that this self-assertion was the creative spirit of the universe. So, in spite of his meticulous correctness and personal respect for existing institutions, the philosopher of Königsberg became a revolutionary force.

Kant's influence was an influence on the philosophers. But Fichte directly influenced the whole German nation.

And this puritan and idealist has had a fate not unlike that of Wilbur Wright, who constructed the airplane to render service to mankind, and lived to see it turned into the most devastating instrument of cruel destruction known in history. Only, as the Word is immeasurably more potent than the Sword, so the teachings of Fichte have been turned to use for purposes immeasurably more terrifying than any destruction from the clouds.

When in December, 1807, the Berlin professor started his series of speeches to the German Nation (*"Reden an die deutsche Nation"*), it was to steel the will of his compatriots never to give in to the tyranny of Napoleon; and large sections of his lectures could be turned against the German oppressors of today and used to cement the passive resistance in any occupied country.* But in his thirteenth speech he gave form to thoughts which have since been utilized to deify the German nation, without any use of critical or moral reservations:

"Only when peoples left to themselves develop their inherent qualities in national community they reflect the Deity as they ought to. And only the man who has no idea of or is an enemy of all lawfulness and divine order can dare to infringe on this highest law in the spiritual world."

This is one of the origins of Alfred Rosenberg's:

"Each race has its soul . . . each soul its race . . . each race ultimately produces one supreme ideal only."

It is easy to recognize Fichte's teaching carried to its vulgar but popular extreme in the profession of Nazi faith in the group *"Völkische Aktion"*:

"I believe in our divinity when millions of Germans are leagued around one Leader. I know God to be in the force ('*Kraft*') of our blood alone."

* As a matter of fact Fichte was used in that way in Norway by the well-known writer Ronald Fangen, a prominent advocate of the Oxford Group movement in Norway; and for quoting Fichte's *"Reden"* in an article in a magazine, he was put in prison by the Nazis and tortured and kept in a dark cell for months.

Fichte's words are very much alive in a pamphlet published for the Hitler-jugend in January, 1942, by Mr. M. F. Schmidt, the vice-gauleiter of Württemberg:

"We can consider the mere fact of belonging to our nation as the purest manifestation of a moral and divine reality. When we say that a man is German or of German blood we acknowledge a divine and inviolable manifestation of creation. In fact this acknowledgment is to us identical with the discovery of God."

And then he continues, as a true disciple of Fichte:

"For whoever lives for his nation with complete consecration and deep loyalty, in the view of mankind, lives in God; but he who carries his disrespect to the point of denying the law of the blood is the emptiest thing on the face of this earth."

Fichte is not only one of the main sources of the German national mysticism which has been made into an unholy religion; in his passionate belief in the mission of the German race * and his consequent complete contempt for individual life and his idolation of death, he is the forerunner of all Nazi philosophers, and he is the supreme schoolmaster who led his entire nation on to an education for death. In an age of humiliating German defeat he glorified sacrifice and victory. He spoke of death as a devout worshipper, as a fanatical priest of Thanatos, the Greek God of death.

"Tell me not of the thousands who fell round his path, speak not of his own early death, after the realization of his idea. What was there greater for him to do than to die? . . . Do you know anything higher than death? . . . Who has the right to stand in the way of any enterprise begun in the face of this peril?"

* When writers and orators in Germany constantly speak of "race" and not of nation, it is, no doubt, largely because there never was a German nation. Germany, das Reich, did not exist until 1871, and until Hitler the various states in the Reich still remained with their legislative bodies, their rulers, their separate stamps and national institutions.

The words of Fichte echo in all the war speeches of the German leader and their spirit flames from the posters put up in every youth camp, in every gymnasium, in every school in Hitler's Reich: "We are born to die for Germany."

In his message of discipline and duty to a nation on the point of disintegration Fichte set up the obligation to the State as a supreme ideal and envisaged an idealistic Germany conquering the world with an army of soldiers inspired with austere and abstract aims. The sole animating principle of history, according to Fichte, is the tendency towards a universal, Christian, European (i.e. German) monarchy, a tendency deeper than the plans of men and stronger than their intentions.

"That a State, even when on the very point of making war, should solemnly assert its love of peace and its aversion to conquest, is nothing; for in the first place it must needs make this asseveration and so hide its real intention if it would succeed in its design; and the well-known principle 'Threaten war that thou mayest enjoy peace,' may also be inverted this way: *'Promise peace that thou mayest begin war with advantage';* and in the second place, the State may be wholly in earnest in its peaceful assurances, so far as its self-knowledge has gone; but let the favorable opportunity for aggrandisement present itself, and the previous good resolution is forgotten."

But Fichte carries his ominous doctrine still further:

"The people metaphysically predestined has the moral right to fulfill its destiny by means of cunning and force."

And

"Between states there is neither law nor right unless it be the right of the strongest."

Here is the nucleus of all the evil teachings of Dr. Goebbels or his master, and Fichte's proclaiming of the absolute will was the birth of the new religion in Germany. Of this new religion Professor Santayana wrote more than twenty-five years ago:

"It passes for a somewhat faded speculation, or for the creed of a few extremists, when in reality it dominates the judgment and conduct of the nation. No religious tyranny could be more complete. It has its prophets in the great philosophers and historians of the last century, its high priests and pharisees in the Government and the professors; its faithful flock in the disciplined mass of the nation." ("Egotism in German Philosophy," p. 69.)

Fichte's successor at the Berlin Academy was Hegel, the second great teacher of modern Germany. To him the State meant even more than it meant to Fichte. He taught that the State was supreme, and the souls of men only accidents, so the individual should be entirely subjugated to the State in the disciplined service of common, impersonal ends; man as an individual exists only through his functions in society, his only reality is the space he fills in the total spectacle. Fichte was a visionary and a poet, passionate, chaotic, the outburst of a volcano; and Hitler is his spiritual prodigal grandson. Hegel was a servile Prussian state functionary, the lava left by the explosion, the mental grandfather of Himmler and his Gestapo. Hegel was taught at every university, college and high school in Germany for two generations; his stamp is left on the whole nation. And he was so easy to understand:

"He despised every ideal not destined to be realized on earth; he respected legality more than justice and extant institutions more than moral ideas; and he wished to flatter a government in whose policy war and even crime were recognized weapons. . . . [He] sacrificed the natural man and all men to an abstract obsession, called an ideal. . . . This imperative is categorical. The . . . war against human nature and happiness is declared, and an idol that feeds on blood, the absolute State is set up in the heart and over the city." *

* George Santayana: "Egotism in German Philosophy," pp. 82-83.

Fichte was a devout Christian; and Hegel, if not an honest personal believer, at least safely at anchor in traditional conventions and conservative veneration for the powers that be. And as long as Christianity still retained its power over the hearts of women and men, the devastating demons of German paganism were still under lock and key, though howling more and more loudly.

Schopenhauer and Nietzsche broke down the shell of veneration for moral conceptions and institutions left over from Kant and Hegel. Instead of order, they worshipped metaphysical anarchy, and turned against Christianity, Schopenhauer half sadly, Nietzsche triumphantly. The pathological prophet and poet who always balanced on the brink of madness until he was finally confined to the asylum where some millions of his followers ought to have been given a long rest, has been promoted to the great authority for present-day Germany. His worship of power was the escape of the impotent; his cult of the superman the pitiful, imaginary *Ersatz* (surrogate) for life of a physical and moral invalid. But his gospel that the strong man should be *"Jenseits von Gut und Böse"* (beyond Good and Evil) has been welcomed as an apology for every variety of wickedness and vice; and although his masterpiece *"Also sprach Zaratustra"* aptly has been described as belonging "in the medicine cabinet of the adolescent" (Crane Brinton in his "Nietzsche"), for the ordinary German (who has never read his books) he still has the halo of sanctified inspiration; and when he apostrophizes cruelty because it is beautiful, when he turns violently against truth because it is ugly, he is devoutly followed by millions of Nazis who are beyond the beautiful and the hideous because all their evil instincts are let loose.

To follow him as a prophet is like following not even Oscar Wilde, but Dorian Gray.* Still his words form one of the ingredients of the potion that has intoxicated Ger-

* "Conscience and cowardice are really the same things."

man mentality; he is one of the apostles of the new German religion.

For Nazism does not pretend to be only a political ideology. It pretends to be something far more. Ambassador Dodd quotes the official philosopher of Nazism, Alfred Rosenberg, lecturing (in 1938) to the South Germans on their loyalty to the sacred State:

"No religion shall be permitted to weaken the hold of the State on the people. Only what is useful to Germany can be regarded as true, and we claim the absolute right to remold all things in Germany as they should be. National Socialists in Germany will form in the future a social order with all the holy mysticisms of the Medieval Age." (See Dodd's diary, 1st edition, p. 199.)

Some years ago this was found more strange than dangerous, and when diplomats discussed such things in Berlin, they shrugged their shoulders and smiled. But in the reawakening of this half mystical, half barbarous Medieval spirit lies the secret of Hitler's power and the drive for war.

The Nazi leaders have always been keenly aware of the importance of stressing the religious element in their movement. What Rosenberg said in 1938 could not have surprised any observer in Germany outside the diplomatic corps. The striving to make into articles of mythical faith the worship of the German race and the Destiny of Germany had been manifest for years. The deep undercurrents in the German mind, named by Fichte, have been brought to the surface very openly. But European politicians did not study the works of the German Messiahs. They were interested in trade statistics, exports and imports; and diplomats were constantly making salaams to the economic superstitions fondly believed by the followers of Marx and the great army of economists to be the ultimate words of human wisdom. Some of the greatness of Hitler lay in his supreme contempt for accepted

financial and economic dogmas. He and those around him
felt instinctively and inarticulately that nations are not
willing to die for material gain alone. No promise of somewhat higher wages, some more cents for the cinema, some
more bottles of beer a week, somewhat more expensive
clothes, will make millions of men ready for the ultimate
sacrifice in a war of aggression. Compared to leaders of
the type of Chamberlain, of Tardieu, of Blum, they were,
in their own way, idealists. They realized the necessity of
giving the masses *panem et circenses* to keep them content,
but they were perfectly clear that the spirit of conquest
cannot live on bread and baseball alone.

"We know that a genuine outlook on life can not confine
its expression to theoretical principles or confessions of the
soul, but that it must assume a form of cult."

The words are taken from Alfred Rosenberg's *"Ordens-
staat"* (1934) and they indicate the spiritual program of
Nazism turned Hitlerism.

From the very beginning of Nazism the professors of
Hitler's theology have worked with patience and passion
to build up such a cult. It was not so difficult as might be
supposed. That restraining talisman, the Cross, was falling
to pieces in Germany, corroded by Marxism on one side,
fretted away by the learned professors of German theology
and the high-priests of arrogant science on the other. There
had been a growing tendency in Germany to create a separate German God as distinct from the God of the Gospel.
There was only a step from Fichte and German romanti-
cism to Wilhelm Stapel:

"Religion is a revelation of the living God. God reveals
himself Jew-like in the Jew, German-like in the German.
. . . The Jesus, the Virgin Mary of the Germans, are German."

Ernst Bergmann, one of the clearest of the religious
leaders in the movement, emphasizing the utility of a

German religion which means a worship of everything set up as German, declares:

"A nation which in the great struggle of nations that is coming, either thinks it is impossible to dispense with religion and church altogether, or abides by a religion and church that are not the supreme expression of its will and endeavor—will lose that struggle. We need a faith that prays to a national God, not an international God of reward and punishment. . . . The God of Christendom has forsaken us Germans. He is no just God, no supernational God; he is a political party God of the others. . . . Did this God for one thing prevent the war? Did he prevent the Treaty of Versailles? Then what reason have we to build our church on him? . . . The cause of our defeat in the great fight was that we believed in him and had abandoned our German God. We are willing to cast out God from our Church. But we will not lose our Church. Not the German National Church."

Ernst Niekisch is still more direct:

"Either a German God or none at all: The international God of Christendom is a patron of the Treaty of Versailles. We cannot bend our knees to a God who neglects us for the French."

Franz Haiser says: "We are in need of a mighty, severe and stormy God." And reverting to the ravings of Nietzsche he exclaims: "Only Wotan (Odin), foaming with rage, can fight Jahve."

The *"Schwarze Korps,"* the official organ of the German police force, commented as follows on the so-called attempt on Hitler's life in the Rathhauskeller in Munich in 1938:

"Whoever feels a glimmer of faith in God himself, must recognize Providence in the drastic and evident preference shown for the German cause because of the Fuehrer, which should teach even a blind man. . . . This man is not like any other man. . . . he is Germany and the incorporation of our faith and will. He is our Father. . . . I don't believe in a totem which grimaces, but I believe in a German God."

The Nazi minister of Justice, Dr. Frank, in a speech
in October, 1935, made the following statement:

"We are under great obligation then of recognizing, as a
holy work of the spirit of our Volk, the laws signed with Adolf
Hitler's name. Hitler has received his authority from God.
Therefore he is the champion, sent by God, of German right
in the world."

It is on the background of words like these that one
must see Hitler's contempt for religion, and read Rauschning's account of his words in "Hitler Speaks," pp. 57-58:

"The religions are all alike, no matter what they call them-
selves. They have no future, certainly none for the Germans.
Fascism, if it likes, may come to terms with the church. So
shall I. Why not? That will not prevent me from tearing up
Christianity root and branch, and annihilating it in Germany.
. . . Leave the hair-splitting to others. Whether it is the Old
Testament or the New, or simply the sayings of Jesus, according to Houston Stewart Chamberlain, it is all the same old
Jewish swindle. It will not make us free. A German Church,
a German Christianity is distortion. One is either a German
or a Christian. You can't be both. We don't want people who
keep one eye on the life in the hereafter. We need free men
who feel and know that God is in themselves."

The spirit of Hitler's words are found in the pamphlet
by the German vice-gauleiter quoted before:

"We have no right to the realization of our pretensions to
control Europe, until we have shown the courage to surmount,
by revolutionary means if need be, the theory of community
of peoples in Christianity which has outlived itself in the past
2000 years."

Hitler outlined to Rauschning how propaganda should
be directed against the Church, both Protestant and Catholic. The Catholic priests should be selected as special tar-
gets for the first attack:

"We shall brand them as ordinary criminals. I shall tear
the mask of honesty from their faces. And if that is not enough

I shall make them appear ridiculous and contemptible. I shall order films to be made about them."

Nobody would deny that Hitler and his prophets have acted along the lines laid down in 1934. But, after all, it is a complex task to uproot the conceptions of religious and moral laws in any country.

It took another world war to make the apostles of the new religion, or anti-religion, come out openly. Mr. Ernest E. Pope in his "Munich Playground" has given those interested an idea of what the new German rites were like. He describes his tour to Hesselberg the "Holy Mountain" of the Franconian Nazis where every year the last week-end in June Dr. Streicher preaches a sermon at midnight by the light of a blazing bon-fire. More than 200,000 Germans had climbed the slopes of the mountain to attend. "The boys and girls of the Hitler Youth Organizations bring blankets. They spend the night bundling for Hitler." And Streicher speaks: *

"We need no men in black to make our confessions to. We have become our own priests, and get closer to God by climbing this mountain.

"We do not need the churches. God has always been with Germany, even hundreds of years before there were prophets or saints.

"All our sins were forgiven last night. The German youth on this mountain is much nearer to God than his Protestant or Roman Catholic parents were before Hitler came and united us. And the girls are beautiful with a godlike, natural beauty. Ugly girls and girls with lipstick or rouge should stay away from this holy mountain. . . .

"Streicher reminded his audience that their holy mountain had been the scene of Germanic rituals long before Christianity.

"Hitler Youths and Storm Troopers kept throwing pieces of wood from a huge pile of fuel on the flames, as Julius Streicher raved on ecstatically, telling them that all of their

* From *Munich Playground* by Ernest E. Pope, courtesy of G. P. Putnam's Sons.

sins for the past year had been transferred to this wood and were being purified by the Germanic god of fire. The entire mob of Hesselberg pilgrims worked themselves into a pagan frenzy. Streicher spoke of the German war machine as of some supernatural magic, more powerful than any witch-craft of Germany's enemies, including the 'hypocritical tom-foolery of organized Christianity.' . . .

". . . I was glad to get to sleep in a bed, rather than in the wholesale open-air flophouse of Hitler boys and girls on the bare rocks of a Nazi stamping ground. I suppose they were hardened—and preoccupied—enough not to mind the rain-storm that night. And if the adolescent couples felt a bit guilty about their unchaperoned bundling, they did not even need to confess their sins to a priest. They merely threw another stick on the fire to be purified from their carnal transgres-sions."

On New Year's Day, 1942, Alfred Rosenberg published his thirty-point program for the new German church. This program, submitted to Hitler for his approval, only codifies what has been going on in Germany for a num-ber of years among the youthful adherents of Hitler. Still, some of the points are of great illustrative importance, because they make concrete what a good many honest people were not willing to believe on the evidence of others:

"1. The National Reich Church specifically demands the immediate turning over to its possession of all churches and chapels, to become national churches.

"2. The German people have no call to serve the National Reich Church, but that church itself is called to serve its single doctrine:—race and people.

"5. The National Reich Church is immutably fixed in its one objective: to destroy that Christian belief im-ported into Germany in the unfortunate year 800, whose tenets conflict with both the heart and the men-tality of the German.

"13. The National Reich Church demands the immediate ces-sation of the printing of the Bible, as well as its dis-semination, throughout the Reich and colonies. All

Sunday papers with any religious content shall be suppressed.

"14. The National Reich Church shall see that the importation of the Bible and other religious works into Reich territory is made impossible.

"15. The National Reich Church decrees that the most important document of all time—therefore the guiding document of the German people—is the book of our Fuehrer, 'Mein Kampf.' It recognizes that this book contains the principles of the purist ethnic morals under which the German people must live.

"17. The National Reich Church stipulates that the future editions of 'Mein Kampf' shall contain its present number of pages and contents unmodified.

"18. The National Reich Church will remove from the altars of all churches the Bible, the cross and religious objects.

"19. In their place will be set that which must be venerated by the German people and therefore is by God, our most saintly book, 'Mein Kampf,' and to the left of this a sword.

"28. The National Reich Church refuses to recognize the usual day of penitence and prayer. Only one religious festival will be allowed—the day on which the National Reich Church was founded.

"30. On the day of the foundation of the National Reich Church the Christian sword shall be removed from all churches, cathedrals and chapels inside the frontiers of the Reich and its colonies and will be replaced by the symbol of invincible Germany—the swastika."

The *New York Times,* commenting editorially on this program, writes (January 2, 1942):

"If the world did not stand in such deadly peril, we might regard some of the more grandiose Nazi projects as erratic eccentricities of rather harmless lunatics, because so many of them are so fantastic that they never could appeal to a people both sane and free. A case in point is the scheme, concocted by Dr. Alfred Rosenberg, Reich Minister for the East and one of the members of Nazidom's inner circle, to abolish Christianity and substitute in its stead a new religion with a ritual which seems to stem from the adolescent hocus pocus of prep-school fraternities and the initiation ceremony of the Ku Klux Klan."

It may be objected that lunatics are never harmless but always constitute a potential danger, especially when moving among a people that has not been sane or free for many years. But the words of the *New York Times* very adequately describe the attitude taken by cultured spectators looking at Germany from a distance. When ten men move in a ritual like the initiation ceremony of the Ku Klux Klan, it may seem ludicrous. But when sixty millions are swaying to and fro in this ritual, it becomes indescribably sinister and terrifying.

Some lines from Gregor Ziemer's "Education for Death" will give an idea of the reality of the world-menace arising from this cult in Hitler's Germany. He was allowed to visit one of the sixty-odd "mother-and-child" homes in Germany, and was present when the mothers should have their luncheon; this is the picture he gives:

"After the white-clad nurses had arranged the food, everybody turned toward the wall where hung an imposing picture of Hitler above a huge swastika. The women raised their right hands and spoke in chorus: 'Our Fuehrer, we thank thee for thy munificence; we thank thee for this home; we thank thee for this food. To thee we devote all our powers (*Kraefte*); to thee we dedicate our lives and those of our children!' "

Even more impressive is a scene from one of the homes for the Hitler *jungmädel* (the young girls). Dr. Ziemer knew and liked the matron, who pointed with pride to a girl who was the spiritual leader of the camp and told of her nightly prayers:

" 'Beautiful prayers they are—in which she offers the bodies and souls of all the girls to Hitler.'
" 'To Hitler—?'
" 'Yes, of course. Her nightly prayers are to the man whom

she considers the savior of Germany. You didn't think she was praying to the Old Testament God, did you?' "

But perhaps the most enlightening incident Dr. Ziemer relates was a visit to a B.D.M. camp (*Bund Deutscher Madel*—the Bund of German girls above fourteen). One of the girls, seventeen years old, unmarried, had given birth to a boy and she was the heroine; but the day happened to be the birthday of Horst Wessel and the group of young girls were celebrating him in a dance:

"I was informed that it was a ritual. Horst Wessel was a martyr who had died for the Party. The Fuehrer had made him a saint. They were calling upon the spirit of Horst Wessel to make them good Nazis, worthy of the Fuehrer.

"Somehow I felt they were holding something back; that there was more significance in the rite than this. I refused to be satisfied, and asked more childish questions. It finally transpired that the Fuehrer had asked all BDM girls to become mothers of future soldiers. But there was something every BDM girl dreaded more than death—sterility! And so, on the birthday of Horst Wessel, they were calling upon his spirit to make them good bearers of children.

"They had made of the notorious pander a deity of Fecundity!"

Finally, the girls marched to the temple of honor and knelt down in prayer to Hitler.

It does not help to shrug shoulders, and it does not help to refuse to believe. If this is lunacy, it certainly is not harmless; it is systematical, it is wonderfully well organized; it is on the background of this lunacy that the cohorts of German young men are hurling themselves against the enemy, that they have been climbing the mountains of Norway, swimming the rivers and canals of Belgium and France, crossing the plains of Russia and fighting their way through the dust-storms of the desert.

Consequently and logically Nazism is trying to imbue every occupied country with this spirit of lunacy. The German authorities and their Quislings in every country are passionately fighting and counteracting religion and religious influence in national life. Particularly illuminating has been the situation in Norway with the primate in prison, all the bishops resigned and more than eleven hundred pastors threatened with the concentration camp.

In many countries clergymen of different denominations have been actively or passively helping Nazism, some from fear of Communism, others because of national affiliations and others from more obscure reasons. Many of them have been in good faith, which may sometimes be an explanation, but hardly an excuse for men who are offering to guide public opinion in domains where they are utterly unqualified to give guidance, and where they can only arrive at their conclusions by closing their eyes and their ears to the facts they do not like.

As Nazism, politically, has made use in the democratic states of every democratic privilege to overthrow democracy; as, economically, it has played up to the sanctity of private individual property as against the threat of Communist expropriation in order to be able to confiscate in due time all private property; as it has, nationally, proclaimed the right of minorities to self-determination and used them to deprive the majorities of the right to any determination whatsoever; as it has, diplomatically, called attention to the supreme importance of sovereignty and sent in armies "to protect" the sovereign rights of small nations and national groups, in order to try to wipe out both the sovereignty and the nation—so in the religious field the agents of Nazism make use of every religious doctrine in any church in order to undermine it from within, and blow it up or take it over and pervert it to Nazist practices when the hour has come.

The aim, not only of Rosenberg, but of Nazism, is to confiscate all churches, body and soul.

This whole program has been openly professed for years. But diplomats and politicians usually have preferred to read the biographies and diaries of other diplomats and politicians to studying the school system of totalitarian states, or the manuals of Nazi party philosophy with their program for a future where the conception of any Christian or universal God has been as dexterously removed as any necessity for keeping up an old-time diplomatic service.

If that had not been the case, no single government in Europe or America could have doubted that the war was coming, and what kind of war it would be. For parallel with the deification of the Fuehrer went the glorification of the German race *and* the consequent beatification of war. And to have been ignorant of the spiritual facts was more dangerous than to be ignorant of the facts of armaments. The failure to keep up a moral, an educational, and intellectual intelligence service was fatal.

VI: Education for Death

Treitschke had preached war—but he was no mystic and poet. Nietzsche proclaimed war as a religious commandment:

"Ye have heard men say: Blessed be the peacemakers; but I say unto you: Blessed are the war-makers for they shall be called, if not the children of Jahwe, the children of Odin who is greater than Jahwe."

This dithyrambic glorification of war is not the exclamation of a "rather harmless lunatic"; it is the voice of the innermost Germanism; even if the expression given to it may seem extravagant, it is the education of Fichte in full bloom.

In that very remarkable book *"Wenn ich der Kaiser wär"* ("If I were the Kaiser"), published in Leipsic in 1912, the anonymous writer, who called himself Daniel Frymann, violently criticized the too peaceful attitude of German politicians:

"It is of need that all those interested in public life should learn to revise their ideas and demand *that we lead an active Foreign Policy or let us coolly say an aggressive Foreign Policy."* *

In later editions the author corrected "aggressive" to "attacking"—*"angreifende";* he also laid aside his pseudonym and made public what all those interested in Germany knew, that he was Heinrich Class, the successor of Peters

* The italics by the German author.

and Hasse as president of the Pan-German Bund. His book went through one edition after another and was spread in Germany before the war as was no other work on politics, except Rohrbach's. The book is written with the dangerous patriotism of a mad fanatic, and is of a particular interest, because most of the chapters of *"Mein Kampf,"* except those dealing with Bolshevism, which had not yet been born, are directly molded on *"Wenn ich der Kaiser wär."* We find here the Nazi conception of the Jews, of the role of women, even of "degenerate art," of the superiority of the German race, and so on:

"We know what our people is—Humanity we do not know, and we refuse to care about it or in any way to be enthusiastic about it" (p. 186). *"We are conscious that every establishment of a state in Europe, all civilization in Europe emanates from Germans"* * (p. 182).

With a sigh Herr Class looks forward to a coming war with England—the object-lesson of a Teutonic State polluted by Jewish influence, corrupted by democratic ideas —and then adds:

"But we can safely say that we serve the noblest part of humanity when we strive with every means to better and strengthen our own people." * (p. 187).

In his book, Class not only predicts the great war of 1914, but the defeat of Germany's first attempt at world domination. And he explains that during the period of defeatism in Europe after such a war, Germany would secretly arm and prepare and after twenty years be ready to conquer the world.

In the spring of 1918 when Germans were still believing in victory, Oswald Spengler, whose meteoric influence was very like that of Nietzsche, quite openly wrote in his famous *"Untergang des Abendlandes"* ("Decline of the West"):

* The italics by the German author.

"The democratic nations must disappear, because they put their trust in illusions, more particularly the illusions of truth and justice. There is only one reality in the world—force. If you listen closely you can already hear the tramp of the Cæsars who are coming to take over the world."

It is not Versailles that has called forth the spirit of war in Germany; but the Versailles Treaty has been a useful pretext.

And in the light of this documentation, which could be made interminable, it will also be understood that the message of Hitler was not new in Germany, it was not startling to the Germans. Only to non-Germans, ignorant of German philosophy, of German political amorality, of German tradition, did his book seem new and startling, original, disgusting and incredible.

To the Germans, who had already accepted Spengler's doctrines, *"Mein Kampf"* was no more terrifying than H. G. Wells's "Outline of History" was terrifying to British readers.

For long years the average German had been pining for a dictator. More than a hundred years before Hitler, Goethe wrote (*"Dichtung und Wahrheit,"* Vol. IV) that this people is ready to accept as their dictator any man who will kick them in their pants and explain that he has been called upon to rule them with absolute power.

Not only was the average German longing for a leader who would rid them of the embarrassing responsibility of freedom; but many upper-class German patriots, fervent in their belief that Germany was predestined to rule the world, looked with concern on Kaiser Wilhelm II as too liberal, too friendly to England, playing with pacifist ideas and unable to coördinate every effort in Germany toward war. They were longing for the man with absolute power to marshal the people to aggression and attack.

Heinrich Class wrote in 1912:

"Only a dictatorship can ultimately save the German people from complete ruin." (p. VII)

And again:

"Today things have gone so far that only a dictator can save the fatherland." (p. 221)

He speaks of the "Führer" to come very much as a fanatical muezzin a hundred years ago might have spoken of the next Mahdi who would crush the Christian powers for good and ever. One of his last chapters is called: "In Expectation of the Führer." "The ranks of fighters for the new order are closed—they are waiting for the Führer."— In another chapter:

"When today the Leader arises he will be astounded at the number of faithful followers expecting him—and how valuable, unselfish men will flock to him."

After the smarting defeat of 1918 the longing for the Fuehrer in many minds became a half-religious obsession. The new Mahdi should redress the wrongs Germany had suffered; he should be the avenger, at the same time vulgar and unintellectual enough to be understood and beloved by the Germans, and amoral enough to be the *Ubermensch*—the superman of Nietzsche—*"Jenseits von Gut und Böse."*
In 1923 Franz Haiser wrote: *

"A nation which lacks a ruling class of pure stock can only be governed by an absolute master. . . . All Germans await such a master: and the rest of the Occident will soon come to their view of thinking. Germany needs the man who will knock down all unmanageable fellows, all personalities."

The expectations of Haiser were made corporate in Hitler, and with his coming the doctrine of war became supreme in the orthodox confession. In his *"Wehrwissen-*

* *Die Sklaverei, Ihre biologische Begründung und sittliche Rechfertigung.*

schaft" ("Military Science"), published in 1932, Professor Banse states:

"War means the highest intensification not only of the material means only, but of all the spiritual energies of an age as well; it means the utmost effort of the Volk's mental forces and the will of the State towards self-preservation and power. Spirit and Action linked together. Indeed, war provides the ground on which the human soul may manifest itself at its fullest height, in richer forms and surging from more profound wells than it might in any scientific or artistic exploit as such. Nowhere else can the will, the achievements of a Race or a State rise into being thus integrally as in war. War is a purifying bath of steel breeding new impulses, and an infallible test of fitness."

In *"Deutsche Wehr"* it was announced that a state of war was as natural as a state of peace:

"War has become a form of existence with equal rights with peace. Every human and social activity is justified only if it helps prepare for war. The new human being is completely possessed by the thought of war. He must not, he cannot, think of anything else."

And in a speech as early as in May, 1933, von Papen declared that the greatest achievement of Hitler was "to have restored German soldierdom to the center of national thought and given back to the German people the German soldier as a model."

But Hitler was no university professor, not even a scholar. He had no learning and very little knowledge. In his mind there were no critical correctives to the vulgarized edition of the ideas of Fichte, of Hegel, Treitschke, Nietzsche and of Class which he had assimilated and made his own. His imagination was limited, and he saw nothing else. But his greatness has been that he alone of great-power statesmen in Europe understood that the thought precedes the deed, that the spirit is stronger than any material conceptions can measure. That was the strength of his appeal to German idealism in *"Mein Kampf."* He realized that the strongest appeal to the boys and the young men of Germany was not to promise them a good time, but to give them the opportunity of dangerous action, of sacrificing everything for an idol which must appear great to them. He led them up on the high mountain and showed them all the kingdoms of earth and their glory and told them that all this should be given to them if they would kneel and worship him. And they embraced the temptation.

His genius was that he eliminated from the minds of his followers the conception of impossibility. Hundreds of professors had taught the same thing; thousands of teachers had confided them to their pupils; hundreds of thousands had been listening to them—but always in the spirit of wishful thinking, with a self-conscious feeling that these individual and national desires did not belong to the world of realities.

In Hitler's mind there was no doubt. I will it; so it must be. And the millions followed him because he made no reservations, he accepted no compromise. He willed what they had all been dreaming. And they accepted him that their dream might come true.

If those who shall one day formulate the terms of a peace do not understand, as Hitler understood it, that the thought precedes the deed, that the fundamental question is not the manufacture of arms, but the manufacture of a spirit, every sacrifice made by the Western world will have been made in vain.

The practical application of this word by Heine has been entrusted to the German educators, and under the Hitler regime they are more deadly dangerous to the future of any country than is the firing squad.

Consistently and systematically the Nazi leaders everywhere try to get hold of the children and the young girls and boys. The ideas which Aldous Huxley played with in "Brave New World" have been realized in the totalitarian states. Any mass-perversion of children was imperfect as long as homes were castles. But it was assiduously undertaken in Germany.

For years before Nazism, before the last war, children in schools in Germany had to study what was called "Heimatkunde" — "homestead-knowledge." They start quite small by telling about their home, sketching the kitchen, the dining-room, the little garden. Then from class to class the scope is widened; they tell about the village or the town; they sketch the byways and highways of their parish and their county. And as they grow into adolescence they are taught to describe the roads leading to the frontier, to study the bridges, to know what facilities there are in various towns for billeting troops, and so on. And when they pass on to the highest grade, they have to study as "Heimatkunde" the roads leading to Paris, to sketch the strategic bridges, to tell about the crossroads, to explain how many German troops could be quartered in various villages and towns.

Why it was all done was clearly expressed in "Der Deutsche Gedanke in der Welt" ("The German Idea in the World") by Paul Rohrbach (1912).*

The young Germans were all prepared for attack years before Hitler.

It may sometimes be useful to remember that Prussia attacked Denmark in 1848 and in 1864, attacked Austria in 1866, France in 1870. And then in 1914 Germany invaded Belgium and attacked France again, devastated their neighbor states, as no states had been devastated since Carthage. In the hundred years since Napoleon there was

* This book was sold in several hundred thousand copies in Germany, something previously unheard of, and preached that the German idea ought to permeate and finally rule the whole earth, and as the Germans were not popular, German expansion could only be accomplished by force—"Macht," and only those who openly embraced the idea of "Macht-Politik" ought to have any say in Germany.

never war waged on German soil, but the Germans waged war in Denmark, in Russia, in Austria, in Roumania, in Belgium, in France, in Serbia! That they never were "strafed" in their home country may have something to do with their present mentality.

And still there are people who cling to the legend of the peace-loving Germans.

What had been planned in the old Germany, was made possible in the Third Reich with the coming of the state-controlled radio, a dictated press and news-system and the iron-hard state-monopoly of education. It has been made practicable to sacrifice a whole generation to the Moloch of Nazism, and mould the minds of millions of innocent children to the ways of the crook and the criminal.

And all those children are brought up to be spies and soldiers, to be killers, obedient pawns in the hands of the minions of the dictators.

From the earliest days of the totalitarian fight to gain supreme power it was clear to the leaders that schools and universities were strategic points; and that one primary problem was to educate the nation to believe that it was a great blessing to be relieved of the burden of thinking. For years devout Fascists have been accustomed to declare, with an expression of satisfaction: *"Il Duce* thinks for us." The rapidity of the Italian retreat in Africa is nothing compared to the spiritual and intellectual retreat behind the lines pierced three hundred years ago when Descartes started a new advance in the intellectual history of mankind by writing: *"Cogito ergo sum"*—"I think, therefore I am."

A few years ago the former minister of education in Bavaria stated in an address to the schoolteachers of Bavaria:

"We are all zeros; and you can add as many zeros as you want to, they will remain zeros, but put the *Führer* to the left of them and you will get some amount."

And Hitler's famous press chief, Dr. Otto Dietrich in a speech delivered at the University of Cologne in 1935, made the following statement:

"Our fundamental position is: Collectivity against the individual. But that does not apply to the *Führer*. He alone has a right to personality and individuality." *

The strangling of schools and universities started in Italy (in Russia there had never been free or liberal institutions of education). The Fascist minister of education, Mr. Ercole, in November, 1932, sent a circular letter to all leaders of schools, academies and universities in Italy stating:

"The didactic and scientific autonomy of universities has no connection with any kind of tolerance of political and cultural agnosticism, which would be absolutely contrary to the spirit of our régime."

He warns them that every lecture at a university will be under strict control; and in a subsequent circular letter he makes it clear that only members of the party will henceforth be appointed professors and from them would be demanded not lip service, but active work for Fascism.

In September, 1932, the organ of education in Germany, *"Die deutsche Schule"* ("The German School"), stated in a leading article:

"Scientific objectivity . . . is only one of the many errors of liberalism. . . . The liberal man is only an artificial construction. He does not exist in reality; there are only men who belong to a nation and to a specific race."

In the same spirit Dr. Krieck writes in his standard work "National-socialistic Education":

"The epoch of pure science, of science for science, of disinterested science is over."

---

* Quoted from Professor L. Rougier's: *"Les Mystiques politiques contemporaines et leurs Incidences internationales,"* Paris, 1935, p. 90.

And in his speech of inauguration when he was made president of the University of Frankfort-on-the-Main, he declared:

"The idea of humanity has to give place to the idea of race. It is not any objective science which will in the future be our principal objective. The University should be militant and form soldiers."

And Mr. Werner Rudolff, executive director of the organization of professors of higher education, wrote:

"We have to liberate the higher education from the idea that science, as such, is international. . . . We must re-integrate in the race-state scholarly research and education. It can not be permitted any longer that the university has an individual life and that the higher education is free. . . . It is necessary to give to every professor the conviction that the nation is above science and that the scholar has to be German first and scholar afterwards." (*"Der Tag."* "The Day." May 16, 1934.)

In China in the old days the binding of the feet of the girls started when they were eight years old—to keep the feet small and prevent too much liberty of movement among the women of the upper classes. In the empire of the Incas the heads of babies were encased in wooden molds to form them externally in accordance with the idea that particular mental faculties were located at particular spots in the skull, and could be artificially fostered or repressed. On these patterns children are treated in countries claiming to be the most modern. The children are turned into Communists or Nazis long before they start being thinking human beings—in the hope of preventing them from growing up to be such public dangers. Any free human development is prevented in totalitarian states; the government directs a mass production of mental deformities.

The ancients sacrificed children to honor Moloch. The babies were laid in the open arms of the idol; then the hollow statue was made red hot from within until every baby had been consumed. On a grander scale and in a more sinister way this sacrifice of children has now been organized. Their sacred souls, their hope of salvation, are given to Moloch.*

The education in evil starts in the Kindergarten, and is intensified from grade to grade in school. Sometimes it is called "games," sometimes "sport." If Sir Nevile Henderson had one day had a stroke of imagination, he could have seen just outside Berlin the training of the potential invaders of England. The editor of the American quarterly, *Foreign Affairs,* gave his impression in the following words:

"It is hard to think of any part of the program as 'sport.' The twelve-year-old boys I saw one Sunday morning near the Wannsee, gathered in trenches, and solemnly throwing dummy hand grenades at each other, seemed very far away from baseball on the back lot, hockey on the village pond, even from that thin upper crust of spectacular American sport which is publicized and promoted for cash." ("We or They," 1936.)

Things have been moving quickly. When the Nobel Peace Prize for 1926 had been awarded to M. Briand and Mr. Stresemann † Mussolini felt aggrieved that he had been left out; those were the days when Locarno was remembered. And to emphasize his claim, Italy suggested at the League of Nations that all the member states should forbid the manufacture of toy soldiers, because playing with such things tended to cultivate evil and dangerous qualities. When brutality and vulgarity came to supreme power in Germany with Hitler, Italy hurried to follow pace. A notice on the Turin exposition of toys for children in *Gazetta del Popolo* (June 25, 1936) states:

* "Nor does the Moloch ritual really merit contempt." (Franz Haiser.)
† Sir Austen Chamberlain had been awarded the prize for 1925 with General Dawes.

"We are shown many and new products, such as machine-guns for children, mounted on tricycles, small armored cars instead of the usual toy automobiles, and a variety of war material, not expensive, but really amusing."

The fashion was catching. A picture-text sent out by one of the international press-bureaus in 1937 states:

"The most modern plaything for the young generation is a model of an anti-aircraft gun, complete in every detail. That kind of toy will make the citizens of the future airminded and ready to meet any attack, but also brings up the question of the desirability of giving the children real arms of war instead of giving them a more peaceful education."

The desirability, not the moral and social danger, of educating in children a conscious war-mentality!

In one country after another children are taken from their homes and given such an education, are impregnated in such a way that they will probably never be peaceful, thinking citizens. And the small disciples of Moloch are called in Germany *"Jungvolk"* and *"Hitler-jugend"*; in Italy *"Figli della Lupa," "Balilla"* and *"Avanguardisti"*; in Russia *"Octobrists,"* "Pioneers" and *"Komsomol."*

The whole school system has been remodeled to serve the same purpose.

Early in 1941 an Associated Press dispatch from Cairo stated that the Egyptian Ministry of Education had forbidden the use of Italian textbooks of arithmetic in Egypt, because they had a deplorable influence on the minds of the children. And a good many people exclaimed: 'Allied war hysteria!" They should study the documents. The Italian textbooks have been modeled on the German pattern, and their way of teaching children to do sums is remarkable. Here is one typical instance from a German schoolbook:

"Daybombers can move with a speed of 280 kilometers (175 miles) an hour. Night bombers can only make 240 kilometers (150 miles) an hour. How many hours would be needed for each class of bombers to cover the distance between: 1) Breslau and Prague; 2) between Munich and Strasbourg; 3) between Kiel and Metz?"

And, of course, in the German textbooks in science there are special chapters called "school experiments in war-chemistry."

The official German teachers' manual, published by the minister for schools and national education, Dr. Bernhard Rust, explains:

"Democracies base their education on the doctrine that man is a being who has reached perfection through culture. This grievous mistake, monstrous as it is, is superseded by another —the illusion that spiritual culture can provide a nation with the stability which in reality can be obtained only through the political deeds of a great personality." *

On another page the manual states:

"A wide cultural knowledge, a broad education in various phases of learning, dulls the senses; a general assortment of information weakens, does not strengthen; too much universal learning tires the mind, paralyzes the will-power and the ability to make decisions."

Those who are desirous of more details will find a wealth of interesting information in Gregor Ziemer's "Education for Death" (Oxford University Press, New York, 1941).

Those men and women who are still fighting for appeasement, for what has been called "a negotiated peace" —they have started calling it a "democratic peace" now— do they desire every nation to educate its children on the German pattern and look upon bombing, machine-gunning, gas-poisoning as natural things to be taught at school? Do they think that democratic countries can ever

---

* It is not Hitler as Hitler who is essential to the German conception. It is Hitler as Führer—it is the *leader-principle*. And if Hitler passed away today the principle would go on and the next leader be deified.

be safe when a great power is systematically and intensely giving all children what Dr. Rust calls an education "of Might"? Or do those "mothers" who unwittingly have been organized as a spearhead-guard for the cult of Moloch, do they believe it possible for any free civilization to exist when in one group of states children are educated to aggression, assault, manslaughter, and in another group to a whimpering refusal to sacrifice any item of their convenience to defend the ideas and principles for which their forefathers fought and died?

Is it still impossible to make them understand that the German leader means it literally when he states:

"Must not the struggle continue until the final domination of a single nation? . . . At the back of Germany's continental empire stands the will of absolute domination of the world, the technical means of which are no longer lacking as hitherto."

So the Germans try, in every country they have invaded, to permeate the church, the school and the universities. Even if Dr. Rosenberg proclaims that only Germans can be members of his new "Reich Church," in occupied countries independent ministers of the gospel are dismissed where there is a state church, as in Norway, or they are sent to concentration camps, or they disappear. The Bible is "purged" and in every way it is attempted to make renegade priests preach Nazism. University professors are persecuted if they refuse to teach what they are ordered to teach; new men, scholarly and scientifically utterly unqualified, are appointed to take the places of those who are honestly seeking the truth. In the schools young Nazi bandits force their way into the classrooms and flog teachers and students; a system of school-espionage is introduced. And boys and young men are invited or ordered to go to Germany, study the new order and come back to their home countries as emissaries of the Goebbels-Rosenberg gospel.

In every territory invaded the Germans have given power to cranks off their mental balance, and to the most contemptible persons who have followed the Nazi invitation to coöperate with the oppressors against the free institutions of their native land. They attach the highest importance to leading the minds of the children into the authorized channels of Nazi thought—and it can not start early enough *—educating them to their own standards of international responsibility and reliability and making the moral language of their fathers a foreign and unintelligible tongue to them.

That is why the American Commission to Study the Organization of Peace has put as a separate post on its program "False Indoctrination." Millions of young persons have been indoctrinated during the past decade into beliefs contrary to the moral principles upon which civilization has been builded; they will be twisted in mind and in spirit. And the Commission agrees that "there will be a great problem of reeducation: many teachers must be trained, many others must be re-trained."

And, since the German system of education is the life-nerve of Nazism, no agreement can be made and no peace is possible until this whole structure of Nazism is broken down, the reign of terror of Hitler, Himmler and Heydrich forced to an end, and the ground cleared in Germany once more for the slow upbuilding of those fundamentals of civilization which have so ruthlessly been demolished by men to whom the very idea of the moral obligations of civilization was abhorrent and a meaningless obstruction.

* The youngest child to have been called in and examined by the Gestapo in Oslo, was a three-year-old boy who had thrown a withered flower against the windshield of a German car. His parents were solemnly admonished to inspire him with the Nazi spirit.

VII: German Lebensraum and the Americas

The Fichte-Hegel-Nietzsche conception of *the German Mission,* of a state with a divine right to demand everything from the individuals, of the blond, German superman * who is called upon to rule the world, has been the *Leitmotiv* of German sentiment since the victory over France in 1870.

After the arrival of Hitler and his satellites, it has become an obsession, part of their general demonolatry, inoculated in the blood of the children, but the pre-Nazi literature proclaiming the law-bound necessity of unlimited German expansion is overwhelming. Only the leaders of opinion in America, England and France were eyeless in Gaza, they did grind in the prison house of the doctrines of materialism, studying statistical data and small political moves, but never asked what spirit was preparing the whole German nation for action.

From 1874 von Treitschke was lecturing at the University of Berlin and thundering in the Reichstag; his popularity was enormous and his influence even more so. He coolly declared that since Germany will never be able to understand the world, "the world must be conquered and reformed so that it will be able to conform to German thought." (*"Die Politik,"* 1876.) But he doubted that other

---

* Who is not necessarily very blond. When jokes were still tolerated in Germany, they used to describe the typical Aryan: Blond like Hitler, strong like Goebbels, slender like Goering.

94

nations were reformable and later wrote that Germany can never have peace with the world because to the German way of thought it is "a foreign world which cannot be reformed, but can only be overthrown." He was the first great open exponent of the mailed-fist doctrine; he claimed that Germany's destiny was to conquer and dominate the world and to hold the nations in thralldom ("the geographical predestination"). There is no other force than the will of the State, and a Germany "rightly constituted can recognize no earthly power, and might is right only when a German wields the sword." (*Die Politik.*) "Germany must make it a duty to employ traitors in the enemy state for its own interests," and "every good German subject is a latent, and when opportunity arises, an active spy."

And Treitschke, advocating that lying and deceit are foundation stones for German foreign policy, declares that treaties are mere scraps of paper and urges that they "can and must be denounced by Germany whenever the promise they hold becomes unprofitable to her." In such a case a treaty becomes automatically obsolete, and "German honor" demands that it be broken.

One of the results of his influence was the action taken in 1881 by the German General School Association to spread the cult of Germanism in foreign countries. This organization, which still exists as the notorious German "Ausland Organization," well known to the F. B. I., was later maintained by the Pan-German league. The league (as mentioned p. 80) was started in 1886 by the famous explorer, Dr. Karl Peters, as *"Der alldeutsche Verband"* (the all-German League) to propagate the teachings of Treitschke wherever Germans lived.

It seems symbolic that Peters should have been the father of this Bund. He was Gestapo brutality incarnate before the Gestapo, and in 1897 he was courtmartialed for cruelty and dismissed.

Professor Ernst Hasse in 1891 succeeded him as president of the League, which in 1894 changed its name to the Pan-German League (*Pangermanische Bund*). The whole time it has been active for world-conquest by Germany, and its program of action was taken over, nearly unchanged, by the Nazis.

One of the principles of the Bund was that "Germanism across the seas must be preserved and fostered by every possible means." (Adolf Lehr: *"Zwecke und Ziele des alldeutschen Bundes,"* "Ends and Aims of the Pan-German Bund"). And "across the seas" more than anything else meant America. For half a century now, with patience and consistency, the Germans have tried to build up in every country in the Americas what is today called a fifth column.

The number of German books predicting the triumph of this work is legion, and they go back to years long before the last war. One writer, publishing his book in 1895 (*"Germania triumphans, Von einem Grossdeutschen"*), foresees a German world victory as early as 1915, when it has become necessary for Germany to wipe out "the doctrine of Pan-America"; and the peace following after this war he describes as follows:

"Germany took Mexico, Guatemala, British Honduras, all Brazil south of the Amazon, Uruguay, Paraguay, Bolivia, Peru and northern Chile. France took Brazil north of the Amazon, British Guiana, Venezuela, Colombia and Ecuador. Italy took what was left of South America, including the Argentine. The West Indies were divided between Germany and France. Gibraltar was restored to Spain, Malta given to Italy, Cyprus to Turkey. The English had to pay an enormous indemnity. There was great discontent in England because the entire British navy was held by the Germans as a guarantee of payment. All England's Suez Canal shares were confiscated and distributed among the victorious nations. The Kimberley diamond mines were seized by Germany and all English and American capital invested in Brazil and South America was transferred to German hands. The cable lines were taken by

Germany and all English and American colonists were ordered to leave South America within a year, never to be permitted to settle in any country on that continent again."

Another "Great German" writing in 1900 does not think the final triumph will come until 1950 when there will be a Great World-Germany and "everybody is happy because all the Germans are now united and are ruling the world." (*"Gross Deutschland und Mitteleuropa um das Jahr 1950"*—"Great Germany and Central Europe in the year 1950").

During the last fifty years German men of letters and of politics * have been constantly assaulting the Monroe Doctrine. The great Mommsen called it "an empty pretension"; Professor Hasse declared in the Reichstag that if the Monroe Doctrine should be allowed to be enforced "the grave of Germanism lies in America."

In 1903 Johannes Volert declared (*"Alldeutsche Blätter,"* Jan. 17): "The Monroe Doctrine is indefensible. It is a direct impertinence and all the more so as America is lacking the means to enforce its application."

Time and again the factual policy of Germany gave evidence that the words of Mr. Volert expressed the leading current in Germany. The Kaiser tried to prevent the Spanish-American War and first planned a Great Power mediation. When that failed he turned to the Pope. It is not a trick of this war when the enemies of all religion try to make the churches work for them. "It is now known that the proffered mediation of the Pope was urged at Rome by the German Foreign Office which was anxious to prevent the war because it might interfere with the German project for purchasing the Spanish islands in the Pacific, including the Philippines." (Walter Flagg Bemis: "A Diplomatic History of America," 1936, p. 447.)

---

* It is sometimes hard to know when a professor speaks ex cathedra or from the rostrum. Treitschke, Mommsen, Hasse and v. Schmoller were all members of the Prussian or Reichs parliament.

And Germany acquired part of Samoa in 1899.

In the following years German interest was focused on Venezuela: "The attention of Europe and America was drawn to Venezuela a second time in 1902 when Germany made a carefully planned and determined effort to test out the Monroe Doctrine and see whether we would fight for it." (John A. Latané: "A History of American Foreign Policy," revised edition, 1934, p. 488.)

It might also be worthwhile to remember that at the Hague Peace Conferences it was the German delegation that worked against universal enforced arbitration because Germany was so well armed and had so efficient and quick-working a machinery of mobilization that Germany would lose by accepting the principles of arbitration.

A generation ago Americans knew their facts and Germany was not popular in Washington. The Pan-Germans had to change their tactics. But no prophetic gifts were needed to look through the camouflage. One of the leaders of public opinion, Dr. Paul Rohrbach, wrote in his book *"Deutschland unter den Weltvölkern"* ("Germany among the World Nations"):

"Does any one think that Germany likes saying nice things to the United States, or that they are the outpourings of a loving heart? She only says them because Germany must eradicate the suspicions with which Americans regard her policy."

German headquarters instructed their compatriots in the United States to lie low and "so organize and educate the German element in the country that political power will finally fall in its lap." (Professor Hasse.) "Germans must abandon all attempts to take sides on Democratic and Republican matters and form themselves into a national political party." Professor Münsterberg, who lectured at Harvard for years, added that the Germans should build a state within the state in the United States, and Dr. Julius Goebel in his *"Das Deutschtum in den Verein-*

igten Staaten" (Germanism in the USA) advocated that the Germans should try to infect Americans, especially those of Irish extraction, with their own hatred of England.

But if the Germans were advised to take it comparatively easily with the United States, not so in South America. "The more Germany is condemned to an attitude of passive resistance towards the United States, the more emphatically must she defend her interests in Central and South America. For this purpose we need a fleet capable not only of coping with the miserable forces of the South American states, but powerful enough to cause the Americans to think twice before making any attempt to apply the Monroe Doctrine in South America." (Professor Schulze-Gaevernitz, *"Die Nation,"* March 5, 1898.)

Dr. Paul Rohrbach made it clear that the strategic country in South America was Brazil:

"Although the United States may possibly prevent the acquisition of South American territory by Germany, it cannot prevent the creation of a state within a state, and that when the Germans have finally accomplished that deed, they would rule the roost in Brazil and rule over the inferior peoples of that country."

Dr. Kappf in his booklet about "German Schools" advocates the same line of policy:

"Germans in South Brazil had better become Brazilian citizens as that is the quickest and surest way to obtain political power. The danger to Germanism in South America comes from North America, and it is not only a question of commercial interests. Is Germany going to stand idly by if America sets about the task of Americanizing that continent? Germany cannot; she must proclaim, *urbi et orbi,* that she is determined to maintain her rights in South America. And Brazil holds out the most buoyant hope for the German and the spread of Germanism."

In his *"Handels und Macht-politik"* ("Trade and Power Policy") Professor Gustav von Schmoller declared, "At all cost a German country must grow up in the twentieth century in Brazil." And Professor Wolf expressed as his opinion: "South America for the German is the land of the future, for that land holds greater promise for the Germans than Europe or Africa."

And as long ago as in 1899 Dr. Unfold predicted:

"The time will assuredly come when Germany, during the confusion caused by some international conflagration, will have the opportunity to acquire colonial territory in South America." ("*Das Deutschtum in Chile.*" "Germanism in Chile.")

All the efforts in the various countries were coördinated in Berlin; and with the triumph of Hitlerism it became one of the main points on the agenda of the German consulates everywhere to become centers of the underground work for German infiltration.

Those who did not understand that the danger to America was real, did not want to understand. When German leaders had planned to seize Uruguay as a German colony in the fall of 1940, and the plan leaked out, the prosecuting attorney drew up an indictment against the Nazi party in Uruguay (here quoted from the *New York Times* of September 23, 1940); and some of the paragraphs of this illuminating document have a particular interest:

1. The German National Socialist Labour Party, N.S.D.A.P., exists in Uruguay.
2. This party is a section of the same party which under the same name functions as the only party in Germany.
3. The union between the two is maintained by the foreign organization of the N.S.D.A.P. through the German Ministry of Foreign Affairs.
4. Our country, for the territorial purposes of the party's organization abroad, is considered as a district ("Gau").
7. The party is one with the Government in the same way that the Government is one with the will of the Fuehrer. The party is the Government itself.

18. Members of the party take an oath of fidelity and obedience to the Fuehrer and to the party leaders chosen by the Fuehrer. The oath is administered even in this country, by the party's chief (Gauleiter).

20. In the political and territorial organization there exists the district of Uruguay, which forms a part of the overseas Gau. Within this district there are the subparty of Montevideo and "support points" at Penarol, Rincon de Bonete and Paysandu. Within these organizations are the minor groups of cells and blocs.

21. The political leaders—the district Fuehrer, sub-party chiefs and support-point leaders—who are considered to possess sovereign power over party members, are appointed by E. W. Bohle, head of the party's foreign organization in Germany.

22. Within this territorial and political organization there functions the sectional parties and associated groups, such as the Storm Troops, the Hitler Youth Movement, the German Women's League, the League of Nazi School Teachers, the Winter Relief Movement, the Movement for the Aid of German Minorities in Non-German Countries, the German Engineers Association and the German Labour Front.

24. Teachers of German schools operating in Uruguay are appointed by the party's foreign organization in Germany.

25. It has been proved that in at least one school in the interior of Uruguay Nazi holidays are celebrated and pupils are taught reverence for the names of party leaders in Germany, almost to worship the Fuehrer, and also the dogma of Germany's greatness.

28. The plan for the attack against Uruguay contains measures tending to insure the functioning of our country as a German agricultural colony without delay or quibbling, the plan being similar in this respect to those put into effect by the Germans in their recent conquests.

29. In our country there are united in one person the duties of Fuehrer for the district of Uruguay and those of attaché of the German Legation.

Does anybody believe that the rules of German overseas organization apply to Uruguay alone? Does anybody dare to profess that North America does not belong to a German Gau, or that the work of preparation, as in Uruguay, has not been going on for years?

The rounding up of spy rings in the U. S. A. in 1942 has given a confirmation that should hardly have been needed. But until Pearl Harbor, influential circles refused to admit that Nazism could constitute a danger to the U. S. A.

Can anybody doubt that the German ambassador to Argentina has been a careful student of the various books on German infiltration and of Deutschtum in South America, when in the beginning of 1941, after a visit to Germany, he made his statement to the press in Buenos Aires? "He warned Argentina that her trade relations with the United States have no future and that American aid to Great Britain is only a British dream. The Ambassador cautioned Argentina not to forget Japan, which is now on 'our' side." (Quoted from the *New York Times* of February 27, 1941.) And having explained that Germany and not the United States will conduct the principal trade with Argentina in the future, the Ambassador hardly veiled the threat to Argentina in the last words of his message to the press:

"For these reasons I hope there will be maintained here an indispensable common respect for our nationals, who have contributed to the creation of industries and commerce and have given their active life to this young nation."

In the light of recent developments it is of some interest what happened at the International Labour Conference in 1933 when the notorious Dr. Ley had his credentials challenged and the South American delegations led the opposition against Nazism. The incident is told by Mr. Harold Butler in the following way:

"The position was not sweetened by an interview which he gave in an exhilarated post-prandial mood to the German-speaking press, in which he described the Latin-American delegates as 'niggers out of the primeval forest.' Not a word of this diplomatic pronouncement was allowed to appear in the press of the Reich, but the cat was let triumphantly out of the bag by a labour paper in Danzig, which was not under Nazi control. Then the trouble began. After an angry meeting the Latin-American governments threatened to leave the Conference unless the German delegation apologized.

"Hectic telephoning to Berlin ensued and the Germans issued a total denial of Dr. Ley's utterance. But the Latin-Americans knew too much and refused to accept the démenti. A deadlock was reached and many confabulations followed. The Germans accused everyone else of a breach of diplomatic etiquette on the characteristic ground that whatever their government said must be true. In the end, however, they returned hurriedly to Berlin, after the first open clash between the doctrines of freedom and totalitarianism." ("The Lost Peace." pp. 21-22.)

Gregor Ziemer in his book gives a fairly good idea of the way in which Nazism looks upon America and tells that the Hitler jugend have organizations in fifty-two foreign countries including the United States—and the great South American countries. The Hitler Youth Foreign Office annually sent 6,000 boys to foreign countries. He tells of the S. A. groups * meeting in the beer halls and drinking the toast: *"Bomben uber New York"* (Bombs over New York)! And he quotes one of the most popular songs about America which gives a fairly good picture both of Nazi humour, of Nazi refinement and of Nazi sentiment. Some stanzas will illustrate:

"America, America,
     Oh, Jewish land, America.
     You certainly conceited are;
     A big fat pig, that's what you are.
     America, America,
     Oh, Jewish land, America.

"America, America,
     Oh, Jewish land, America.

* S. A. means *Sturm Abteilung* (Storm Troopers—Brown shirts.)

You are diseased, you are a dupe,
You are naive, a nincompoop.
America, America,
Oh, Jewish land, America.

"America, America,
Oh, Jewish land, America.
New Germany sends warnings clear,
The day of vengeance is quite near.
America, America,
Oh, Jewish land, America.

"America, America,
Oh, Jewish land, America.
New Germany is calling, Fie!
Democracy, you cur, you'll die!
America, America,
Oh, Jewish land, America.

"America, America,
Oh, Jewish land, America.
And with you falls, remember now,
Your Rosenfeldt, the Yiddish sow.
America, America,
Oh, Jewish land, America."

VIII: Freedom from Mental Disturbance

If there shall be any hope of a lasting peace it will be necessary to establish among nations that freedom from mental disturbance which is an indispensable condition for international stability. Not only in the world of abstract philosophy and in education but also in the sphere of practical politics the thought precedes the action. Only when this is recognized will come the realization that more important to the world order than the fixation of political boundaries will be the fixation of educational boundaries. Lines of demarcation must be established to ward off the systematic offensive of school systems which would lead to mental disturbance on a national scale.

Years ago Hitler stated his educational objective in these words:

"I shall eradicate the thousands of years of human domestication. I want to see again in the eyes of youth the gleam of the beast of prey. A youth will grow up before which the world will shrink."

The world has shrunk; and the world must take steps to keep the Hitlerian young men and women in the reformatories until they are domesticated once more. Reluctantly and belatedly politicians and diplomats have been forced to realize the fact that as children are taught at schools and universities, so will they act in national and international life; and it will be a fundamental task for those responsible for the post-war order to find ways and means to stem the tides of war at their tiny springs.

These things cannot be discussed with the present-day rulers of any totalitarian power, or any delegate representing a Nazi system, any more than the tints and the values of a great picture can be discussed with a color-blind person. It is not that he does not understand our standards; he denies their very existence. Similarly we do not understand the German conception of the world or the Japanese conception.

When the Japanese solemnly and literally believe that they are the descendants of Amaterasu-O-Mi-Kami, the Sun Goddess; when their soldiers at war in moments of distress turn toward Japan and invoke the intervention of the Goddess and commit hara-kari if Amaterasu-O-Mi-Kami turns her face away—our minds can not follow them. What is normal to them is mental disturbance to us, or rather it seems an atavistic return to conceptions extinct in our mental world for more than two thousand years.

During the time when the Manchurian Commission of the League of Nations was at work in the Orient, a pamphlet was distributed to all Japanese soldiers and officers giving the national version of an incident that happened on September 18, 1931, when Chinese soldiers, unsuccessfully, had tried to blow up a railway line. A Japanese lieutenant, "a direct descendant of an uninterrupted line of Samurai ancestors of forty-eight generations," then turned to the Goddess and asked her to intervene:

"His humble and fervent prayer was heard. The train reached the spot where the lines had been destroyed, raised itself in the air, and having passed the dangerous point, gently came down again on the other side of the railway line and continued on its way. The testimony of the driver and the fireman of the train, as well as of Lieutenant Kawamoto and his six soldiers, who saw this event with their own eyes, is sufficient to prove the truth of this supernatural fact—a fact which has once again demonstrated for the whole world the divine origin of the Japanese people."

Such official declarations of the divine character of the Japanese are current in Japan. In a pamphlet issued in the summer of 1925 by the Japanese Naval Ministry it is stated:

"If the other powers fail to recognize the Mission of Japan they may well be said to disobey the will of Heaven."

In another pamphlet distributed to Japanese soldiers with instructions for using dope to corrupt the Chinese functionaries and officers it is stated:

"The use of narcotics is unworthy of a superior race like the Japanese. Only inferior races that are decadent like the Chinese, Europeans and the East Indians are addicted to the use of narcotics. This is why they are destined to become our slaves and eventually disappear."

It would be a dangerous illusion to believe that any peace can be durable as long as nations are being brought up to this idea that it is their heavenly mission to enslave the rest of the world.

In many interested quarters there is a growing realization that one of the main reasons why the last peace was never really won was the lack of adequate education: school education and adult education. In the Weimar Constitution given to Germany after the First World War, Article 148 stipulated as one of the educational aims of the German school "the cultivation . . . of the spirit of international reconciliation." This very wise provision, if it had been carried out, might have proved a paving stone toward the winning of the peace. But the Weimar Republic was given no support by the Allied Powers, and Article 148 was looked upon as high treason by the teachers and by the military caste in Germany. After Weimar came Hitler. He, at least, understood the importance of education. The mental development in Germany is well summarized by Mr. Harold Butler, one of the few Englishmen with a thorough and intimate knowledge of German life:

"The kernel of his whole effort has been to uproot every democratic seedling in German life. He has done it with characteristic thoroughness and ruthlessness, and it would be foolish to suppose that he has not largely succeeded. Every official, every university teacher, every schoolmaster with a tinge of liberal sentiment, was summarily ejected, unless he could give plain proof of his conversion to the Nazi creed. No newspaper, no book, no film, no play was tolerated which did not harmonize with the Nazi view of life. Every instrument of education and propaganda was turned to its inculcation. Fairy stories and schoolbooks were rewritten, science was falsified, economics and history travestied, in order to ensure that no word of any other doctrine should penetrate into the minds of the young. . . . The whole object of their system of education was to eradicate individualism and independent thinking." ("The Lost Peace," p. 115.)

As a result of this process the world is faced with the double-sided problem of curing, if possible, an existing epidemic mental disturbance and of preventing the outbreak of new epidemics:

"After the fighting stops, young Germans with their warped minds and misshapened ideas and attitudes, will present one of the most tragic and difficult problems in post-war reconstruction. Their reëducation will be among the most crucial tasks of those determined to insure a lasting peace." (Walter M. Kotschnig: "Problems of Education after the War," "International Conciliation," 379, p. 243.)

While the massing of German youth for mental disturbance was allowed to go on unimpeded and unnoticed, no constructive educational effort in the international field was made in the great democratic countries; and, as Mr. Butler points out, the new world order which should have been inaugurated with the organization of the League of Nations "could only have been effected by an intensive and persistent campaign of education conducted by the national leaders."

In this field of national and international education, what we have called the peace intelligence service will have its first and most obvious task. The existing International Institute of Intellectual Coöperation with its network of Committees in practically every country must be reorganized and strengthened and establish its own peace patrol. Nations have united to fight dangerous drugs and have established a most successful organ of worldwide control. Spiritual dope, the use of which can only result in mental disturbance, constitutes an even more mortal menace to mankind than narcotics derived from poppy, from coca and from hemp, but it will be easier to control any large-scale traffic in spiritual dope; for in this case the illegitimate trade that can be carried on would not be very extensive: great publicity is indispensable for widespread obnoxious effects. A system of reports from national supervisory bodies to an international central board must be instituted. And this board must be coördinated with other organs of international control and power.

Part of the work will be a superintendence of textbooks used in schools. This, of course, is no new idea. In most countries no such book can be used without being duly authorized by the national department of education. Even the idea of some kind of international control of certain categories of textbooks is not entirely new; and to a certain extent an experiment has already been made.

No countries of Europe have waged war against each other for a longer period than the Northern countries. For more than a thousand years no century passed without long and devastating wars between Norway and Sweden, or Sweden and Denmark, or Denmark and Norway. The last war terminated in the fall of 1814.

One of the natural results of this long-standing enmity

was that the histories of wars and warriors were not taught in exactly the same way in Denmark, Norway and Sweden. Prejudice, resentment, seeds of hatred, were cultivated at school when children were taught history.

Some years ago a joint commission of scholars was appointed in those countries to study the textbooks of history used in the schools. It was found that there were some slight differences in the presentation of facts. The results of the investigation carried out was a recommendation that any line in any such book which might hurt the feelings of children in any of the other two countries, should be suppressed or rewritten, and that historical facts should be presented in a similar way to schoolchildren in all those countries. These recommendations were carried out with excellent results.

A good deal of interest for the action taken in the Northern countries was created on the League of Nations, and especially at the International Institute for Intellectual Coöperation working in Paris under the auspices of the League of Nations. Everybody could see the implications of universal action taken along this line. There was no difficulty in seeing what it would mean for international relations, if, for instance, the factual history of the war of 1870-1871 and of the last great war, could be presented in the same way to students in German and in French schools —or in anticipating some improvements in Anglo-Irish relations if the same facts in Anglo-Irish history were told in the same manner in schools in England and in Ireland. A wise man has said that the difficulties in Anglo-Irish-American relations arise from the fact that the English can never remember history, the Irish can never forget history, and the Americans were never taught history. Now, if they all had to learn the same history taught in the same spirit of understanding, it would not take any unconscionably long time before the difficulties would be minimized.

Of course, the idea of any kind of international control of certain aspects of education was not accepted with enthusiasm by Great Power representatives when discussed in League circles. It was suggested as an alternative that in French and German textbooks of history should be printed on one page the French version of the Napoleonic wars, the War of 1870 and the Great War of 1914 to 1918, and on the opposite page the German version, to give the students the valuable knowledge that historical facts can be given different interpretations. Or that the books could be printed with three columns, giving in the middle the objective and factual story of what really did happen, in accordance with the Chinese saying "that there are three sides to every question, your side, my side and the right side."

There is a long way from agreeing in principle to certain theories and putting them into practice. National feelings can always be whipped up against any idea of international control in what is deemed internal matters. But, unwillingly, the world has had to learn that it is not a matter of domestic policy if in Germany, systematically, the entire youth of that country is brought up to the conviction—and it may sometimes be said enthusiastic and idealistic conviction—that Germany is called upon to rule the world and subjugate every other nation, or an internal Japanese concern if all young men are taught that eventually, under the will of Heaven, all other nations must become their slaves.

It is not an internal matter if any great nation ruthlessly is educated to believe that between states there exists no moral, no right, no binding obligation.

Nazism has set out to create "a new order" in the world; if the old order had been perfect, no such attempt would have had the slightest chance of success. But it is not unreasonable to admit that things might have been better ordered, nationally and internationally. No active pro-

gram can be successfully combated only through a nega-
tion. If democracies want to survive, they must remember
that democracy is yet in the making—and will always be in
the making. Democracy must be recreated in every generation and adapted to new requirements, must constantly
strive towards a new order. National democracies must
combine to establish an international democracy. And one
of the first steps towards a better international order is to
prevent, through enlightened education, the artificial
breeding of hatred and prejudice.

Not only supervision of textbooks will be needed. It
will be necessary to give schoolchildren an idea of world
solidarity, international collaboration and the whole network of conventions and treaties which are the fibers of
modern civilized life. So much is told of wars and battles;
the importance of military action is usually vastly exaggerated in the minds of young people. But in very few
countries are the modest but far-reaching peaceful vic-
tories of the constructive spirit of mankind recorded in
textbooks and taught at school.

It should be obligatory for teachers to be well versed in
these things; and in all textbooks of history should be told
how, for instance, the Universal Postal Union and the
Telegraphic Union were brought about, how the Jay
Treaty was the first treaty between sovereign states to
stipulate that if friction arose over questions of frontiers
and borderlines, they should be arbitrated and not decided
by belligerent action. Something should be told them
about the Hague Conventions that are still the international law of warfare, and about the Permanent Court of
Arbitration at the Hague and how it was brought into
practical existence by an action of the United States Government. They should know the thrilling story of international drug control and how it materialized, about the
League of Nations, the International Labour Office and
the Permanent Court of Justice, about such things as the

London Convention for Safety of Life at Sea and the International Health Service.

It is only because there has been a void in education that Isolationalism has become a power in certain countries.

"Criticism, whether friendly or unfriendly," wrote the then Secretary General of the League of Nations in the London *Spectator,* in November, 1928, "can not endanger the League; ignorance may." His words apply to all international collaboration.

And education is not confined to schools and universities. It is a continuous unconscious process and can be influenced in many ways. In all the allied countries was instituted after World War I the cult at the grave of the unknown soldier. It was an educational program well conceived. When this war is over the monuments to be erected should be to honor the victim and not the victor, monuments to the unknown homes that have been bombed and annihilated, to the unnamed men, women and children who have been tortured and slain, monuments that will create in the mind of the spectator the instant and spontaneous, passionate, if inarticulate, desire that "none of the nightmare may happen again."

Not only children have to be educated, but ordinary men and women.

Mr. Harold Butler in his book describes one aspect of this problem in the following words:

"The man in the street had been taught at school to look on the world as a collection of perfectly separated states, each of which ran a lonely, selfish race against all the others. Even if some devil did occasionally catch the hindmost, every runner felt that all was well as long as he escaped. The average citizen of every nation had never been taught to think of himself as a member of a world society with obligations to it similar to those which he owed to his town or his country." ("The Lost Peace," pp. 35-36.)

Education is a slow process. But it must be one of the first items on the program of action of the United Nations. It cannot wait for a final peace conference. It must be included in the terms of an armistice, if indeed there shall be an armistice. Maybe, fighting must go on until Nazism can fight no longer. And it will take a long time before the final terms of the complex of peace treaties can be established. There will be treaties of a universal character. And there must be a *de facto* council of administration for great parts of the world. Every single question will have to be studied scientifically, in the light of the fullest possible information and in an unbiased, disinterested, and completely unsentimental way. And from the very start it must be made clear that this time full consideration will be given to moral and educational questions. In their solution, in the earnest desire to solve them will be the only possibility of a dynamic peace, a just and durable peace.

If delegates meet with the preconceived idea that politics is the art of the possible, they had better not meet at all. Hitler has proved to an astounded world that a policy can triumph just because it never stops at the possible.

The program of the peace conference must be to do the impossible. And those who lose the first conflicts of the peace should be shown no more consideration than generals who lose their battles. Mankind is on the march toward a new and better international order. Delegates must know beforehand that if they lag behind, the march will not be stopped. They are under the orders of the French Foreign Legion to "march or rot."

IX: Education for Democracy

It is not difficult to see the shortcomings and the crude fallacy of the totalitarian philosophy. It is easy to understand that there can be no stable peace if nations are allowed to make their education the base and the runway of aggression, the inexhaustible arsenal of international hatred and disturbance. But something more is needed than merely taking note of this fact.

Let no man believe that the German armies are fighting because they are forced to by the Gestapo, that the young men attack so ruthlessly because they are desperately in fear of being shot by their officers. They fight because German education has succeeded in creating the spirit which renders a people capable of bearing arms. They fight because German education has taught them to believe without faltering that life can offer them nothing greater than to die for Germany. They fight; they do not evacuate and they do not surrender. Their education has bred in their blood the passionate conviction that it is worth fighting for German domination of the world.

If democratic education does not succeed in rendering our peoples capable of bearing arms, if it does not breed in the blood of the young men and women a deeper and more passionate conviction of the eternal values of life than that instilled in the totalitarian youth, democracies will not survive as democracies when this war is won. If democratic education cannot produce valiant soldiers of peace, builders of new freedom, men of willing and glad sacrifice, we can never win a lasting peace.

A well-meaning clergyman was preaching in a youth camp somewhere in the U. S. A., to a gathering of boys, and the leitmotiv of his sermon was "and all this Christ will give you just for nothing."

Hundreds of ministers and of teachers are telling young people the same story. And in that story lies the whole failure of democracy, the disease of democratic education; the secret of democratic unpreparedness. Well-meaning politicians have been so busily discussing how to make the world safe for democracy that they entirely have forgotten the importance of making democracy safe for the world. And as long as popular leaders believe and announce that the final aim of our efforts is to get something for just nothing, as long as they try to sell both democracy and religion on this idea, democracy is not safe for the world.

In most democratic countries people have taken democracy for granted, they have taken the four freedoms for granted, as part of their heritage. Their forefathers at one time were willing to pledge their property, their lives, their sacred honor to win a democratic freedom; and so no sacrifice can be demanded from their grandchildren and grandchildren's grandchildren. But a man can no more be born to democracy than he can be born to a religion. He may be born to certain dispositions, facilities and usages, but he has to acquire for himself the vital truths and the vital force. Democracy can never be static. What was democracy a hundred and fifty years ago, may be a fossilized tradition today; the liberty of old may be vested privilege now.

In the springtime of democracy when our forefathers were drafting their declarations of independence and their liberal constitutions, they turned their thoughts to the State in terms like these: What can I give to make this new Commonwealth of ours strong? What shall be my contribution? What sacrifice is demanded from me?

When modern legislators in democratic countries turn

their thoughts to the State it is to ask: What can I get out of the State? For my constituency and for myself?

When a candidate for nomination goes round electioneering it is not customary for him to tell his constituents that they may be requested to give up something; that they have to make a contribution toward the welfare of the State; that they have to contemplae what they can sacrifice. His prospects of being elected would be small indeed in most democratic countries if he made that kind of speech. But the man who can come back from any capital and bring to his constituency a new penitentiary, or a bridge, or a post office, or a munition plant, or a lunatic asylum, is considered a good and smart representative.

It is common in democracies to hear people complain of the kind of representatives they have got. The term "politician" has a derogatory implication. More particularly in the United States of America it is confusing and rather disconcerting for any believer in democracy to listen when people are discussing their politicians. A recent article by the serious and interesting columnist Samuel Grafton was opened with the following statement:

"This Congress bleats piteously that it does not get enough respect from the country, and, in sober truth, we have reached the point where the only man who takes off his hat to the average congressman is his secretary."

Even if this bitter paradox has a comparatively high percentage of exaggeration it certainly shows that something is very wrong with the system of educating for democracy. And it brings into high relief an opinion held by a good many people and supported by such authorities as Mr. Herbert Hoover and Mr. Hugh Gibson in their "Problems of Lasting Peace": that only countries with a representative government should have access to an international organization of states. Does anybody believe that it will be easy to persuade nations whose pattern of government is

different from our democratic pattern that they must win
this war in order to get the kind of representatives Mr.
Gratton describes? Or do we recognize that making democracy safe for the world starts at home?

Not only the congressmen are criticized. It is a constant
complaint that the church has lost its influence; that if
only the churches had been what they should have been
the present war would have been impossible. If democracies had been what they should have been a world conflict would have been impossible. All this is quite correct.
And if human beings had been perfect and without sin
the world would have been an entirely different place.
But these people who complain, what kind of representatives would they like? The man of unimpeachable integrity who would tell them that sacrifices were needed, or the
kind of man who would be amenable and "see reason"?
And the people who complain—what kind of church would
they prefer? Most likely the church that is a democratic
crossbreed of a social club and an endowed corporation.
Preachers are catering for a large following; and they
think that the large following wants a comfortable religion. People do not want to be confronted with disagreeable facts in their own lives and in human life as a whole.
They want "a good time"; and a religion that will promise
them a good time for nothing—or for very little—a good
time for ever and ever, amen. Hell has become a kind of
hot springs where diplomats and other dignitaries of dam-
nation are kept for an indefinite period before they are
sent to their final destination.

But Christianity is not comfortable. The Sermon on the
Mount does not promise anybody a good time. As a matter
of fact Christianity will make any honest man pretty un-
comfortable until, like the corn of wheat, he is willing to
die in order to bring forth much fruit. "He that loveth
his life shall lose it."—That has been the peril of democracies; and certainly we are passing through a holocaust

making it pretty clear in the hardest way that nations who love their lives too much are losing them, while the nations that are willing to die shall survive. And even at a peace conference it ought to be pretty clear in the minds of delegates that ye cannot serve God and Mammon.

It may not be quite so easy to sell that idea as to sell a good many other ideas. And so it is sometimes kept in the closet as a kind of family skeleton of Christianity and never painted over the doors of churches which advertise how much it has cost to build them.

The great Danish Christian philosopher Soeren Kierkegaard tells a story: It once happened in a theatre when a popular show was on that a fire broke out backstage. In the midst of a farcical act the curtain was lowered; the manager stepped out in front of it and announced: "There is a fire backstage; your lives are in danger."—There was an uproar of laughter. People thought it was an excellent joke, and quite original. The manager sounded the gong and repeated: "I am serious, in five minutes if you don't get out immediately, you may all be ashes." He was received with the most spontaneous clapping of hands ever heard.—So I think the end of our civilization will come, says Kierkegaard, amidst thunderous applause from a well-dressed audience that will persist in thinking that the whole thing is a joke.

If this is not to be the end of democracy, we shall have to face disagreeable facts openly and honestly. They may be distasteful, but they are doubly dangerous when we do not look squarely into their ugly face.

German philosophy and the education impregnated by German philosophy were awe-inspiring in many ways and the modern school system of Germany made life beastly, hard and rigid; but it did not promise something for nothing. German students used to know certain verses by heart. One of them is by Nietzsche who was a better poet than philosopher:

*"Tief ist die Nacht
und tiefer als der Tag erdacht."* *

German teachers were not afraid to admit the dangers, and the dark, and the night. And their students were enabled to meet them with less risk than those who have only been told to go out and have a good time and try to get something for nothing.

Those who completed the Nazi plan of education understood one thing which for quite a time had been forgotten in the big democratic countries. They understood that what makes the strongest appeal to every normal young boy is not to be promised fun but to be promised adventure, danger, the highest excitement of life: to face death. This noble and heroic urge was twisted and tortured to suit the aims of the leader and is the parent of the perverted and aggressive idealism we meet among young Germans. The quiet life, the undisturbed enjoyment of an ever-to-be-continued good time held little temptation for them.

There is a famous poem by Goethe:

*"Wer nie sein Brot mit Thränen ass,
Wer nie die kummervollen Nächte
Auf seinem Bette weinend sasz
der kennt Euch nicht, Ihr himmlischen Mächte."* †

Democratic education has shunned mentioning tears and sorrow and nights in pain without sleep. It has taught children the most commonplace worship of success, which again led to an open sympathy for the man who could get away with it, a feeling that has been the parent of graft and gangsterism and produced the congressmen of Mr.

---

* "The night is deep
And deeper than the day thinks."

† "Who never ate his bread with tears,
Who never sat weeping on his bed
through long nights of pain and sorrow,
he does not know you, ye heavenly Powers."

Grafton's article. In the international field the cult of success has led to the openmouthed admiration for Hitler which swept thousands of people, who did not always call their instinctive reaction by that name. This again has made possible the organization of battalions of fifth columnists, of spies and helpers of spies in every country on every continent.

Those who have been educated never to face disagreeable facts, were entirely unwilling to believe in the possibility of war. A most peculiar kind of fetishism was developed during the nineteenth century and still has a strong hold on the minds of men in democratic countries —a half religious belief in something, vaguely called progress, coupled with a devout worship of something termed material welfare.

In one of the earlier years of this epoch of progress an enthusiastic believer exultantly told John Ruskin that the first telegraph cable to India had been completed. And Ruskin looked at him and said: "What message shall it carry?" (A question still asked in India.) It sometimes seems that democracies have forgotten the message in their ardent devotion to the cable.

One of the great exponents of the cable creed was Woodrow Wilson when he said:

"All through the centuries there has been this slow painful struggle forward, forward, up, up, a little at a time, along the entire incline, the interminable way."

This creed crumbled in the last world war, and those who had believed in it were reduced to mental disturbance, because they had built their house upon the sand and it fell. And they did not understand why. In spite of the terrifying backsliding, nations and leaders of nations were loath to give up their convenient creed, and they tried to build upon the sand once more. Even now, when committees and commissions in so many countries are studying the organization of peace, we meet the overemphasizing of material welfare, the social aspects, the economic aspects of peacemaking. They are extremely important; but material welfare has never created the spirit that made nations capable of great deeds. "The seed of reform does not grow in the soil of comfort and abundance," wrote one of the fathers of the Norwegian Constitution in the years of distress and starvation during the Napoleonic wars.

Human beings with troubled minds have been fed on the gospel of progress; and it is sand on their lips. They have listened to lecture after lecture on the blessings of an improved standard of living, until it has become pretty clear to them that no chewing gum for victory or draft-beer in bottles, or the best washing-machine can satisfy the craving soul of man. They sometimes ask to what goal Mr. Wilson's interminable way will finally lead them. And there is some dread in their minds that the heaven of material welfare and improved standards of living will be the peace described in a familiar anecdote:

A man passed away who had always been a firm believer in progress, a self-righteous man, who had never broken any law, who had always done the right thing and was deeply convinced of his own goodness and usefulness. When he woke up on the other side he found that he was where he had always known that he would come and everything was just as perfect as he had expected it. He was surrounded by an abundance of everything he had appreciated in his previous career. The chef was excellent and prepared every day the dishes the deceased man had always liked best. His eye met the conventional beauty he admired, everything was absolutely, perfectly to his taste; every desire fulfilled even before it had been clearly defined in his conscious mind. The first few days he was extremely happy, after a while he started fretting, and when some weeks had passed he found himself suffering from an inexplicable spleen he never had thought possible. At last he could not stand it any longer. He went to the superintendent's office and explained that he was in need of some variation, of something less perfect, in short, before he quite realized what he was doing he asked for a pass to hell. The superintendent looked coldly at him and said: "My dear sir, where do you really think you are?"

Surely, if democracies do not grasp the meaning of Ruskin's words, if their educational system is built on a cable and not on a message, they will head for the same kind of final destination. Only by understanding the oneness of body, soul and mind, only by recognizing the spiritual forces in human history, by administering to the immaterial needs of nations, can we learn to build upon the rock.

In his great address on Memorial Day Vice-President Henry A. Wallace stated:

"I would like to speak about four duties. It is my belief that every freedom, every right, every privilege has its price, its corresponding duty without which it cannot be enjoyed. The four duties of the peoples' revolution, as I see them today, are these:

1. The duty to produce to the limit.
2. The duty to transport as rapidly as possible to the field of battle.
3. The duty to fight with all that is in us.
4. The duty to build a peace—just, equitable and enduring. The fourth duty is that which inspires the other three."

Those duties do not stop with the war. But they will be given a different peace interpretation.

Something very strange is happening in all the occupied countries of Europe. Spontaneously, without reflecting very much, millions of men and women, just ordinary men and women in every walk of life, are facing starvation, the firing squad, indescribable torture, not to uphold their standard of living or improve their material welfare, but to preserve their liberty of mind and conscience.

They are proving, through their suffering and their death, that infinitely more important to human beings than freedom from want and freedom from fear are freedom of speech and freedom of religion. It is the greatest thing in this war. It is the redemption of democracy. And if peacemakers do not understand it, they will fail. If the nations who are not redeeming democracy through their sacrifice do not bow their heads in awe before this unsophisticated demonstration of the spirit, the war will have been fought in vain. And if democracies cannot incorporate this lesson in their systems of education, they will go to their doom. Children must be taught to see and admire what is great. Their inarticulate, but divine and serious and ardent longing for an existence worthwhile, for creation, for beauty, must be directed toward the unattainable things that alone make life worth living. The duties of democracy must be interwoven in the very texture of education.

This must be the background of every discussion of a future world order; the unwritten and maybe unspoken, but inflexible march order for delegates. It is the primary material for peace.

PART TWO

X: The Pace of Peace

As the present war has been different from any previous war, so the whole process of peace-making must be different from any previous pattern.

The time-honored conception has been that between countries there existed either a state of war or a state of peace. But to an international world where moral principles were no longer current coin this conception was purely technical and was used as a decoy for public opinion. Towns have been bombed, countries invaded, populations enslaved—and the aggressor nations declared that technically this was not war. This sham was accepted by international statesmen and lawyers alike, and the nations are paying the price of it today.

Japan did not declare war on China. Italy did not declare war on Ethiopia. Germany did not declare war on Poland, or Denmark, or Norway, or Holland, or Belgium. There is no obvious reason why the United Nations should declare peace on the totalitarian powers. It may be questioned whether they should even grant them an armistice when the last battle is won, or demand an unconditional and complete surrender. It will be a matter of expediency to be decided at their convenience. But if the victorious democracies should find it natural to grant Germany, Italy and Japan an armistice, it must be with the right of full occupation of their countries; and the patent of surrender must be signed by the responsible rulers of the totalitarian states, or by the generals responsible for the conduct of war, if the dictators shall have disappeared.

It was one of the mistakes after the Great War 1914-1918 that the victors refused to accept as representatives of the German people those who were responsible for the war, and forced the potential leaders of a democratic Germany to give their signatures to the declaration of war-guilt, thereby discrediting them in Germany and nourishing the Nazi myth that Germany had never been beaten but was betrayed from within.

No peace conference can be called until a tremendous work of clearing, of salvage and of reconstruction has been done. It may be well to make perfectly clear that a long period of transition will be needed before nations can discuss officially the terms of peace treaties to come.

There are practical and political, as well as psychological, reasons why this must be so. The men coming to a peace conference immediately after a bitter and devastating war can never be expected to meet in a spirit of impartial judgment, of dispassionate deliberation and careful weighing of facts and evidence. They will be delegates of governments, subject to the influence of popular sentiment and political propaganda. Those who remember what was called the "khaki election" in England will also know that the delicate and complicated problem of making a peace that can mean something more than an armed truce, needs to be discussed in a serene and cool atmosphere. Delegates whose minds are obscured by the smoke from their bombed and ruined homes and in whose ears still reverberate the cries from the torture chambers of the enemy will be poor peacemakers. What has been termed a cooling-off period will be sorely needed.

Two of the men particularly well equipped to discuss peace-conference problems, because they are rich in experience from the last peace-making effort, two men of widely different political views, have both given their support to this idea.

Lord Davies, who was principal secretary to Lloyd

George during the Versailles Conference, states in his book
"Foundations of Victory" (p. 174):

"There should be a cooling-off interval before the peace
plan can be finally settled. . . . Perhaps more than one transitional period will be necessary."

And Mr. Harold Nicolson, who was a member of the
British delegation to Versailles, in his "Why Britain Is at
War" declares that among the lessons to be learnt from
the errors and misfortunes of Versailles is this:

"The negotiators must draw a sharp distinction between
the Preliminary Peace which must be *imposed* upon the enemy
and the Final Treaty which must be *negotiated* with the
enemy. The Preliminary Treaty should deal only with the
physical facts of the situation. . . . The Final Treaty should
deal with the future political and economic structure of the
world. The Preliminary Treaty should be imposed and signed
immediately after the armistice. The negotiations for the Final
Treaty should not even begin before one year had elapsed
since the conclusion of the war. Admittedly such a suspense
will keep the world in delay for some eighteen months; this
is an inevitable disadvantage; even prolonged uncertainty is
preferable to decisions come to in a mood of hatred and
without sufficient consideration and calm. . . ."

In this connection it is also of interest to note that in
a "joint declaration" issued by Democratic Socialists of
Several Nationalities (Rand School Press, 1941) it is stated
(p. 5):

"We favor a preliminary peace treaty after the military
defeat of the Axis. This will, on the one hand, obviate the
necessity of delaying the peace pending discussion and settlement of frontier questions, and make it possible to arrive at
a final decision after hatreds and rancors have cooled off."

And, no doubt, in every country at war labour leaders
and trade unions will take the same view, fully realizing
that only slowly, cautiously and gradually can the re-gear-
ing of concerted national efforts be managed if there shall

be no explosions and if the machinery shall not break down in the process. Those asserting that labour cannot wait do not speak for the workers. Ordinary men and women have great power of patience, but a dictator can never wait. He wants immediate results; he has no past and no future, only a present. He has no dimensions; he is not even a line—a generation. He is just a point. Democracy is the very life-stream of the nations, timeless and always flowing on. That is why democracy can wait. That is the greatness of the people. And two things are essential to the establishment of a just and durable peace. Time and patience. Let no man try to steal them.

Time and patience will be needed to heal the wounds of war. And if any peace conference should meet prematurely, it would gravely endanger the process of world convalescence. A number of the great problems to be solved will still be latent when the war is over, or they will be in a state of chaos or amorphousness, not crystallized to such an extent that they can be properly dealt with. When the Versailles conference met, the delegates and their governments had not yet discovered a number of the real difficulties. They were so preoccupied with purely political problems that the peace treaties contained no economic provisions whatsoever (except to impose unspecified reparations on Germany). And, in spite of the fact that the International Labour Organization was set up at Versailles, no government had prepared to meet the social problems which arose when millions of men were suddenly demobilized. Unemployment on an international scale dates from the period of demobilization; and bitterness, sullen disappointment, a strong feeling of deception and futility filled the hearts of hundreds of thousands of men who had been willing to make the ultimate sacrifice during the war and found no jobs, no niche in an ordered society to go back to when the war was over. There was a fertile soil for every variety of revolutionary propaganda in their minds.

This time it is evident that the outcome of the terrible fight will to a large extent be determined by the war of production. And no single government can be blind to the colossal problem of readjusting industrial and economic life from war production to peace production. To complete this process without social unheaval and financial calamities will need the coördinated efforts of governments, of labour and of industry. By itself this fact will make it a social and economic necessity to proceed to demobilization slowly and by steps so as to make possible the absorption in productive and constructive life of the many millions of drafted men and volunteers.

Not only for this reason will it be wise not to expect any immediate demobilization. For purely military reasons it will be necessary to keep the allied forces under arms for a considerable time when the war is over. And it is well that this is now being generally recognized.

Few persons in the allied countries can fail to admit today that it was a disastrous mistake not to occupy Germany after the last war. If the peace had been signed in Berlin, it might have saved the world a lot of sweat, blood and tears; and it might have given the German people a fuller realization of the meaning of war and made it easier to build up a new social order in Germany.

The same thing must not happen again when this war is over. Even the calmest and most objective observers cannot fail to see this point:

"It seems probable that the military occupation of portions of the territory of the aggressor governments for a considerable period would be the best means of convincing the Germans, the Italians, the Japanese and other people that military aggression does not pay." (Professor Quincy Wright in "Second Report of the Commission to Study the Organization of Peace," p. 267.)

But the military occupation of the territories of the aggressor nations will not primarily be a defensive or a punitive measure. It will serve a greater purpose and be part of the universal plan of organizing and reconstructing a civilized community of nations.

A military defeat will mean political and social disintegration in the totalitarian countries; it will mean chaos and probably civil war. An international army will be needed to protect the lives of potential administrative and democratic leaders in Germany, Italy and Japan. Only under shelter of such an army will it be possible for a nucleus of political and social intelligence and broad-mindedness to develop the organs of a modern national self-government.

Not only in the totalitarian countries will it be necessary to have an international army to keep order, police the territory and protect the population. The same thing will apply to large sections of the world, how large no man can foretell today.

In some countries it will be comparatively easy to establish law and political order when the enemy troops are driven out, or have to retire, although it remains an open and fearful question what havoc of destruction and what human atrocities the German armies and their hated and contemptible local collaborators will perpetrate when they know that all is finished. Legal and constitutional governments still existing will take over. There is no deep split in the nation; those who have been traitors will be dealt with under national law. Holland, Luxembourg, Norway are such countries and what applies to them to a certain extent also applies to Belgium and Denmark, although no two cases are identical. But even in these countries there may be great difficulties. Constitutions have been suspended; elections have not been held; governments will have to be confirmed, and their authority renewed by the nations in question. In every case those who stayed at home and whose sufferings made victory possible, will have the final word of decision.

All the time we shall have to bear in mind that this war was planned by the Germans, Italians and Japanese as a civil war in every other country. Puppet governments have been organized, subversive activities staged, treachery engineered and promoted. In a number of countries, both in Europe and in Asia, the totalitarian aggressors have succeeded in creating a national division and sowing a seed of hatred that might well cause a general conflagration as soon as the forces of occupation and the army of enemy agents disappear. A civil guerilla would be threatening, different in character from the international civil war waged by Nazism, a national guerilla between parties, factions and individuals, more sanguinary, cruel and unrestrained than any regular fighting. Such a civil war to the point of extermination may be feared in France, possibly in Greece, in Roumania, in Jugoslavia, and there may be explosions in Bulgaria, in Finland, in Hungary. There may be armed conflicts in Thailand, in Burma, in Java.

There is still another group of states where national and political difficulties will be even more complicated: Czechoslovakia; Poland. And there is the enigma of the Baltic states.

A general synopsis of the situation is given in a statement from all members of the American Commission to Study the Organization of Peace:

"Terrible forces will be released when military control ceases—forces of revenge, of ambition and lust for power, of hunger and desperation. Upon the military forces of the victors the world must depend for the maintenance of order. Their forces, in coöperation with those of the governments in exile, and such stable forces as can be found among liberated peoples will have the task of policing almost the whole of Europe, and perhaps other parts of the world, until constitutional regimes can be set up and the wishes of the people expressed as to the form of government they wish. It cannot be permitted that interminable and bloody conflicts arising from rivalry of political leaders, territorial ambition, or anything else, should hamper the convalescence of a worn world, no matter what feelings of national sovereignty or national pride may be involved. . . . These strong international forces must be ready to assume control wherever needed." (pp. 155-156)

But the task of the international armies of protection will not be a purely military or policing one. The problems of fighting starvation on a worldwide scale, of reëstablishing means of transportation, rebuilding, at least provisionally, bridges and railroads and ports, of repatriating millions of refugees and prisoners of war can be tackled only by disciplined, regimented forces and will need an organization on a tremendous scale.

Millions of people have been uprooted from their homelands, and by the totalitarian war-lords sent to strange lands as industrial or agricultural slaves. Whole populations have been forced by the Japanese and by the Germans to give up their farms or their business, whatever it may have been, to make room for the "master-races." Hundreds of thousands of Jews have been taken from their homes by force and deported to new ghettos created by the Germans; these people will have to be restored or to be moved to such areas where they can live the life of civilized human beings in liberty and dignity.

And there will be the problem of fighting the epidemics following in the wake of retreating armies, waiting for the right moment of disorganization to sweep over the earth. With the coming of spring, 1942, all the papers of the world could tell how the German armies had detached battalions of men to act as scavengers, to burn all the corpses uncovered by the thaw and check the process of putrefaction all along the front. Any health officer will understand what that means and what enormous dangers to human life are indicated in the short statements. But maybe few realize that in most wars far more people are killed by epidemics and starvation than by military action.

During and after World War I—more than thirty-five million human beings died from starvation and from those epidemics which follow in the wake of war. This time we are faced with the probability of mortality on a scale that would make the Spanish flu, the spotted fever and the malaria epidemics of 1918-1922 seem bucolic idylls. The health services of Europe and Asia have broken down; what had been built up during twenty years of international effort has been destroyed, at least temporarily. The Institute of Tropical Diseases at Singapore, that most important center of epidemiological warning, is gone; the world's stock of medical supplies exhausted, factories destroyed. At the same time the unprecedented migrations, the congestions of refugees, the wholesale destruction of human homes have multiplied the danger of epidemics and the difficulty of combating them. It can be done only by regimented, disciplined forces.

Lord Davies and Mr. Harold Nicolson agree that the transitional period, or "cooling-off period" as they have termed it, should last for twelve months or eighteen months. Professor Quincy Wright in his "Political Conditions of the Period of Transition" quite casually remarks:

". . . it is believed a period of four or five years should be envisaged during which most of the changes should be made."

Then he goes on, somewhat surprisingly:

"This has been the normal period for an administration to last in England and in the United States. It is the period usually allowed for carrying out large-scale economic plans in Russia, Germany, and elsewhere. It has apparently been considered long enough to enable an efficient regime to carry out major political plans, but not so long that such a regime will lose its contact with public opinion and its elasticity of action."

The parallels are not convincing, and they would not have been more convincing if the "five-year-plan" in Russia or Goering's four-year-plan in Germany had been entirely successful. Living organisms, organic growth cannot be made subject to mechanical temporal plans. Rather the plans will have to be adjusted as the laws regulating the process of growth are made clear. The task of creating a new world order is so tremendous that no precedents are to be found; and very little light can be shed over the problem by studying the history of national administrations or parliaments. But perhaps a slight indication of an experienced truth of statesmanship may be found in a word by the great Napoleon:

"It is better for a country to have one bad administration for ten years than to have ten good administrations in one year."

The whole problem is well put by the eighty-sixth signers of the "Second Report":

"It is impossible to say how long a period will or should elapse between the cessation of hostilities and the establishment of a permanent world order. It is clear, however, that the traditional methods of ending a war—armistice, conference, and treaty—are inadequate, and should be abandoned. A period of control, between war and peace, is now essential, so that it will not be necessary to rush decisions; so that there may be time for careful thought, for experimenting and testing, for the rebuilding of national governments, the formation of public opinion, the discovery of what peoples want, after their sufferings, in the way of a permanent settlement. Time for study and deliberation is essential in the democratic process, and for the solution of vast problems. It is not necessary to estimate in advance the time required for this process, but it is essential to establish the community means of control for the period."

It is perfectly true that it will not be essential—and it will not be possible—to establish beforehand how long the period of transition should be. But it is of some importance to make clear what Professor Quincey Wright has seen, that the period of transition has already begun, that the British Commonwealth of Nations and the United States of America are already readjusting their constitutional, economic and social life under the tutorship of necessity; and they are making their arrangements of far-reaching readjustments, not only for the duration of the war, but in many cases fully (though not always openly) aware that the clock can never be put back again. Gradually democracies are moving away from stale traditions, petrified practices, time-honored red tape; they are mounting a telescopic ladder that has already carried them over some walls and deep into the land of transition. The vision and patience of statesmen, the adaptability of democracies, the practical common sense of nations will decide how soon they shall be able to traverse this region and cross the frontier to the new world of international order and security.

XI: Discordant Interlude

If it is our desire, as expressed in the English verse, that "we shall all have a hand in the peace we have won," we have to watch our step carefully and be well aware that during the years of transition will be prepared the conditions of the final peace settlement.

In their statement of peace-aims, the two great spokesmen for democracy declare:

"They respect the right of all peoples to choose the form of government under which they will live; and they wish to see sovereign rights and self-government restored to those who have been forcibly deprived of them."

But the Atlantic Charter has not been ratified by the United States Senate or by the British parliament. It is not a binding document. And there is no denying that a good many of those well-meaning and prominent men and women who are now discussing publicly the new world order for which the United Nations are fighting, seem to have forgotten the pledge of the Atlantic Charter. Not only are eager ideologists in the English-speaking countries pressing their governments to impose upon the world the kind of new order they advocate, irrespective of the wishes of nations; but in many quarters there is a tendency to forget that even if the war as waged in 1942 is, primarily, a war between armies, navies, air forces and giant industries of the Great Powers, fundamentally and morally it is not a Great Power war, but something new and far more important. It would hardly bode well for the future if those who take a keen interest in the post-war settlement start their work by overlooking completely the countries which have suffered most under the hands and heels of the totalitarian aggressors and oppressors.

There is a growing feeling of uncertainty among men and women from occupied countries. Not only do they feel that their war-efforts are minimized or not mentioned by the official information machine, but they are well aware that one new organization after another, leading over to the transition period, is established without any representation for the small powers. They do not demand much, but on the other hand, they have no intense desire to remain, on the day of final reckoning, just a group of forgotten nations. They think that they have a right to a hand in the peace we have won. Maybe they are touchy, maybe they are unduly suspicious. But they have every reason to be so. They know that unless the small nations are given a voice and a vote in the council of the mighty, there will be faint hope of any international democracy and of any democratic control of foreign policy, and without democratic rights in the international commonwealth, no peace can be won.

To more than one representative of the small Allied powers it may be a sad surprise that the very fact that they are Allied powers, that their men are fighting and dying at every front, is non-existent for Anglo-American writers of authority.

This does not apply to the men on top. No doubt they all realize what Vice-President Wallace, in the speech from which we have quoted above, expressed in the following terms:

"Those who write the peace must think of the whole world. There can be no privileged peoples. We ourselves in the United States are no more a master race than the Nazis."

But experience proves that more than once the moderation and wisdom of the informed and responsible people will have to bow to the impact of massed prejudice, of short-sighted chauvinism and demagogic propaganda, on the day of reckoning.

It is a remarkable fact that even men of great perspicacity and with an open eye for the shortcomings of their compatriots, are suffering under this innate illusion that only their own country is fit to govern the world. Few writers have criticized British statesmanship or lack of statesmanship in recent years so severely and so convincingly as Lord Davies. In his last book "Foundations of Victory" (London, 1941) he passes judgment on Neville Chamberlain, Lord Halifax and some other British leaders in terms that could hardly have been stronger. Having made it very clear that there has been neither adequate political nor military vision in England, and that British statesmen were incapable of protecting the interests of the British Empire, he proposes to hand the entire world over to a British-American Commonwealth. In the transition period he further suggests: "British-American Commissions should be established in the capitals of Europe." These commissions should be responsible for the disarmament of the rest of the world and they "would arrange between themselves the provisional boundaries of the states or territories for which they were responsible during the first transitional period."

If Lord Davies himself is unaware of his own charming lack of logic, he can be perfectly sure that the nations whose future fate he disposes of will not fail to comment on it.

When Lord Davies, in so many ways a distinguished pioneer in the work for international collaboration, can be led so grotesquely astray by his patriotic enthusiasm, it is not surprising that men without his political training and experience and without his intergity of criticism should discuss the future of the allies of their country as if they were carcasses on a dissecting table to be disposed of for the benefit of pure science.

An English writer, who is, no doubt, an authority in his own field, Professor Julian S. Huxley, in an article on "Peace Aims as War Weapons" (*Common Sense*, June, 1942), talks condescendingly about "the thorny problems presented by the Governments in Exile." (He puts "Governments in Exile" in quotation marks.) What would have been the fate of England if those governments had chosen the expedient way of least resistance and had not gone in exile? If any single one of them had sided with Germany where would England have been? And what would the reaction have been in the United States? When it became possible for the United Kingdom to obtain lend-lease aid, the opposition to the Lease-Lend program would unquestionably have been stronger but for the confidence engendered in the United States by the continued resistance of the governments in exile. One of them, the Norwegian, while in exile, has fulfilled all its international obligations and paid in full interest and regular amortization quotas on all its external loans. Not every government which never had to go in exile has the same record. And, surely, if peace aims shall be war weapons, few things could be more unwise than to slight and deride allies whose aid is needed.

The culmination, so far, of professorial detachment from political facts, common sense and critical judgment has been reached by Professor G. T. Renner in an article in *Collier's*. Now the aberrations of an immature mind, the Hitlerian rant of any person great only in his own imagination, usually is of very little interest; but when such a man as a professor at Teachers College, Columbia University, officially acting as an instructor to hundreds of young men and women, destined to be the educators of the nation, promulgates such ideas and they are circulated in one of the most widely read magazines in the world, it is not a matter to be treated only as a bad joke. At a time when the United States, as one of a group of allied nations, is fighting for her very existence and for the existence of those nations, at a time when the Government of the United States is solemnly pledged to restore to these allied countries their liberty and territories, an instructor of teachers publicly advocates that most of the territory of these allies should be given to Germany, more than even Hitler ever has asked for, and that a number of allied nations should disappear altogether. Belgium should be partitioned between France, Germany and the Netherlands. The Netherlands, Mr. Renner then goes on to incorporate in the British Commonwealth of Nations, giving them as a consolation the assurance that they will get a "full dominion status." Luxembourg, Professor Renner donates to Germany; he also presents Hitler with Hungary, a fat slice of Roumania, a large part of Poland, the whole of Austria and the greater part of Czechoslovakia.

But Mr. Renner is not content with disposing of the countries that actually are at war. He does away with Switzerland, which should be divided between Germany, France and Italy. Portugal he gives to Spain; on the other hand he gives a section of Spain to France, and presents England with Calais.

At a time when the continued neutrality of Portugal, Spain and Switzerland is of the greatest importance to his own country, this professor proclaims as one of the war aims to get rid of them. No doubt Dr. Goebbels has appreciated the valuable service he has rendered to the Nazi propaganda machine in these countries whose nationals still have an old-fashioned desire to continue to exist.

And Mr. Renner is not a completely isolated phenomenon. Even on the pages of the Second Report from the American Commission to Study the Organization of Peace, we meet, quite naïvely expressed as something that goes without discussion, the conception that it is all right

for Anglo-Saxons to dispose of other nations and their
territories.

Dr. Quincy Wright takes it for granted that Great
Britain and the United States will assume responsibility
and direct world affairs during the transitional period and
that they will "establish provisional institutions to deal
with regional and functional problems as the need arises."
And benignantly he remarks:

"Doubtless in the Scandinavian countries, the Low Countries, and in France and Spain, new governments may be
provisionally recognized earlier than in Central and Eastern
Europe."

The statement must be quite interesting to the Queen
of the Netherlands and the King of Norway and their
armed forces on sea, and land and in the air, and stimulating to the sailors of their merchant marines which, until
December 7, 1941, carried about fifty percent of oil and
supplies to the war theatres. And to the governments of
those countries it must come as a peculiar sensation to
learn that they are abolished without more ado, and will
no longer be recognized when they have done their duty.
It will give them some new ideas for their definition of
the term "allies." The King and government of Denmark
are not in exile, and Sweden is not in the war at all. But
to Mr. Quincy Wright that is no difficulty, nor is it one
that these four countries have been generally considered
the best governed countries in the world. Spain is not in
the war either; but if many American professors should
discuss what they think should be done with Spain when
the war is over, perhaps it will be found that this is a
question which does not leave Spain entirely neutral; and
unwittingly the learned gentlemen might increase the
number of their country's enemies. The rearrangement of
the entire world may be easier on a blackboard in the
schoolroom than in actual political life. But too much

blackboard lecturing may endanger the peace before it is in sight.

The same writer, in the same report, institutes a "European Constitution" and declares that:

"National legislation in violation of the European constitution should be null and void."

The President of the United States, in his radio address of February 23, 1942, mentioned as the essence of the kind of peace we seek "self-determination of nations and peoples."

Can any person with some experience in practical political life imagine that nations which are braving torture, starvation, indescribable suffering and death rather than acquiesce in one kind of dictated peace and world order, would gladly and silently accept another kind of dictated peace and world order in which they have no voice?

Not only private individuals, but also official representatives of Anglo-Saxon interests have been speaking along somewhat similar lines. The British Minister to Uruguay, Mr. R. C. S. Stevenson, in an address at Rivera in May, 1942 (printed from the manuscript in the *Buenos Aires Herald* for May 19th), made the following statements:

"I believe that the peace and prosperity of the world can only be assured by close and whole-hearted collaboration between the peoples of this Continent and the peoples of the British Commonwealth of Nations and in no other way. The hope of the world lies in our hands and yours. Between us we have the power. . . .

"We, that is the freedom-loving peoples of this Continent and the free nations of the Commonwealth, must make up our minds that we will be content with nothing less than a world consecrated in the words of President Roosevelt to 'freedom of speech and expression, freedom of every person to worship God in his own way, freedom from want and freedom from terror.' These four freedoms are the basis of the only kind of life which you and we think worth living. We, and as history has shown, you also, are ready to fight and if necessary to die to preserve them. We must see to it that after this war they are attained for all the world and if you and we are determined to bring this about it will surely happen."

It may be unpremeditated, but it may also be according to plan that the popular diplomat failed to mention President Roosevelt's words about "self-determination of nations and peoples." Anyhow, any interested observer will note that Mr. Stevenson, in his hope of the world, does not include any of the nations that have been fighting shoulder to shoulder with the peoples of the British Commonwealth of Nations since before Pearl Harbor. He does not mention China or Russia, Poland, Norway, Holland, Belgium, Greece, Jugoslavia. Can anybody imagine a diplomat making that speech in China, or in Russia, or to any allied audience? Is there one diplomatic hope in the Western Hemisphere and another in the Orient and a third in Europe? Or is it the grand official idea to leave out the nations that have been the victims of war and may appear exhausted and impoverished to the diplomatic eye?

Professor Julian Huxley, in his article, institutes a European Commonwealth but admits that "there remains, of course, the problem of getting action" on his program, and then he adds:

"Purely private discussions, both in the United States and in Britain, among officials, and between officials and responsible non-official persons may prepare the ground. . . .

"A more formal, joint conference, non-official, but with some officials in it, and with representatives of *say Russia, China and Holland sitting in, would be a definite step which could be arranged before long."

It does not seem to occur to him that Russia, China, Holland, every fighting ally has just the same right to hold an opinion and take its part of the decision as has Great Britain or the United States of America. To "sit in" is not a privilege bestowed as a grace in a subsidiary clause by any Great Power, or by any two Great Powers. It is the primogeniture of free nations. And until this is realized by those who speak for great nations there will be a poor prospect of winning the peace. The crucial question for the problem of a just and durable peace is confidence. Without confidence between nations and confidence in international justice, there will be armaments, international intrigue, and always a pretext for aggression at hand. And there can be no trusting confidence until all nations and the leaders of every country realize that no single nation is called upon or has the qualifications needed, or has any right to decide for other nations or for any other nation.

It seems to be a very hard truth to grasp for those brought up in an imperialistic or even a nationalistic school of political mentality and sentiment, but nevertheless this truth cannot be bypassed on our road toward a better future. Right of representation for those who pay not only their taxes, but in blood, sweat, and tears, is one of the fundaments of democracy. In a civilized state even a minor is entitled to be heard and express his opinions through a guardian when vital decisions are taken concerning his fate and future. And, still, people who fondly believe that they are working for a democratic victory, unwittingly advocate that small countries should not be heard.

It is well known how exceedingly difficult it has been found to establish any united war strategy. It should not be quite so difficult and complicated to organize a united strategy of peace. And it is desperately needed. For the establishment of any second front it is necessary to consult the representatives of the nations whose countries are to be used as basis for a second front. Every single nation has a vital interest in the peace front and a right to be heard.

It may be inconvenient, it may be cumbrous and bothersome to have to consult representatives of a number of countries. But that is the way of democracy; the road to progress is the resultant of the given composition of forces.

Transitional organizations have been instituted in the relations between Great Britain and the U. S. A. and between Canada and the U. S. A. But there are no real interallied organizations except for questions of relief, and the greatest innate reluctance among the mighty to give a vote to any other country in any undertaking.

As a typical instance might be quoted the British-American Maritime Commission. For more than two years Norway has been operating for the allied cause, with a fleet of more than 6,000,000 tons deadweight and has carried more than forty percent of the fuel used by Great Britain and more than twenty-five percent of all provisions reaching England; and the Norwegian Merchant Marine has suffered relatively higher losses than any of her allies. But it took more than two years for Norway to obtain a seat on the Joint Adjustment Board, although it can hardly be denied that in this particular field the experience of Norwegian shipping men might have been most valuable, and great satisfaction given to those 25,000 Norwegian sailors who, cut off from their homeland, and with their families in German hands, have been serving in the danger zones day and night.

In World War I Norway was neutral; but her ships sailed for the allies and she lost 49.7 percent of her fleet, a higher percentage than Great Britain lost. It was never remembered, outside Norway, and Norwegians do not complain. Not even when they are given the impression that deliberately they are sent to posts of Uriah. Willingly they have gone to Crete and to Malta, to Singapore and in every infested sea. They had only one desire, that their ships should be used to the fullest capacity. And they felt that this was not done and could not be done as long as the unique experience of Norway was set completely aside.

They felt that this might involve a danger of creating the suspicion that only the interests of two nations were looked after.

The point of view expressed here is not merely national; it is widely understood. And many intelligent American observers have seen the same weakness in the Washington-London set-up. In his book "Prelude to Victory" (New York, 1942) Mr. James B. Reston writes:

"Nor have we learned, even now, the full lesson of our failure to co-operate with our allies. When we established the machinery for running the war, we set it up not on an allied basis, but on an Anglo-American basis. This is not an Anglo-Saxon war. The Norwegians alone, for example, have been delivering in their ships to Great Britain about one-half of all Britain's oil and approximately one-third of all her other imports, yet Norway is not sitting on the committees that settle the Allied shipping problems. We and the British are geographically on the edge of the central conflict. The decisive theater, for us or against us, has always been at the center of this World War, and the center is clearly on the Russian Near and Middle Eastern fronts."

In the first months of 1942 there were held in London a number of inter-allied conferences. Mr. Trygve Lie, the Norwegian Foreign Minister, in a statement printed in the *Inter-Allied Review*, March, 1942, remarks:

"They might, perhaps, be developed into a real Inter-Allied Committee, holding regular meetings and having, so far as possible, executive powers."

He goes on to recommend the establishment of such a body and states:

"For the time being the Inter-Allied Committee will deal only with questions of supplies in the immediate post-war period; but there is nothing to prevent its being developed into a permanent organ. Steps should be taken now to extend the inter-allied machinery, pending the inclusion of other states after the war."

In such a way the period of transition would naturally melt into the final peace period. And, as Mr. Lie says, there is nothing to prevent it—except the traditional aversion in Foreign Offices of Great Powers to admit anybody to their trade-union.

But to any international work the small nations and their men and women are needed. They are brought up to be internationally minded. Ignorance is the privilege of great countries. It is a luxury small nations cannot afford, if they want to survive. They are educated, not in one language, but in many languages. They have to study the history, the literature, the mentality of all the great nations. Their existence ever since Frederick the Great and Napoleon has been precarious. They have to be on the outlook constantly, their very independent life is always in danger. And as they cannot rely on their power, on armies and navies, they have always been the protagonists of international efforts, eager to serve any idea of universal collaboration, not because they were more unselfish but, logically, because collective action and collective security were their only protection.

The contagion of self-sufficiency might assail the small countries, but could never get a foothold, as it was too obvious that they could never be self-sufficient. Isolationism might appeal to them as it will always appeal to strong-willed, ignorant and prejudiced individualists; but they were brought up to understand that in material, in moral and in mental life, isolation spells stagnation and decay. Their terms of existence forced them to adopt the policy of the open door. Therefore, the small countries and their nationals were trusted, and they were used because they were not dangerous; they were not under suspicion. Between the jealousies of Great Powers, the small countries were oases of innocence. It was not accidentally that The Hague was made the seat of the Permanent Court of Arbitration and the Permanent Court of International Justice;

Berne of the Universal Postal Union and the rest of similar international unions; Geneva the seat of the League of Nations; Basle, of the Bank of International Settlement. A large majority of international organizations of the world, hundreds of them, had their headquarters either at Geneva or in Brussels. And most of the great international movements of modern times have originated in the small countries. The Red Cross organization started in Switzerland and got its status by the Geneva convention. The work for an ecumenic world alliance centered in Sweden, and hand in hand with the "Stockholm-movement" has gone the "Lausanne-movement." It was a Swede, Nobel, who founded the most impressive institution for the furtherance of international intellectual life; and he turned to the Parliament of Norway for the distribution of the Peace Prize. The first time scholars and scientists from the countries which had been at war from 1914 to 1918 met in joint discussions and to pick up again the threads of intellectual collaboration was in Oslo in 1919 at an invitation from the Institute for Comparative Cultural Research Work.

In every field of international activity the small countries and their nationals have been pioneers; and in every international organization they have taken a part far greater than their populations and territories would indicate. For years a Norwegian was president of the Mixed Courts of Egypt, the only president to be re-elected unanimously. When Iran started on its modern career a Swedish officer was called in to organize the national gendarmerie. In the international postal service, custom service, lighthouse service in China a number of Norwegians held the highest positions. When Kemal Pasha set out to rebuild Turkey he called in Danish engineers to construct the railroads. In them were no germs of any imperialism.

The part played in the League of Nations by delegates from small countries can hardly be exaggerated. They made the League a reality. "There were no abler men in the Assembly than some of those who represented the smaller states." *

"Much of the strongest and most consecutive leadership in the Assembly has been furnished by these lesser powers." †

Sir Alfred Zimmern declares that the fact that the doubts of the Assembly's value were so swiftly and triumphantly dispelled was primarily due

"to the energy, the public spirit and the statesmanlike equipment of the leading delegates of some of the smaller European States. M. Hymans of Belgium, who was elected to the Presidency, had at his side Mr. Branting of Sweden, Dr. Nansen of Norway, Mr. Motta of Switzerland, Dr. Benes of Czechoslovakia, to mention only the most outstanding figures in a group on which citizens of Great Powers have not seldom had occasion to look with envy." ("The League of Nations and the Rule of Law," p. 458.)

When these men and women were active in international work it was because they believed in international democracy; it was their national ambition to fulfil every duty under the Covenant, to make the greatest possible contribution to the Commonwealth of nations.

It is still the ambition of the lesser states. Their limited resources in manpower, territory and material wealth does not leave room for any other national ambition on their part. To think that the preliminary spadework for a future peaceful world-order could be made without their experienced help would be a fatal mistake, a criminal and a stupid negligence of facts.

Even for the planning of the transitional period their active collaboration is needed. They have no axes to grind. They want to serve.

In the face of so many over-officious peace-schemers, it

* Margaret E. Burton: "The Assembly of the League of Nations," Chicago, 1941, p. 92.
† *Ibid.*, p. 208.

is well to speak openly and honestly. Only by openness and honesty can a peace be won.

When writers, diplomatists, men of action and men of imagination so loudly discuss an Anglo-American direction of world-affairs they will be met with these questions: What should entitle those two powers to act for all countries and particularly for the small nations? Is there anything in their near political past that gives them the full confidence of the rest of nations? Have their politicians and their diplomats shown a wisdom, a foresight, a moral courage to which the world can look for guidance? Were they prepared? Could they read the script on the wall? Or is the present holocaust largely due to the sins of commission and the sins of omission of those responsible for Great Power policy since the last war?

In every small country there is the greatest confidence in the present leaders of American foreign policy. Few men have given more hopeful inspirations to recent international planning and thinking than President Roosevelt, Secretary of State Cordell Hull and Undersecretary of State Sumner Welles. But such leaders are exceptional; they are not the rule. And no man can guarantee for how long a time their wisdom will prevail. Every nation wants to have a say in decisions concerning its own fate and future. But let there be no mistake.

No small nation has any particular desire to have a seat at the conferences of the big. It is an onerous task to disagree with the mighty. Good advice is less welcome and popular than might be thought, and it is not always considered tactful to point to the naked truth. Hans Andersen never mentioned what happened to the little boy who cried out that the Emperor had no clothes on. Maybe the boy did not survive. The weak as a rule go to the wall. And if small nations could have confidence in the Great Powers and know that they would feel and think for every nation and not just for their own, that they would work for the common weal and not for their particular national interests, the small nations would gladly keep away from the council chamber. But it is hardly an exaggeration to say that such a conviction has never been strongly expressed.

It is the natural tendency for every representative of a small nation to start out in international life, believing that even as some countries are bigger, more populous and more powerful than his own, so representatives of such countries must be infinitely wiser, more broadminded, richer in knowledge than he himself or any of his compatriots. And, instinctively, this seems to be a prevalent idea among Great Power politicians and diplomats. But not even in the most modest mind could such a faith survive any international conference. Reluctantly and remorsefully any observer will have to confess that the greatness of an individual is entirely independent of the extensiveness of the territory from which he hails, and that sometimes the soil of the greater territory is less fertile for international growth than the scant lands of a smaller country.

Only in the coördinated and harmonious interplay of nations and interests can a solution of the peace problems be found. All instruments are needed for the great ensemble; tremendous patience will be required from those who shall be entrusted with the orchestration. It is of need that the good work should be started immediately and the rehearsals begin.

XII: Before the Minds are Made Up

The opening of the great play for peace is of such supreme importance because it will decide whether initial peace discussions between the United Nations shall be conducted in an atmosphere of confidence or of distrust. And if from the very opening we move in an aura of misgiving and distrust, there will be little hope of winning the peace.

Today every small country, whether neutral or allied, lives in fear of being selected as the pawn sacrificed in the gambit by one of the Great Powers. And as long as the approach to peace discussions is reported to be through diplomatic channels, and with only three or four principal allied powers represented, that fear will not be alleviated because such an approach would be the sin against the very spirit of international democracy.

Of course, governments are discussing peace-problems and post-war reconstruction. It is the obvious thing and a clear duty for every government to do so.

But the task of governments is primarily to make up their own minds, not to make up the minds of other governments. The war is not decided in the Cabinet rooms of the great capitals, and the peace should not be decided there either.

The venerable John Bright, one of the most broad-minded and instinctively wise men to be a member of a democratic government, once showed the then young John

Morley the Cabinet Room in Downing Street, and remarked:

"More crimes and blunders have been committed within its
four walls than in any other place in the island." (Viscount
Morley: "Recollections," I, p. 218.)

The same words could probably be applied to the Cabinet Room in any Great Power capital. And if they have
not the same application in the Cabinet Rooms of the
lesser powers, it is only because their opportunities for
sinning have been more modest.

But this time there must be no crime committed and as
few blunders as humanly possible. The future of all nations, of the entire human race, is at stake. The task of
winning an intelligent, a just and durable peace is the
most tremendous which has ever faced mankind. The
preparations should be made in a realistic, a practical, a
matter-of-fact way, but also in a spirit of awe and veneration.

And before governments make up their minds in this
initial and transitional period, there is a double-sided
work to be done. One is concerned with the political outlook, the elaboration of new systems of international law
and international collaboration, the social and economic
planning which can result only from exhaustive studies of
the needs of nations, from tentative and provisional attempts and most careful steering. The other is the work
of collecting and sifting facts, of preparing that documentation which will be needed, not only for a final peace-
conference, but should be required for every decision
taken.

Governments often arrive at their conclusions, even the
most far-reaching ones, on very superficial examination of
facts. Viscount Morley relates that he was surprised to see,
when he had become a member of His Majesty's Government in the United Kingdom, in what manner decisions

were made in cabinet meetings. John Morley was a trained journalist and leader-writer, and he states that very often the Government took action on information so incomplete that no responsible editor would have dared to involve his paper in any leading article, if his knowledge had been so insufficient. And there is no reason to believe that Mr. Gladstone's cabinet was less conscientious and more superficial than later governments have been.

Certainly, at Versailles, very often decisions were taken in a hurry and on so scant a documentation of facts that it made leader-writers gasp. Mr. Harold Nicolson summarizes his judgment of the Versailles conference in the following words:

"The conference was conducted in an atmosphere of angry and hysterical rush." ("Why Britain is at War," p. 146.)

Lord Davies, in his "Foundations of Victory" (London, 1941, p. 173) declares:

"At Versailles there were no negotiations or discussions. A future peace settlement must not be done at the gallop as was attempted twenty years ago because our rulers were in a hurry to catch a train or a steamer or win an election."

It has been common and it has been made commonplace to vilify the Versailles Treaty as one of the major causes of this war. A marvelously well-conducted propaganda campaign, unwittingly helped by a number of possibly well-meaning, but most unscholarly politicians, has to a large extent succeeded in making the name of Versailles a popular bogey. This propaganda against Versailles was the spearhead of the Nazi campaign of infiltration, not only in a number of countries in Europe, but still more so in the Western Hemisphere. Under cover of this campaign Germany rearmed to an extent the world began to realize somewhat late; and under cover of this campaign the Nazification of immature minds in many countries was made possible.

It is not difficult to criticize the Versailles Treaty. But to avoid making the same mistakes over again, it is necessary to know exactly what was wrong with Versailles. The main faults were not on the political side. And in the light of history it can hardly be claimed that Germany was given an unfair deal. With some justification it may be maintained that hardly ever in the known history of the world has a country been utterly defeated after having committed more crimes of war than the world had witnessed for over a thousand years, and been let off at so cheap a price. Nearly one-third of France and large sections of Belgium had been laid waste as no country had been devastated since Carthage. And no war was waged on German soil, no retaliation was made. Ships belonging to neutral states, as well as to belligerent states, had been torpedoed and sunk without warning, women and children had been killed, open towns had been bombed from the air. But no moral retribution was enforced.

On the other hand, the Versailles Treaty, instead of facilitating a democratic resurrection of Germany, made it nearly impossible. Instead of forcing the men or the representatives of the regime responsible for the war to sign the peace and so expose them to the German nation, the victors refused to negotiate with the friends of the Kaiser and demanded that the peace should be signed by the men who had been opposed to the war policy of Germany. And these men were also forced to attach their names to a declaration of war-guilt that had no political importance whatsoever; they were discredited in Germany and rendered unserviceable for the cause of democracy. To humiliate a foe without making him powerless has always been considered a very risky policy, and will continue to be so. "Germany was neither conciliated nor suppressed. She was wounded, but not slain." (Harold Nicolson.)

On two other important points the Versailles Treaty was a political failure. Russia, the greatest empire of the world and the most populous state of Europe, was left out completely. Russia had been an allied power. Russia had gone to pieces on account of the war. Russia had suffered more than any other country. But as a result of the revolution in Russia the former ally was unrepresented at the peace conference and was looked upon as a derelict ship.

No sane man could doubt that as soon as Russia had nationally and financially recovered, no matter what government there happened to be in that country, it would be a natural ambition and aim for the foreign policy of the great Slav state to regain what had been lost and win back the former frontiers of the Empire.

Next, the splitting up of the old Austrian-Hungarian empire without any attempt to create on the ruins some kind of Danube confederacy, or plan the necessary organic financial coöperation between the new states created and the old states ruined, proved a fatal mistake and a cause of constant inflammation.

What was wrong with Versailles was that peace problems had not been studied, that Governments were unable to make up their minds because they simply did not know what kind of difficulties the post-war period would have to face. As mentioned in a previous chapter, only so-called political questions occupied the thoughts of the men of Versailles. They were blind to the moral, economic and social, to the industrial, monetary, commercial and agricultural problems and did not even understand that at any given moment such a problem may become an acute political and international question.

In various ways we shall be better equipped to face the future when this war is over, because governments will be in the position to know what they should make up their minds about.

There was no general secretariat at the Versailles Conference, and there was no regular organization. Every national delegation had its own secretaries, but there was no coördinating bureau, no staff of trained international civil servants collecting information, preparing correct statements of facts, representing the objective, dispassionate, scholarly equilibrium of mind.

Whether there shall be one big peace conference this time or a number of smaller conferences it is of importance that now, immediately, existing agencies should be utilized for this preliminary work. Mankind cannot afford more decisions which are not based on thorough investigation.

The International Labour Office, now located at Montreal, Canada, since the outbreak of the present war, has been busily engaged in studying certain aspects of the peace problems. In close collaboration with representatives of governments the trained staff of experts have been occupied with the problem of readjusting industrial life from war-production to peace-production, the relationship between unemployment and demobilization. Studies have been made of possible new labour regulations, labour legislation, new social-security systems to take care of the millions of women who have been doing the work of men during the emergency.

At the International Labour Conference held in the City of New York in October-November, 1941, a resolution, drafted by the American Government delegation, was unanimously adopted by representatives of thirty-five governments.

This resolution requests the Governing Body:

"to call the attention of the Governments of all Member States to the desirability of associating the International Labour Organization with the planning and application of measures of reconstruction, and to ask that the International Labour Organization be represented in any Peace or Reconstruction Conference following the war."

In the light of this resolution we may expect governments to apply to the International Labour Office for ex-

pert secretarial help and advice on a series of questions
which have to be dealt with in the present period of planning and transition. And at a meeting in London in April,
1942, of the Emergency Committee of the Governing Body
of the International Labour Organization, further action
was taken along the lines indicated in the resolutions
adopted. Governments have been requested to make special contributions to the International Labour Organization to enable the Office to increase the volume and the
speed of its work, and two countries, members of the
I.L.O. but not of the League of Nations, Brazil and the
United States, in the early months of 1942 gave supplementary grants.

In a similar way the Secretariat of the League of Nations should be called upon by governments to undertake
other kinds of preliminary work, more particularly the
Economic Intelligence Section, located for the duration
of the war at Princeton, N. J., and the Health Section,
which has not been officially transferred to the Western
Hemisphere.

As a matter of fact, important studies are being made
of demographic and economic conditions in all the territories involved. Exhaustive comparative studies of such a
kind and of such a scope have not been undertaken before
and will be essential, not only for transitional settlements,
but for the question of removal and migration of populations and a final regulation of demographic questions.

All these various studies have to be made simultaneously
and must be coördinated by a joint committee, or by a
special committee of statesmen and experts appointed for
this purpose.

This work will, to a certain extent, be specialized; it
will be a work of experts, unspectacular and unsensational.
It will be a work carried out in the studies of research
scholars, but in its application as important as research

work carried on in the great laboratories of the greatest industrial and scientific institutions of the world.

There will be legal problems, some of them of far-reaching international importance. A number of them may be referred to the Permanent Court of International Justice for an advisory opinion. All the best insight and trained experience of the world should be utilized.

There are also technical committees of the League of Nations which may be called upon and whose advice may be highly valuable. Some committees are in function, such as the Economic Committee and the Fiscal Committee. Other existing committees might be instructed to meet again and continue and extend their work, such as the Health Committee and the individual Nutrition Committees.

All these various instruments of work have the confidence of those who know and are not under suspicion of those who do not know. It is one of the remarkable and hope-inspiring things of the moment that among the Governments of the democratic nations at war there is a growing feeling of the present and future importance of the work planned and accomplished by such international agencies.

The Permanent Central Board of Opium for the first time after the outbreak of war met in London in September, 1942.

There was a joint meeting of the Economic and Financial Committees of the League of Nations in London in April, 1942. Besides the ordinary members of the committees, experts from all the United Nations not represented in them took part in the London meeting, which was continued in Princeton, New Jersey, in August, 1942. The United States, without being a member of the League, has for a long time been represented on these important committees. Mr. W. W. Riefler is a member of the Financial Committee and Mr. Henry Grady, former assistant

Secretary of State, is chairman of the Economic Committee.

The reports from these meetings have gone to the Governments of all the United Nations—and to the Governments of other countries, members of the League. They will have practical importance in defining the questions, in laying out a definite line of planning, and in ensuring intimate collaboration among all the nations in question.

Twenty countries, several of them not members of the League, were represented at these meetings; complete agreement was reached concerning the planning of preparatory reconstruction work and the fact was emphasized that the rebuilding of the economic life of the post-war world can only be effected on a basis of close international coöperation.

Secretary Hull, in his great radio address of July 23rd, 1942, stressed that the United Nations should "from time to time, as they did in adopting the Atlantic Charter, formulate and proclaim their common views regarding fundamental policies which will chart for mankind a wise course based on enduring spiritual values." But he also made it clear that it was not sufficient to proclaim such policies. It is necessary to find the mechanisms by which they may be most fully and most speedily attained and most effectively safeguarded:

"The manifold tasks that lie ahead will not be accomplished over night. There will be need for plans, developed with careful consideration and carried forward boldly and vigorously. The vision, the resolution, and the skill with which the conditions of peace will be established and developed after the war will be as much a measure of man's capacity for freedom and progress as the fervor and determination which men show in winning the victory."

But the conditions of peace cannot emerge spontaneously from an international conference. The adequate mechanisms cannot be improvised; no enthusiasm will suffice. Governments cannot even make up their minds on the line of action they want to take without knowing exactly how to pose the problems. That is why time and patience are needed, and the establishment of the right kind of instruments to pursue the factual investigations.

And, maybe, after all, some guidance can be found in the Versailles treaties.

XIII: Visit to Versailles

Before we look at some of the constructive work that sprang from Versailles, it might be well to bear in mind how insufficient was the time given to the negotiators at Versailles. The world was impatient, parliaments were restive, democracies were uneducated and undisciplined. Immediate results were requested, not a study of problems.

Mr. Bevin, when discussing the objective of the war, writes:

"A future peace must not be influenced by a couple of hundred M.P.'s in the House of Commons sending a telegram to a Prime Minister at the Peace Conference, as was done at the time of the Versailles discussions. That must not influence us. What must influence us is principle, and I want a lively consciousness this time on the part of the masses of the people whose children always have to pay the price of war." ("The Balance Sheet of the Future," p. 17.)

That there is a real substance in this hope was proved by the resolutions adopted by the International Labour Conference.

This consciousness of the masses must not be exploited by political rabble-rousers whose vulgar minds smell a chance for promotion in crying for revenge and retaliation, but given ample time to develop into the conviction expressed by Mr. Bevin in the following terms:

"What we know as Western Civilization, cannot survive except upon a basis of liberty and equality among the peoples of the earth, giving to others what you claim for yourselves and getting in return a feeling that there is something to fight and live for."

It will not be too easy to make delegates and parliaments accept this view in a moment of triumph, but, perhaps, it will be made somewhat less difficult if they are made to understand what a slow and laborious work peacemaking has always been. And measured by the standard of the history of nations, some years more or less do not count when the question is to give the most careful preparation to a worldwide peace.

The conference at Versailles lasted not quite six months. The Congress of Vienna in 1815 was in session for more than nine months. The Congress of Utrecht (1712-1713) that had to rearrange Europe after the wars of the Spanish succession lasted for fourteen and a half months.

The Thirty Years' War, which in many ways bore more resemblance to the present war than any later conflict, took long years of conference to end. The peace negotiations were opened in 1636; after preliminary deliberations in Hamburg in 1637 and 1640 it was suggested in 1641 to move the conference to Münster and Osnabrück; by the end of 1641 this was agreed upon, and the opening of the conference set to July 11, 1643. The peace treaty was signed in Münster on October 24, 1648.

And in one way it was much easier to conclude a peace under the political conditions of earlier centuries. The wars before 1813 were not primarily national wars. They were dynastic wars. The plenipotentiaries who met for peace-making were responsible to their monarchs and not to any parliaments. There were no heated public discussions of peace terms. There was no radio and no press to whip up emotions. To be a soldier was an honorable profession and not a national duty. Troops of many nationalities were fighting for the ruler who could afford to pay them. There were no nations fighting nations. And even the emotions raised by the religious conflicts were simple compared to those stirred up by the creed-wars of today.

The whole growth of social machinery, the vast complexity of modern society, the interdependencies linking country to country, make the problems of war and peace infinitely more intricate than in any other epoch; and even if it may be asserted that the means and powers of regeneration have multiplied and are far stronger than they have been, it is of importance to remember that the human material has not developed at a par with state machinery or mechanical inventions. Neither human intellect, human conscience, nor human character has been able to keep pace with technical development. So time is needed more than at any earlier moment, ample time before the involved problems can be solved.

But in spite of the hurriedness at Versailles something new was created which will, perhaps, in the light of history, in a certain measure, vindicate the peace makers of 1919. The League of Nations, the International Labour Office, the Permanent Court of International Justice were instituted; and out of the practices of these organizations has grown an experience highly valuable and most instructive for the planning of the peace to follow this war.

When after the victory we come to the question of occupation of the totalitarian countries we have this accumulated store of experience which may prove more important than has been generally realized.

The traditional idea of occupation presupposes a military administration or a German hybrid of military and gestapo administration. Such a system may be necessary for some time, but it is hardly the kind of administration which, if made lasting, would appeal to democratic nations, and hardly the kind of administration that would accelerate peaceful national recovery and re-creation in occupied territories.

Conditions and possibilities of local organization and

local self-government differ from one territory to another; and we may hope that some new form of central national government can be developed from the organs of local self-government. But two of the experiments made at Versailles have proved so useful that they may serve as a model for the long period of transition which will be needed in the totalitarian countries.

Government by some kind of international commission was instituted in various forms after Versailles. The most important experiment was tried out in the Saar district.* It worked for fifteen years and worked remarkably well.

Still more important was the mandates system introduced after Versailles.† And it will appear to many that

* The Saar district is one of the richest coal-mining districts of Germany. Lying close to the iron ore deposits of the Lorraine, it was coveted by France after the last world war. President Wilson refused to grant France the transfer of sovereignty of this territory inhabited by Germans. A compromise was found whereby France got the control of the economic interests of the coal mines and whereby the territory was to be administered by an international commission for fifteen years. The five members of this governing board were appointed by the Council of the League and were responsible to it.

On January 15, 1935, a plebiscite was held and the population by a vast majority (more than 95 percent) voted for return to Germany.

The international government was on the whole very successful and the plebiscite, held under the protection of an international police force—consisting of soldiers from Great Britain, Italy, the Netherlands and Sweden and police officers also from other countries—was probably the best organized and supervised international plebiscite ever held, in spite of the fanatical moral pressure from Germany across the frontier.

† As a result of the First World War the Central Powers lost all their colonies to the Allied and Associated Powers. It was decided at the Peace Conference that these territories should be administered by certain States—all of them from among the Allied and Associated Powers—as "Mandates" under the League of Nations. (The U. S. A. did not wish to become a "Mandate-Power.") All these territories were under the supervision of the League through the machinery of the Permanent Mandate Commission and the Mandate Section of the Secretariat. Article 22 of the Covenant of the League lays down:

1. "To those colonies and territories which as a consequence of the late war have ceased to be under the sovereignty of the states which formerly governed them and which are inhabited by peoples not yet able to stand by themselves under the strenuous conditions of the modern world, there should be applied the principle that the well-being and development of such peoples form a sacred trust of civilization and that securities for the performance of this trust should be embodied in this Covenant.

2. "The best method of giving practical effect to this principle is that the tutelage of such peoples should be entrusted to advanced nations

the best solution of the problem of Germany, when a military occupation is no longer necessary, will be to make of Germany a mandated territory until such a mentality and such institutions have been developed in the Reich that the German people is no longer in need of international tutelage and can choose for themselves a constitutional form of government under democratic responsibility.

Maybe the best alternative would be to combine the system of an international governmental commission with the ordinary mandate-form of administration.

It is of interest to remember that the mandate system was widely felt to be so important an innovation in international life that in 1937 proposals for the extension of this system to other colonies were laid before the British Government by the Advisory Committee of the British Labour Party, which had definitely adopted this policy for implementation, if and when it again resumed power. Mr. Baldwin, replying for the Government, could not accept the proposal, but his statement on the other hand made clear that the mandates articles of the Covenant of the League were considered a ponderable reality. He ob-

who, by reason of their resources, their experience or their geographical position, can best undertake this responsibility, and who are willing to accept it, and that this tutelage should be exercised by them as Mandatories on behalf of the League.

3. "The character of the mandate must differ according to the state of the development of the people, the geographical situation of the territory, its economic conditions and other similar circumstances.

4. "Certain communities formerly belonging to the Turkish Empire have reached a state of development where their existence as independent nations can be provisionally recognized subject to the rendering of administrative advice and assistance by a Mandatory until such time as they are able to stand alone. The wishes of these communities must be a principal consideration in the selection of the Mandatory."

(An example of this group, called A-Mandates, is Iraq which later was recognized as a sovereign state and became a member of the League. —To this group also belong Syria and Palestine.)

7. "In every case of mandate, the Mandatory shall render to the Council an annual report in reference to the territory committed to its charge.

9. "A permanent Commission shall be constituted to receive and examine the annual reports of the Mandatories and to advise the Council on all matters relating to the observance of the mandates."

jected to the proposal that it would mean the creation of a kind of international colonial office to replace the present Permanent Mandates Commission. Today, it seems not entirely improbable that such an international colonial Commission may be created as part of a final world settlement. And undoubtedly the spirit of Article 22 of the Covenant did influence colonial policy far beyond the mandated territories.

Although the mandates system, on the whole, turned out a greater success than might have been expected and has proved a great constructive contribution to international life, there were setbacks, and the weakness of the system as originally planned was manifest. But it was also made very clear how the system could be improved.

Under the Covenant, Mandates fell under the jurisdiction of the Council—which (in the beginning) meant, practically, the mandatory powers. But every year, in the Assembly of the League, at the request of the Norwegian delegation it was decided that the report on Mandates should be considered by the Sixth Committee of the Assembly. The report, as a rule, was fully, sometimes violently, discussed in public, and on various occasions action was taken by the Assembly.*

The discussions were of particular interest, because here again the constellation was: The Great Powers against the rest of the states. England, France, Japan heartily disliked

* It is stated in "The Problems of a Lasting Peace" by Herbert Hoover and Hugh Gibson: "In effect, no action of the Assembly could become binding without the approval of the Council."—This assertion must be based on a peculiar misunderstanding of the League system. No action of the Assembly needed the approval of the Council. No decision taken by the Assembly went to the Council. Under the Covenant and the peace treaties the decision of certain questions appertained to the Council. Other questions, a very great number, appertained to the Assembly. All budgetary questions, for instance, were discussed and decided only in the Assembly. And the general tendency was for the Assembly to take over more and more power, as illustrated in the case of the Mandates Report. The peculiar mistake in the book quoted gives a fundamentally wrong impression. What complicated League procedure was the very fact that the Council and the Assembly moved in different orbits and that sometimes it proved difficult to obtain the needed coördination.

any efficient control of their mandatory stewardship. Nevertheless, in the Fourth Assembly of the League a vote of censure was adopted, criticizing the way in which South Africa had behaved to the Bondelswarts tribe in Southwest Africa.

Under the system that had been elaborated the population of any mandated territory had the right to send petitions to the Mandates Commission; the Commission felt that this was not sufficient and proposed the granting of permission to petitioners in mandated areas to appear before the Commission in person. The Commission also wanted to have prepared a more elaborate questionnaire to guide the mandatory powers in the preparation of their annual reports. The powers in question opposed both proposals violently and once more demonstrated their shortsighted unwillingness to give up any vested privilege, even if it was entirely usurped, or any shred of ill-acquired prestige.

"On the occasion in question, four of the most influential of the fourteen Council members suddenly and almost simultaneously addressed that body in their capacity as mandatories —a role in which they revealed little of the unbiased point of view expected of Council Members when that body is acting as arbiter on questions related to the administration of mandated areas. (Margaret E. Burton: "The Assembly of the League of Nations," p. 219.)

What the Mandates Commission had desired was not granted it. But the Jewish agency in Palestine was permitted to present petitions in person. The British administration of that country was very freely criticized in the report of the Mandates Commission in 1930; and in recent years the discussions of Mandates in the Assembly centered on Palestine. Conditions in that country have made the task of the mandatory power extremely complicated. But the British Government, on various occasions, has expressed appreciation of the Commission's criticism.

The real difficulty was the mandatory power that tried to keep the Commission in the dark and showed no willingness to coöperate. On one occasion Lord Lugard, for many years member of the Commission, remarked:

"[If the Mandatory power] derided the system and took no notice of what the Mandates Commission said, serious friction would be inevitable, resulting in all probability in the Mandates Commission declining to discharge an obviously futile task."

His words applied to Japan, whose non-coöperation with the League produced the ultimate result that no report was given at all. The League was powerless, and the country that had a right to act and should have acted—the United States—preferred to stand aloof in splendid, but as events have proved, grossly expensive isolation. The United States had been given the Mandate over the former German islands in the Pacific. But the Senate refused to ratify, and the islands were mandated to Japan. Still the United States retained the right to study the report and control the execution of the Mandate. But the Senate refused to take any action.

The Mandates system has been mentioned so fully because one of the things generally agreed upon that emerges from the preliminary discussion of peace aims is that the Mandates system will continue and will be extended. What should be done to improve it Mr. Benjamin Gerig has summed up as follows:

"Continuation of the Permanent Mandates Commission with new territories brought under its supervision, a supervision to be extended as regards: (1) the right to make inquiries on the spot, (2) easier petitioning procedure, and (3) utilization of administrative officials drawn in part from among nationals of states other than the mandatory power." ("World Organization," p. 229.)

If there is a positive guidance to be found in these results of the Versailles treaties, it will probably be generally admitted that on some other points there is a negative lesson to be learnt from Versailles.

As mentioned before, the only economic provision in the Versailles treaties was the decision that Germany should make reparations. But reparations were not made and for years the political horizon in Europe was overshadowed by the discussions concerning what and how Germany should pay. In Germany the idea that the whole nation, economically speaking, should do forced labour for years after the war created bitterness and desperation, and such currents of opinion helped to prepare the coming of Hitler.

It will probably be felt when this war is won that all indemnities to nations robbed and ruined, that any fine for criminal violation of international law should be taken out of Germany immediately, and that a new generation in Germany should be given the opportunity to rebuild their country without being crushed by burdens of debt. The stability of the whole economic system of the world would suffer under such long-term financial punishment.

At yet another point we have something to learn.

The terms of the Versailles treaties created a new kind of passionate nationalism among many ethnological groups in Europe.

President Wilson in his address to Congress on February 11, 1918, declared: "National self-determination is not a mere phrase. It is an imperative principle of action." On this principle national minorities were given certain privileges under the Versailles treaties; but it was never defined what is meant by a nation nor what should constitute a national minority. The right to national self-determination is so important a part of a democratic system, and the protection of national minorities has often been so badly needed, that the men of Versailles shut their eyes to the danger of setting free violent centrifugal forces in the new territories created by the peace, without providing for any needed corrective. It was overlooked that historical conditions made the application of Mr. Wilson's principle of action next to impossible in the world of hard political realities. For nations are not living beside each other in watertight compartments, in such a way that national self-determination behind one set of bulkheads will not interfere with national self-determination in the neighboring partition. Nations are blended and intermingled and intertwined. For thousands of years migrations and warfare have sent wave upon wave of invaders across all the territories of the European continent: Phœnicians and Jews, Greeks and Romans, Celts and Teutons, Slavs and Mongols, Saracens and Moors, Huns and Turks. And each wave has left behind eddies and backwaters, small "pockets" of populations, foreign to their surroundings in practically every sector of Central Europe.

Extremely few countries have a homogeneous population and no national minorities. The outstanding examples are Iceland, Norway and Sweden, where practically one hundred percent of the population belong to the same nationality and speak the same language; and where even religious unity is very marked. In Denmark there is a German minority; in Finland there is a Swedish minority; their banknotes are printed in two languages —Finnish and Swedish, as in Canada banknotes are printed in English and French; in Belgium in French and Flemish; as in Switzerland they are printed in French, German and Italian. This simple fact graphically illustrates one very important and long-established political experience: For the conception of a state and for the stability of a state, national and lingual unity is not necessary; but financial and economic unity is. All the languages printed on the old Austrian banknotes symbolized this idea: It was the financial and economic system of the state that bound all these languages and nationalities together.

No state can exist if it cannot lead an independent

financial life, and be economically self-supporting. At Versailles new divisions were made and new frontiers set up, irrespective of the financial and economic, of the industrial and commercial requirements of the territories involved. And the proclamation of the right of national self-determination led to the gradual disintegration of the new states set up. If at Versailles British and French politicians and diplomats used this term as a useful wedge for the process of cleaving the German and Austrian-Hungarian empires, they certainly have learned that the wages of sin is death. In the name of national self-determination Nazism mobilized the Sudeten-Germans who had never belonged to Germany, or had any connection with Germany—except as enemies in the war of 1866 and a series of earlier wars. And their claim to self-determination meant the destruction of Czechoslovakia. In the name of national self-determination for the Germans, not for anybody else, disturbances were created in Danzig and Memel, in every neighboring country to Germany. The boomerang forged by President Wilson returned with a bang.

At the peace conference to come it will be necessary to analyze and to X-ray every slogan and every catchword and not take even a proclaimed principle of action at its face value. And, as it will be necessary to microscope the national self-determination, so it will also be necessary to have the term "protection of minorities" adjusted in the critical laboratory and the practical workshop. Under certain political constellations the majorities are in more bitter need of protection than the minorities. And until we have generally accepted rules defining what percentage of the population in a given country, what kind of geographical concentration, of historical traditions shall be deemed necessary for the constitution of an internationally acknowledged minority, we had better beware. Military parachutists would hardly be considered a minority in the country where they landed; and technicians, financial parachutists, commercial parachutists have no more right to claim the protection granted to minorities than have military parachutists.

Leading men in public life in most democratic states have declared their willingness to revise conceptions of national sovereignty. They are ready to sacrifice on the threshold to a new era of peaceful international coöperation some of the prerogatives and privileges of national sovereignty; and, certainly, they cannot enter a new epoch vested in the garb of ancient prejudice. But the unrestrained right of national self-determination, the loud demand for the protection of minorities, are only other aspects of the extreme conception of absolute sovereignty for each individual state.

It might be well to have in mind sometimes that nationalism as we meet it today was made in Germany, and is one of the products of the romantic school in the beginning of the nineteenth century; it was promoted as one of the elements of the German renaissance in the days of Napoleonic glory. But there is no denying that the growth of nationalism during the last hundred years has made the world more narrow and national boundaries more insurmountable. And at Versailles the very creation of new small states in the name of self-determination bred an outré nationalism which again engendered that kind of difficulties and evils which the fourteen points of Wilson had intended to prevent.

In public and private discussions the terms "national self-determination" and "protection of minorities" will always play their part, and quite naturally; without a just and reasonable administration of those rules no stable peace can be secured. But a trained staff of observers will have to prepare for a peace conference the necessary data and to draft the demographic charts needed to understand where minorities are to be found, and of what kind, and to fit into the jigsaw puzzle of nationalities, which is Central Europe, only the amount of rightly conceived national self-government which that beautiful picture can sustain without going explosively to pieces.

And fortunately, even if these revenants from 1918 are mobilized by those whose innermost hope it is to frustrate any universal peaceful settlement, more and more groups understand the complex nature of the problem.

In the "War Aims, Peace Terms, etc.," sent out as "a joint declaration by Democratic Socialists of Several Nationalities," it is stated with full truth:

"Frontiers in Europe cannot be made to coincide very closely to ethnical or linguistic boundaries, nor can they create perfectly balanced economic units. . . . Self-determination must not be identified with the artificial creation of states and frontiers along ethnical lines. The doctrine that each nationality must be a separate state has to be discarded."

But when it comes to the question of minorities even this group is sentimental and not realistic:

"In all cases, full political and civil rights as well as cultural autonomy must be given to minorities where there are compact minorities, and where practical, regional administrative autonomy should be given to them."

Even in this cautious rendering the sentence has to be accepted *cum grano salis*. Are the Poles in Chicago or the Chinese on Manhattan a compact minority that should be given cultural and regional administrative autonomy? Are the Japanese fishermen in British Columbia such a minority? If the Germans who have been rounded up in Brazil claim that they are a minority, will they constitute such a compact group?

The minority clause in the Versailles Treaty was excellent so far as it went, and has proved of great practical and political value; but good-will was an indispensable condition of its working successfully and good-will among various national groups in Eastern and Central Europe is a rare bird indeed.

No procedure was fixed in the peace treaties and minority treaties or declarations for receiving, hearing, rejecting or acting upon petitions from minorities. Under the treaties the Council of the League had to deal with these problems; there is no reference at all to the Assembly in the minority treaties. Still the Assembly asserted its power, regularly requested to have the report on minorities sent to the Sixth Committee, and on many occasions discussed minority questions and adopted resolutions that became law. But under the treaties only a member of the Council could legally put on the agenda of the Council an alleged infraction of the minority clauses of the treaties. In October, 1920, the Council adopted a proposal to constitute a Committee of Three to examine minorities' petitions in order that they might make "a report to the Council upon each petition *at its following session.*" But the influence for evil of the Little Entente was strong enough to oblige the Council to drop from the proposal the words underlined and the Committee of Three—

". . . has too often stifled the petitions without either States Members of the League or the petitioners themselves knowing anything about the fate of them.

"After these early successes the politicians who were strongly committed to maintaining the status quo of Europe and to silence the minorities with whom this status quo was unpopular, lost no opportunity of preventing, so far as it was possible, fair or public treatment of minority petitions." (John Eppstein, "Ten Years' Life of the League of Nations," p. 116.)

Further, we have to bear in mind that the system set up for the protection of minorities, including the right of petitioning to the League of Nations, was not made applicable to minorities within the boundaries of the victorious empires. And in the long run this unilateral application of the principle tended to make it non-operative. Nevertheless, as a result of that clause a vast store of international experience has accumulated. Those who shall discuss minority-problems when the war is over, will be bound to examine the files of the minorities section at Geneva and to study such material as the Finnish system for education of the Swedish minority * or the Danish handling of the minority problem in Schleswig, which has been admitted to have been as fair as efficient and tactful.†

It should also be borne in mind that for the solution of problems of immigration, of opening up new territories to so-called overflow populations, the questions of national self-determination and protection of minorities have a very direct importance. Every country would be afraid of an open-door policy if immigrant groups should be considered as minorities having a right to autonomy and national self-determination. We must not commit over again the fault committed by the League. The minority-practice instituted after Versailles was used as a strong instrument for political fragmentation at a time when economic integration was becoming irresistible.

* Mantere, M. Oscari: *"Conditions linguistiques de l'enseignement en Finlande,"* Vol. I, *Le Nord,* 1938, pp. 101 ff.

† Andersen, Holger: *"Le Danemark et la minorité allemande du Slesvig du Nord,"* Vol. I, *Le Nord,* 1938, pp. 52 ff.

XIV: A Universal Solution

Every problem coming up before an eventual peace conference has an international bearing. No single question can be insulated in such a way that any big nation can declare: "We are not interested."

Minority-questions, the application of the principle of national self-government, questions of colonies and of raw materials, are all twined together and linked to other questions of an international character and of vital interest to every country.

The Hon. Sumner Welles, Undersecretary of State, in his remarkable speech at Arlington on May 30, 1942, states his belief that the "voices of the men who will make our victory possible when there is established that permanent system of general security promised by the Atlantic Charter will demand that the United Nations become the nucleus of a world organization of the future to determine the final terms of a just, an honest and a durable peace." But men of less importance have not grasped the meaning of the Atlantic Charter and are still discussing whether the best solution would not be a Union now between certain groups of states, or a federation or a union of states within certain continents—a European Union, an American Union, a Far-East Union, etc.,—or the establishment of what has been called Regional Agreements.

On the face of it a solution along any of these lines might seem natural and sympathetic, offering far fewer difficulties and problems than any solution on a worldwide basis. But critical investigation will make clear that such a plan, with all that could be said to support it, even if it might appeal to many countries, would in no way be adequate to prevent future wars or to make possible a dynamic peace.

Not only geographical unions have come under discussion, but political unions and linguistic unions, which again mean race-unions that would become political.

That a federation of democratic states automatically would lead to a federation of non-democratic states, is obvious. And an English-speaking union would immediately call forth other unions—German-speaking, French-speaking, Spanish-speaking, a Slav union and what not. The English-speaking nations, after all, only constitute a small minority of mankind. The role of China and of Russia in this war will also make it necessary to revise some old Western concepts. And any formation of any block would lead to the formation of other blocks, would speed up the armament race and divide the world into two or more armed camps, distrustful of each other, each hoping to steal a march on the other group.

Viscount Cecil, who is such an extremely wary and experienced observer of international events, when discussing the plan of Mr. Clarence Streit writes:

"I am afraid that the immediate result of this would be the crystallization of a counter-group of those countries which believe in some form of autocracy." ("A Great Experiment," p. 347.)

It would be difficult to find any statesman of authority who would disagree with him, and on this point statesmen and professors of international law are in full accord. Professor Quincy Wright, in his essay on "Fundamental Problems of International Organization," published in the preliminary report of the Commission to Study the Organization of Peace, printed by the Carnegie Endowment for International Peace, writes as follows:

"If the European democracies organized various authorities with competence over their territories excluding the territories of the Totalitarian States, it is to be anticipated that the latter would organize in opposition and tensions would be increased."

And Professor Lauterpacht, Cambridge, England, writes in the *London Political Quarterly* (April-June, 1941):

"Without the unifying and restraining influence of a League of Nations universal in its potential membership any such united Federations may well become a source of regional friction and far-flung wars."

Even the solution that has been called continentalism would lead to the same results. The interchange of commodities and ideas has never been isolated within one continent. Trade and commerce, finance, social evolution will not only make one continent dependent on the others, but also give one continent a very definite interest in the others, and questions of import and export, of emigration and immigration have brought states to war before now.

If we stop skating on the thin ice of polite speech, and soberly and realistically examine hard facts, we cannot help recognizing that continental interests are not of a very solid substance or trustworthy texture. They have to be built up on sentiment and have no background of continuity. It is, of course, far easier to discuss American continentalism than to imagine a European or even an Asiatic continentalism. But any attempt to divide up the modern world, even in continents, is out of tune with time. As that most experienced international servant, Mr. F. P. Walters, former Undersecretary General of the League of Nations, writes:

"The world is growing smaller. Radio, aviation, and other inventions may be considered from an international point of view as having changed the nature of space and time, and demonstrated the impracticability of a continental organization of the world almost before it had been suggested." ("Administrative Problems of International Administration," p. 12.)

But, nevertheless, we shall meet in many quarters this idea of a continental organization. It will give an outlet to many enemies of international coöperation and be used by opponents of what may be called the Roosevelt-Hull line of policy to create a new and dangerous variety of isolationism in the Western Hemisphere, and to unite all the distrusts and dislikes and jealousies of America in the Eastern Hemisphere.

Nobody would contest that continental interests can exist. And in the Americas a certain similarity and an important simultaneity in history and political traditions make a manifold collaboration natural. But it must not be forgotten that in the course of history oceans have not separated nations and interests. They have linked them together. From time immemorial trade has followed the waterways of the world. Wherever a ship could sail, men could meet, and thoughts could travel with them. The sea is still the cheapest and most convenient autostrada that exists. It is only in very recent times it has become possible to cross the continents; but it has always been comparatively easy to go from one continent to another. Mountain ranges, deep forests, arid plains, wastes and deserts barred the march of man; the oceans carried his ambitions from one coast to another; the history of continents is written in criss-cross lines over the waves and not in curves of splendid isolation. The Seven Seas still carry most of the traffic of the earth; and in 1939 it was still cheaper to send a barrel of fish from Seattle to Hamburg than across the continent to New York.

"Given the same separation in miles there is less economic distance across water than across land. The wheat distance from Kansas City to New York is about three times the wheat distance from New York to Liverpool." (Eugene Staley: "The Myth of the Continents," *Foreign Affairs*, 1940-41, p. 485.)

It is cheaper and it takes less time to send a cargo of paper from Norway to Philadelphia than to send it to Moscow. The interests of the northwestern states of Europe are in the North Atlantic, and link them closer to North America than to the South of Europe.

"As an Atlantic people we want above all a strong organized collaboration between the two great Atlantic Powers: The British Empire and the United States. This is our primary concern and the very condition of our participation in any international order in Europe." (Statement by the Foreign Minister of Norway: *Inter-allied Review*, March 15, 1942, p. 57.)

The Panama Canal means more to the Northern states of Europe than do the Dardanelles. The Mediterranean countries of Europe, on the other hand, are more closely in touch with the near East and with North Africa than with Northern Europe. The interests of Egypt, of Libya, of Algeria, are in the Mediterranean and not in the South Seas; they are north of Alexandria and Tripoli and not South of Capetown and Natal. And in spite of the tremendous distances, Australia, New Zealand and South Africa are linked together by bonds of interests and kinship.

Canada and the United States are much nearer to Ireland and England than to Argentine and Uruguay; and on the other hand, large sections of South and Central America are more nearly in touch with Spain and with Italy than with North America. History cannot be undone; neither can geography. It may be fashionable in certain epochs to disregard the obvious things; but words alone, however beautiful, and fictitious daydreams, however tempting and enticing, cannot support any heavy structure or stand any continuous strain.

It would be more in accordance with political and historical facts to discuss possible oceanic than continental organizations. The present war has made evident—it should have been evident before—that there exists an Atlantic sphere of interest, a Pacific sphere of interest; that every ocean is a theatre of war. Every day we are reading about the battle of the Atlantic, the battle of the Mediterranean, the battle of the Pacific. For more than fifty years there has been a North Sea Convention, there is a Baltic convention and under the London Convention on Safety of Life at Sea a group of fourteen countries has accepted the idea of their joint interest in keeping open the North Atlantic lanes of traffic. It may well be that future regional conventions will be defined on oceanic lines rather than on continental. And it is worthwhile remembering that when a close Pan-American collaboration seems a perfectly natural thing, it is not on account of the continental links but because all these countries have the same oceanic interests and are exposed to the same oceanic dangers.

What influence air-traffic after the war will have on world trade can hardly be estimated today. But, certainly, air-borne trade will make the world shrink still more and discussions of continents seem still more out-of-date.

A durable peace can only be based on facts, and to bridge the way from one fact to another in the quagmire of international intrigue, polite ambiguity, individual ambitions and national aspirations, a circumspection is needed, a perspicacity, a wariness which can X-ray any volume of verbosity and which will have to discard any project of solution which is not anchored in factual realities.

It has become quite fashionable in America to talk of a European union or even a European constitution. It ought to be made perfectly clear in very outspoken words that such plans have no factual background, they are contrary to historical, geographical, demographic, economic and political realities. Such plans are not welcome to any nation; nor are they supported by any responsible statesman. When Briand was an old and tired and hopeless man he tried to set up in the League of Nations a Committee to study the question of a European Union. The Committee never had any importance. Mr. Harold Butler in his book gives it the following epitaph which is a correct summary of political facts and sentiments:

"In 1930 a Committee on European Union was set up at Geneva on Monsieur Briand's motion, but it had no plan, political or economic. From the first it was a suspect child; its early and unnoticed demise surprised no one." ("The Lost Peace," p. 41.)

And this most wise and wary—and critical—observer of international political life sums up his observations of today in the following words:

"The world will still continue to be organized in a number of separate nations. The violence of the reaction against Nazism was due more to its attempt to stamp out national freedom and individuality than to anything else. To suppose that nations which have made unprecedented sacrifices in order to preserve their national identity are going to surrender it once they have regained it is surely contrary to common sense. To remake their national lives will be the first and dearest wish of all of them, even the smallest, and their right to do so is implicit in the conception of democracy. The national ideal is still the source from which the vitality, the culture, and the rich diversity of our civilization will be drawn."

If, on examination, we can find no safety in continentalism, it will certainly be admitted that no variety of regionalism could effectively prevent war, and that any solution within the limited frames that have been suggested, rather would provoke those very conditions of latent warfare which it should be their intention to prevent.

The problem of a dynamic peace can be met only by a universal solution. And the most important fact in the discussion of post-war conditions is the lucidity of the Roosevelt-Churchill declaration in this matter. It leaves no doubt. In summarizing the war-aims of democracy the two great leaders have made it perfectly clear that they aim at a future world organization of a universal character; they mention "all peoples" (point 3); "all states, great or small" (point 4); "collaboration between all nations" (point 5); "safety to all nations" (point 6); "all men" (point 7); "all of the nations of the world" (point 8).

Only through some kind of international agency built up on a worldwide basis can all nations, all peoples, all states, great or small, all men collaborate profitably and in full confidence. The eight points have been drafted with that perspicacity which marks leadership, in knowledge of the fullness of material at hand and in an exhaustive study of the question of universality versus regionalism.

In recent years no single question of international co-operation has been given more consideration by the governments of the world, and on few questions has there been collected such a mass of documentation and of evidence. The problem was considered so urgent that the Council of the League of Nations in October, 1936, appointed a special committee (called popularly the "committee of 28" because twenty-eight states were represented on it) to study the application of the principles of the Covenant. This committee asked Lord Cranborne, then Parliamentary Undersecretary for Foreign Affairs in the British Government, to write a report on the question of universality (participation of all states in the League of Nations), and asked Mr. Boris Stein, then Russian ambassador to Rome, to write a report on regional or continental organization of the League of Nations. These very important documents were discussed in 1936, 1937 and 1938 by more than fifty governments. Surely if the League of Nations had done nothing else, it should have taught nations what were the stumbling-blocks in the path of world organization. Even to those who adopt the expression of Viscount Cecil and look upon the League merely as "a great experiment," it must seem clear that no folly could be greater than to discard the vast store of results in political research accumulated during those twenty years of experimenting.

Mr. Elihu Root, that great protagonist of peace, speaking before the Council of Foreign Relations in 1924, declared:

"It is my deliberate belief that the greatest contributions to the history of world-peace are the negotiations and the exchanges that have failed in their immediate objective."

But such contributions become operative only if we are willing to draw the lesson of the failure.

Nobody can doubt that the work of the League of Nations, and especially the political work, was gravely handicapped by lack of universality. Even if the League was not originally conceived as a universal organization, it was soon made clear that the work it set out to accomplish had to be carried out on a universal plan. And gradually all states, whether members of the League or not, came to participate in the non-political work of the League and to benefit from it.

These League activities reached out over the entire earth, and their results were felt in every class of society and in every country. Traffic in women and children was brought under severe supervision, prisoners of war were repatriated, refugees were given a legal status and protection; traffic in drugs and narcotics was brought under strict control; slavery and slave trade were stopped; hundreds of thousands of homeless and landless people were given the possibility of a self-supporting existence, from the days when the Greeks from Asia Minor were planted in Europe until the recently accomplished settlement of the Assyrians in the Gab district. A worldwide warning system against epidemics was built up. One hundred and forty-eight different states and territories participated in the work. The different types of serum were standardized, so were vitamins; lighthouse-signals, buoyage-systems, road-signals were made uniform all over the globe. Nutrition committees were established in most countries; the International Institute of Intellectual Coöperation was spreading a network of informative and educational committees round the globe. Comparative studies of statistics, of world trade, of balances of payment, of world productions and prices, of money and banking were perfected, and the periodical publications of the League mark an epoch.

"The League of Nations has been responsible for the development of mutual exchange and discussion of ideas and methods to a greater extent and in more fields of humanitarian and scientific endeavor than any other organization in history." (Letter from the Secretary of State, the Hon. Cordell Hull, to the Secretary General of the League, February, 1939.)

But from the very outset the League was suffering as from a kind of infantile paralysis because the United States did not adhere to it. In drug-control, in health-research, in humanitarian work the United States participated fully and made important contributions. But when it came to political action the League was lame and not in full exercise of the powers with which it was intended to be invested.

First Brazil in 1928 left the League, but not the International Labour Office nor the Permanent Court of Justice, of which organizations Brazil has always been an ardent, active and faithful supporter. Then Japan left in the same way, continuing this partial membership, which in itself gives evidence to what an extent international coöperation was deemed important even by states

unwilling to give the League any political support. In
October, 1935, Germany ceased to be a member, and in
December, 1937, Italy gave notice of withdrawal.

To a certain extent, but quite insufficiently, these with-
drawals were counteracted by the entry of Russia, of Iraq
and of Egypt. No government could fail to realize that
any political action of the League, after this reduction in
membership, had ceased to have a universal effect; that
was one of the reasons for the breakdown of the action
against Italy in 1936.

The resulting discussions on the application of the principles of the Covenant and on the participation of all
states in the League of Nations seemed to prove that the
road followed had led to an impasse. A number of states
were unwilling to apply the Covenant in its entirety because the League was not universal; other states declared
that the League was not universal because it had been
proved that the Covenant could not or would not be applied.

Lord Cranborne in his very clear report * summarized
the situation in the following way:

"There appears to exist on this question of universal membership the double paradox that in a coercive League † universality may be essential, but impossible of realization; and
that in a non-coercive League, it may be easy of realization,
but cease to be essential."

As long as statesmen will rest content with only such
declarations of polite impotence we shall never reach a
dynamic peace. In political life, to do the impossible is the
only way to success—a fact which Hitler has fully realized.
And the realization of the war-aims enumerated by the
President of the United States and the Prime Minister of

---

* *Official Journal* No. A 7, 1938, VII.

† A League involving "provisions whereby, in certain events, its members would be obliged to impose so-called sanctions—economic, military,
or both—may, for convenience, be called a coercive League." (*Ibid.* p. 42.)

England cannot be stopped by the double paradox mentioned by Lord Cranborne. Whether the organization to be established after this war be called a World Federation or a reformed and revitalized League, it must be an organization strong enough not only to impose sanctions, but to prevent any outbreak of war. It will also have to be universal, because an organization strong enough to enforce its decisions, but not universal, would reduce the states outside its frame to a state of forced labour, forced law, forced conceptions of liberty, which would be in violation of the promise of the eight points.

In order to understand fully the problem of universality it is of importance to know why states were unwilling to act under a League system which was not universal.

The cause was very ably put by Mr. Undén, speaking on behalf of the Swedish Government before the "Committee of 28" on January 31, 1938, and elaborating on the "impossibility" mentioned by Lord Cranborne:

"A League of Nations cannot in the long run maintain its cohesion or influence international politics if it renounces in principle all means of pressure other than those of a moral character. An organization of states which make respect for peace a fundamental principle of international law cannot regard the violation of that principle with indulgence without exposing itself to the peril of gradual disintegration. It is a sociological fact that violations of law against which action is not taken, in the last resort, by coercive measures, lead rapidly to further violations and soon cause the principles of law to lose their influence over men's minds.

"Nevertheless, it should be realized that the idea of collective security, however sound it may be, cannot be put in practice unless the League obtains a very wide measure of support from the nations, unless—as is so often said—it achieves universality, this expression being taken in the relative sense. It is naturally impossible to indicate in any exact or general way the degrees to which the participation of states is indispensable. But no one, I think, will dispute the fact that a League of Nations which is very restricted in membership is incapable of functioning in accordance with the letter of the provisions of the Covenant."

In a similar way the Federal Council of Switzerland in a letter to the Secretary General of the League had already stated (September 4, 1936): "It would be a mistake to suppose that an inadequate membership could be counterbalanced by the coercive powers provided by the Covenant."

Mr. Rutgers, speaking after Mr. Undén on behalf of the Netherlands, declared:

"There is first of all, the lack of universality of the League of Nations. If all the countries of the world were united, it would be comparatively easy to restrain a single refractory state, but the situation becomes entirely different when the united countries are far from representing the universality which is essential to the League of Nations, and when the majority of the states entitled to a permanent seat on the Council are outside the League."

Mr. Komarnicki expressed the opinion of the Polish Government on this point in the following words:

"If it is to carry out fully the task entrusted to it by the present Covenant, the League of Nations must be genuinely universal and must comprise all the most important states. As long as these conditions cannot be fulfilled, the League will be obliged to adjust its activities to its resources. Furthermore it would be neither fair nor reasonable to seek to impose on the State Members of the League obligations and responsibilities out of proportion with the international responsibilities of the non-Member States, particularly since—as we are bound to recognize if we take a realistic view of the situation —those responsibilities are not in any way balanced by the advantages which the League is today in a position to offer to its Members."

H. E. M. Valdés-Mendeville on behalf of Chile made the following declaration: "Universality was the reason for the League's foundation, and it was in the interest of

universality that Chile became a member." And he further
advocated a return to universality even at the cost of substantial changes in the Covenant.

Mr. Hume Wrong, speaking for Canada, declared:

"The Government of Canada is in favor of every practical
effort to attain the substantial universality which is assumed
in the Covenant and which is necessary for the effective working of the League. It is essential to the adequate working of
any kind of League that its membership should approach
universality. The whole character of the League and the scope
and effectiveness of its activities obviously are radically
changed if a large proportion of States remains outside."

The point is not whether all these speakers were right;
other speakers—Mr. Litvinoff, Wellington-Koo speaking
for China, Mr. Fabela speaking for Mexico—maintained
that the main problem was to strengthen the League by
applying the Covenant, and that universality was only a
secondary problem. The political point is that the majority
of governments asserted as their considered opinion that
only a universal League would have their full support
or would be of real political importance and influence.
This mass of evidence, which could be multiplied, seems
to be sufficient to demonstrate that only a world organization based on universality is politically possible and feas-
ible. And if this was so in 1936, 1937 and 1938, it certainly
is still more so after September, 1939, when a number of
nations, still members of the League, either have sent in
their resignations or refuse to take any part in League
activities because the Axis powers are outside the League.

But the general adoption of the principles of universality does not mean that regional arrangements should
be precluded. On the contrary: a number of treaties, after
their very nature, are regional and should remain so. .
Other practical arrangements, involving geographically determined interests, might be left to wider federations;
there might even be continental unions, but all subject to

legislative and judicial authority exercised by the executive or parliamentary organs of a universal international organization. To use the words of Professor Quincy Wright:

"Regional international authorities should be subject to at least judicial control by a universal authority in order to solve conflicts of jurisdiction and to prevent usurpation of authority."

As mentioned above, all efforts to create a European Union or a Pan-Europa have met with little response. The infant movement started along those lines has been anemic and no medico-political injections have been sufficient to make the baby look natural and healthy.

When M. Aristide Briand sponsored the idea of a European union he insisted that it must be within the framework of the League of Nations. His words were: "There is not one peace for America, one peace for Europe and another for Asia, but one peace for the entire world."

XV: World Organization in the Concrete

Every plan sketched by statesmen or by representative groups has emphasized, directly or by implication, the importance of including among the principal peace-aims some kind of world organization. But very little has been said about the character and the competence of such an organization. Nevertheless, one thing emerges clearly from the accumulated experience of the last twenty-two years of international coöperation: that no matter what kind of constitution is given to this international body, and no matter what kind of executive committee, council or government will be instituted to act on its behalf, there must be some kind of World Assembly. Democratic nations would not agree to be governed internationally by any kind of ambassadors' conference. They will demand the policy of the open door. Whatever may be said about the League of Nations, the world would not go back to any form of international representation which was *less* democratic. An Assembly will meet again, and it must be known beforehand what shall be the jurisdiction of that Assembly, under what principles states shall vote, and how far the authority of the decisions will go.

World organization to secure peace has to be rendered concrete. General principles and moral declarations are very good and extremely necessary; but they do not lead us very far. Practical political international work has to start at the bottom with the cementing of fundamentals; it cannot start on top. And the practical details are not only of technical interest but of constructive importance; they mean the building of the walls that make it possible to live in security within the framework of peaceful international coöperation.

Not only political necessity but also practical experience points at a two-chamber system for any great international organization. In the League of Nations, as it was originally conceived by those in authority, there would have been no two-chamber system—because they did not want any chamber at all.

The British Foreign Office memorandum and the Cecil draft, prepared at the request of the British Foreign Office and submitted by Lord Robert Cecil to the British War Cabinet on December 17, 1918, both envisaged a League with the direction residing in a Council, composed wholly of representatives of the Great Powers. They did not include any League Assembly in their plan, but proposed that representatives of all states included in the League were to meet quadrennially. No single state outside the group of Great Powers felt any enthusiasm for this proposal, and at last the Council was set up with nine members, one representative of each "Principal Allied and Associated Power" and four members appointed for an indefinite period by these powers. The Assembly should meet "at stated intervals." But one of the fundamental decisions taken by the very first Assembly was that the Assembly should meet regularly every year; and gradually this more democratic body made the League depart more and more from the original idea of an extended ambassadors' conference. The membership in the Council was increased, it was decided that the Assembly should elect the non-permanent members, and there was a tendency to make the Council more and more like a Senate, with at last fourteen members. If the United States had been

in the League and Japan, Germany and Italy had not resigned, the Council would have had eighteen members,
with Russia nineteen—and probably at least three more
non-permanent members.

In the International Labour Organization there has always been a two-chamber system of a peculiar order. There
is the Labour Conference, corresponding to the Assembly
of the League, to the House of Representatives of the
United States, and then there is the Governing Body of
thirty-two members, built up on a far more democratic
basis than the Council of the League; sixteen members are
state delegates, eight members are labour representatives
elected by the labour delegations to the Conference, and
eight are employers' representatives, elected in the same
way by the employers' group.

Both the Governing Body of the I. L. O. and the Council of the League of Nations have some of the duties and
privileges of a national government as well as of a Senate.
And the upper house of any world organization set up
must of necessity have some such power, unless an international government should be instituted.

For the discussion of the competence and constitution
of any world assembly it is important to know under what
principles the new world organization should be directed.

Quite often one may hear the term "international government" without anybody's seeming to know exactly
what is meant by this term. On August 10, 1941, Mr. John
Cudahy gave an appeasement address over the radio. In
this speech the former United States Ambassador to Belgium apparently seemed to envisage a world cabinet vested
with extensive authority. He mentioned "an association of
nations and a sovereign international government" without making it very clear what he meant by these words.

Entirely different in spirit is the extremely interesting
"Declaration of the Federation of the World," adopted

unanimously after long deliberations by the General Assembly of North Carolina, March 13, 1941. We find here the words: "Whereas it is necessary at the present juncture of human affairs to enlarge the bases of organized society by establishing a government for the community of nations," . . . But it is evident from the following paragraphs that the meaning of these words is only a community that will "submit to the restraints of law and order." The ultimate aim of the Declaration is to establish The Federation of the World and "write the definite Treaty of Peace in terms of the Constitution of" such a federation. The authors of the Declaration did not have in mind any particular kind of government. They were inspired by a passionate desire for the ultimate victory of democracy and freedom; they had a vision and a dream, and they saw that government is essential to the "existence of communities and that the absence of government is anarchy." But government in international affairs does not of necessity mean a premier or a world president with a number of cabinet ministers in charge of various government departments. We have to envisage something entirely different.

The North Carolina Resolution, usually called the Humber Resolution, after its author, has been sponsored also by the General Assembly of the State of New Jersey. On May 1st, 1942, the following resolution was adopted (the Senate concurring):

"That the legislature of New Jersey, recognizing the interdependence of nations, does hereby memorialize Congress, and in particular the Senators and members of the House of Representatives in Congress from the State of New Jersey, to study the subject of World Federation as embodied in the Preamble of this Resolution."

Mr. Humber himself has declared that his resolution is not a formula but an indication of a line of action. And in a number of states within the Union good men and women with a keen sense of national and international responsibility are endeavoring to get their State Assemblies to adopt similar resolutions. And, no doubt, it would make the task of peace-making less difficult to American statesmen if the interdependence of nations were officially recognized all over the Union.

One of the most peculiar phenomena we have been witnessing during the last two years is the rather ghastly dance of peace executed by fanatical ideologists who take an unholy glee in exclaiming that the entire structure of civilization has broken down, and that without impediments mankind can sail forth in stratospheric altitudes of pure political speculation. But, fortunately, in the year of grace 1942 mankind does not start from scratch, and even if we seem to be witnessing a sort of general cataclysm, more institutions remain than are being overthrown. It may seem a rather macabre paradox to pretend that international law has never played a more prominent part in public propaganda than during this war, and still there is a surprisingly great element of truth in such a paradox. Even the aggressor and the murderer are quoting conventions and treaties, agreements, declarations and protocols to explain and defend their actions, and are willing to employ any shyster of international law prepared to be their counsel and help them to deviate the instincts of justice. Apparently it is a psychological necessity and of importance for the bolstering up of national morale that even modern dictators should employ legal assistance in trying to convince their nations, and by repercussion themselves, that they are not guilty. There is a famous phrase by a British moralist, writing in defense of cant, that people should not be too hard on hypocrisy, but bear in mind that after all, it is a compliment to virtue. In the international world of today we see some such compliments paid and they are not entirely without value.

We are products of tradition, of time-honored practices and usages, we cannot act as if the earth were created afresh, rising from a sea of blood. Eighty years ago the French philosopher Dupont-White in his preface to the translation of John Stuart Mill's "Liberty" printed the wise words:

"Continuity is one of the rights of man, it is a homage of everything that distinguishes him from the beast."

The instinct of continuity is innate in normal men, it is the spontaneous clinging to the concrete, the trustworthy and tried in a dangerous and changing world. Any states-man acting as if it did not exist will find that he has mis-calculated. In international matters, as in national matters, it is an essential advantage to be able to build on what is, and not to raise against constructive efforts the incalcu-lable forces of human inertia, supported by critical com-mon sense. Ortega y Gasset, that clear-eyed observer of political fallacies and failures, remarks in his "Toward a Philosophy of History":

"In revolutions the abstract tries to rebel against the con-crete, failure is therefore of the very substance of revolutions."

Mankind can hardly afford to invite failure once more; we have to build on concrete foundations.

No state living an orderly and normal national life would be prepared to sacrifice its form of tried government to any experiment in super-government. There may be much to criticize in the constitutional uses and abuses in every country, but people are familiar with their own things, and with their own leaders. In every state men are reluctant to accept any kind of foreign authority. Their feeling of continuity is not clearly defined; but neverthe-less it is a tower of strength in their lives; and one, per-haps vulgar, side of this ever-present, even if only latent, feeling, might be described by two stanzas from Kipling, true in every community, but, it may be, particularly so in the English-speaking nations:

> "The men of my own stock,
>   They may do ill or well,
> But they tell the lies I am wonted to,
>   They are used to the lies I tell;
> And we do not need interpreters
>   When we go to buy and sell. . . .
>
> "The men of my own stock,
>   Bitter bad they may be,
> But at least they hear things I hear,
>   And see the things I see;
> And whatever I think of them and their likes,
>   They think of the likes of me." *

The more limited use we can make of interpreters in any world organization, the better; for any nation will like to "feel the mind" of its rulers. But all states having suffered under the scourge of turbulent international insecurity might be willing to make some kind of sacrifice to establish an effective rule of international law and order. And the more modest the framework needed to carry out that rule, the greater the prospects of success.

When politicians, inspired by President Wilson's far-seeing vision, and statesmen like General Smuts fought for a League of Nations at Versailles, one of the great obstacles to a successful realization of that idea was the fear that states and nations should lose their sovereign individuality and become submerged in a world organization. One of the worst impediments in the way of making the League of Nations an efficient organization, and the organic paralytical condition of the League as an instrument of peaceful coercion, were due to this very fear. Mr. H. A. L. Fisher, the prominent British parliamentarian

* From *The Stranger*. Reprinted by courtesy of Messrs. A. P. Watt and Sons.

and historian, United Kingdom delegate to the first Assembly of the League, put it in the following words:

"The rule of unanimity has been devised to secure confidence in the League, and reassure timorous spirits against the
phantom of a Super-State."

There are still timorous spirits fearing a super-state;
there are so many of them in every country that the political weight of their fear cannot be neglected.

And not only the timorous spirits look upon a super-
state as a spectre and a phantom. A good many of the most
intrepid and undaunted spirits of recent years have commenced to look upon the super-state as a kind of awe-inspiring, magnified and multiplied octopus.

Any observer of the nature of states and of concrete
realities has been bound to admit to himself, however unwillingly, that the most imminent danger to democracy
today does not come from lack of government, but from
an excess of government. And the prospect of having a
super-state-structure imposed upon the federal and the
state administrations of the different countries is not al-
luring. In a good many countries the body politic has been
suffering from a long spell of what might be called *com-
mitteeocracitis*—the malady of believing in the rule of
committees, of giving more and more half-responsible and
sometimes nearly uncontrollable power to an ever increasing number of committees, until democracy is on the point
of being devoured by its own products. As an interesting
and graphic case of this disease might be quoted the development of the so-called Coördination Committee of
the League of Nations created during the Ethiopian crisis.
This is the picture:

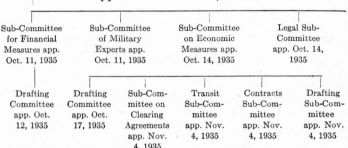

COÖRDINATION COMMITTEE
|
Committee of Eighteen
appointed October 11, 1935

Sub-Committee for Financial Measures app. Oct. 11, 1935	Sub-Committee of Military Experts app. Oct. 11, 1935		Sub-Committee on Economic Measures app. Oct. 14, 1935		Legal Sub-Committee app. Oct. 14, 1935
Drafting Committee app. Oct. 12, 1935	Drafting Committee app. Oct. 17, 1935	Sub-Committee on Clearing Agreements app. Nov. 4, 1935	Transit Sub-Committee app. Nov. 4, 1935	Contracts Sub-Committee app. Nov. 4, 1935	Drafting Sub-Committee app. Nov. 4, 1935

The disease did not originate at Geneva; a number of delegates brought the infection from their home parliaments. Every new committee set up is an evidence that democratic machinery is at a fault. Every new functionary appointed under a public administration is an evidence of some kind of failure in the relationship between the individual and the state. Tyranny cannot be fought by appointing legions of petty tyrants in government offices of hypertrophic tendencies. A steadily growing number of presumably intelligent persons are withdrawn from productive circulation and engaged in non-productive work; the percentage of people creating values and wealth is steadily dropping; the number of those who carry the actual burden of sustaining the commonwealth is gradually reduced. To quote another graphic word by the great Spanish writer:

> "The people are converted into fuel to feed the mere machine which is the State. The skeleton eats up the flesh around it. The scaffolding becomes the owner and tenant of the house."

To preserve democracy we cannot imitate the totalitarian dictators and establish more and more governmental administration, interference and intervention in every walk of life. The new order we are aiming at should need a minimum of new machinery, but most certainly a new spirit.

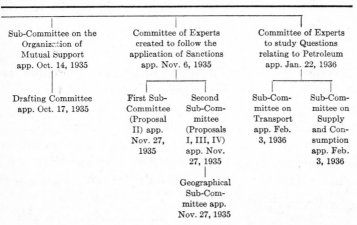

Sub-Committee on the Organization of Mutual Support app. Oct. 14, 1935	Committee of Experts created to follow the application of Sanctions app. Nov. 6, 1935	Committee of Experts to study Questions relating to Petroleum app. Jan. 22, 1936

Drafting Committee app. Oct. 17, 1935

First Sub-Committee (Proposal II) app. Nov. 27, 1935

Second Sub-Committee (Proposals I, III, IV) app. Nov. 27, 1935

Sub-Committee on Transport app. Feb. 3, 1936

Sub-Committee on Supply and Consumption app. Feb. 3, 1936

Geographical Sub-Committee app. Nov. 27, 1935

The cheap and shallow belief that human problems can be solved simply by setting up a new machinery is part of the popular lack of a critical sense of proportions and dimensions. As laws of right and wrong were losing their sharp edge, man gradually became intoxicated by his own mechanical inventions; and under this process of moral erosion, he was also gradually losing contact with fundamental, immaterial realities and becoming a victim to his own megalomania, dispossessed of his native sense of limitations. In certain nations this sickness became epidemic, and the conviction grew strong that there is no difference between human beings and robots, or rather that robots are superior, far more efficient and not subject to the failings of feeble products of feeling and sentiment. The robots and the robotical instincts took command with the result forecast by Goethe in his *"Zauberlehrling"* (The Sorcerer's Apprentice). It was possible to make an S. S. man or a Gestapo officer out of a broomstick, but they could not be changed back into broomsticks. The apprentice has become the slave of his own magic, and when he,

like his precursor in Goethe's poem tries to kill the robot,
it only "goes in twain," and he has double the number of
masterservants. They are going to drown him in the
luxurious bath he has prepared for himself. In vain he
exclaims: *"Ach das Wort worauf am Ende*
                *Er das wird was er gewesen." ***

But only the master has the word, and the apprentice has
forgotten that there is a master.

Many who are working with enthusiasm for the construction of a super-state and some who are speaking
thoughtlessly of a sovereign international government are
believers in robotian ideals and fully convinced that mankind can find happiness if we only can carry organization
and mechanization of national and international life to a
perfection like ant-existence in one single wonderfully
constructed cube. But they are far removed from the
realm of the concrete, and they are measuring and add-
ing and subtracting human beings and human qualities
which are incommensurable and inconvertible. Any structure they are planning in the abstract would prove a house
of cards in the concrete.

A study of the actual problems that would face a sovereign international government will corroborate the philosophical deduction. So far no practical plans have been
proposed for the solution of all the complicated problems
of national and international legislation, of international
and national taxation, involved proposals for the regulation of the relationship between the international super-
sovereignty and the individual state sovereignties. But it is
clear that the very fact that men not entirely without some

---

* "Oh, the word so strong and baleful,
   To make it what it was before!
   There it skips with pail and pailful—
   Would thou wert a broom once more!"

("Poems and Ballads." Translated by W. Edmondstoune Aytoun and
Theodore Martin.)

kind of public, as well as political, experience, men who have held responsible positions, can talk of a sovereign international government, will tend to mobilize all the latent forces of national isolationism against any attempted international organization.

And, certainly, it would be more than optimistic to believe that the rather constrained national unity more widely proclaimed and advertised than solidly manifest under the surface in the countries at war should last when the war is over.

The explosive outbursts of personal and political animosity against President Wilson after Versailles will be repeated on a grander scale against President Roosevelt when this war is over. All the atavistic ideas of savage senators in every democratic country, every power of prejudice, every instinct of individual ill-will will be marshaled against those who with wisdom and foresight try to build up an orderly international world organization. People cannot be expected to understand that the efforts to win the peace are as important for mankind as the efforts to win the war, and that even more self-restraint and discipline will be needed after the war than during the war, if we hope to arrive at a just and durable peace and not lapse into international chaos and anarchy.

XVI: Peace and Payment

If any question always is concrete, it certainly is the question: Who shall pay the bill? And no matter what kind of world organization or international government is put on foot, it will be necessary to give to it a financial reality and elaborate a system of contributions or a set of laws for international taxation, making it possible for the new organ of international coöperation to establish and to balance a budget.

In this field of joint state action we have a rich international experience dating further back than the League of Nations, but brought into the right focus by more than twenty years of difficult financial sailing.

Those who cling to the idea of absolute sovereignty for each individual state, also in principle adhere to the theory that conceptions of sovereignty and equality among states make it necessary that in any joint undertaking each sovereign state should pay the same amount to defray the expenses.

On this idea was based one of the first and most interesting conventions setting up any kind of international administration—the Cape Spartel Convention of May 31, 1865. This convention was concluded between Austria, Belgium, France, Great Britain, Holland, Italy, Norway, Portugal, Spain, Sweden and the United States of America for the upkeep and administration of the lighthouse at Cape Spartel (in Morocco, at the western entrance to Gibraltar). Germany and Russia later joined the Convention.

The Convention, to the sophisticated modern mind, has a certain fragrance of lavender and old lace. Diplomats were more naïve seventy-six years ago. It is stipulated in this document that even in case of war between the signatory powers (*ce qu'à Dieu ne plaise* . . . "Which God forbid") they shall continue to pay their contribution to the upkeep of the lighthouse. It is probably the last international treaty in which the name of God is mentioned; and one of the few honest enough to recognize the fallibility, even of conventions. And until now all the states have continued to pay, each state the same amount as every other signatory power. And they pay even in these years of disgrace.

The Cape Spartel Convention is also the last international convention built on this idea that the principle of equality among states makes it imperative that if they enter upon any joint undertaking, they should contribute an equal amount to the realization of it. National ambition seldom soars to such altitudes that public opinion claims to be taxed irrespective of any law of relativity.

The same month of 1865 that saw the Cape Spartel Convention also witnessed the signing of the International Telegraph Convention; but this convention, in this respect, has significance mainly as a forerunner of the Universal Postal Union. The Union was established in 1874 and its constitution for many years served as the model in practically every other field of international collaboration.

It was obvious that even the strictest interpretation of equality among states could not demand of Luxembourg to have the same bulk of postal correspondence as the United States. So when this Union was established, it was agreed that all the territories participating should be divided into six classes, paying their contributions at the ratio of 25—20—15—10—5—3. And the International Bureau of Telegraph Administration follows its Postal colleague. In the same way the bureaus of the union for the protection of literary and artistic rights, the bureaus for the protection of trade-marks, of patents, etc., repartition their expenses.

As state budgets were growing higher and higher, certain small countries felt that even a ratio of 25 to 3 was very unfair, and when the Universal Postal Union celebrated its semicentennial in 1924, a new, seventh class, was instituted for states that should pay only one unit.

There is no scientific rule or economic principle back of the classification. When a new state becomes a member, the country itself suggests to which class it ought to belong, and the formal decision is then taken by the Federal Council of Switzerland. But the total budget of the Postal Union shall not exceed 300,000 Swiss francs a year, and most of the other budgets are still more modest. When such small sums are allocated between a hundred partners, it does not mean much for New Zealand to pay the same amount as the United Kingdom and twenty-five times as much as the late Austria, and it may give a certain satisfaction because the original convention laid down that states should pay not merely according to extent of postal traffic, but in part according to national rank.

In the first class we now find besides the seven Great Powers, China, Argentina, Turkey, all the British Dominions, India and the Irish Free State, sixteen in all. Nothing can illustrate more strikingly the absurdity of the theory of absolute sovereignty and equality among states, than the fact that some authorities have been greatly perturbed because certain states did contribute more to the Postal Union than other states:

"This classification cannot be used as a proof of inequality among states, because it does not discriminate between Great Powers and other States, but is a purely objective classification based on population or similar factors," writes Max Huber, the great Swiss jurist in his *"Die Gleichheit der Staaten"* (1909). It certainly is tempting to analyze the logic of Mr. Huber's sentence. But in 1921 he was elected a member of the Permanent Court of International Justice; and it may safely be suggested that if he had waited twelve years before he published his essay on "The Equality of States" he would have published an entirely different treatise, or no treatise at all.

The Universal Postal Union attempt at international taxation and assessment was for a long time considered the best attainable. When the Permanent Court of Arbitration was instituted in 1899 (see p. 274), it was decided that the permanent expenditure of the Court should be allocated under the scale adopted by the Postal Union. And when the Versailles Treaty framed the Covenant of the League of Nations, it was laid down in Article 6, point 5, that the State members should contribute under the scale of allocations of the Postal Union.

Only twice, since 1865, has it been attempted to build up an international budget on an entirely different principle.

When the metrical convention was concluded in 1875 between Argentina, Austria, Belgium, Denmark, France, Germany, Italy, Norway, Peru, Portugal, Russia, Spain, Sweden, Switzerland, the United States of America and Venezuela (later Serbia, Roumania, Great Britain, Japan and Mexico joined), it was decided that each signatory power should pay a contribution to the upkeep of the bureau of weight and measurement in Paris corresponding to the actual population of the country. The budget, of course, is very restricted; still the most populous countries on earth, China and India, have not been willing to sign the convention, because it would establish a somewhat pernicious precedent for them to accept figures of population as the basis of international taxation.

The other convention regulating a small international

budget is of particular interest to the United States. The very important London Convention of 1929 on safety of life at sea was drafted and signed at a time when Americans seemed to agree on the idea that the United States had a legitimate interest in the North Atlantic, and found it natural that the United States Navy should patrol the Northern danger zone.

Articles 36 and 37 of this Convention provide for a service of ice patrol, a service for study and observation of ice conditions in the North Atlantic, and a service to ensure the destruction or removal of derelicts in the Northern part of the Atlantic Ocean. Fourteen states are signatory powers, and they agreed to pay towards the expenses for these services: Great Britain 40 percent, United States of America 18, Germany 10, France and Italy 6, Netherlands 5, Canada and Norway 3, Belgium, Denmark and Sweden 2, Japan, Russia and Spain 1 percent. If any of the contracting states wants to have its contribution altered, it can be made "in accordance with their mutual interests."

The convention gives proof that when practical men meet to draft a treaty on practical problems, the arid questions of sovereignty and equality are not discussed, but an agreement made on the basis of mutual interests. And no isolationalist opposed the ratification of the Convention by the United States Senate. It required some years before the ratification took place, but that was because of doubts regarding the relationship between certain sections of the convention and American laws for the protection of sailors. No voice was raised against the responsibility undertaken by the American Government; for all contracting states agreed that the United States Navy should carry out the patrol, and all the contributions be given over to the United States Government.

But those were the days before mighty men had declared impotence at sea and isolation in harbor of Ameri-

can ships to be the highest political wisdom and the best
way to secure the future of the freedom of the oceans.

For the rest, all international conventions involving a
joint budget have been built on the pattern of the Universal Postal Union.

There is an established democratic principle reading:
No taxation without representation; and to this is very
often added as the reverse: No representation without taxation. In national life in democratic states that principle
is no longer unchallenged, or admitted valid, but in international life at present, and as far ahead as we can see,
we have to accept as a law that no representation will be
given without taxation. In other words, those who call the
tune will also have to pay the piper. And to decide the
scale of payment, it might seem natural at the first glance
to accept also in international matters the general national
rule that representation is correlated to population. A
moment of reflection will show the impossibility of such
a rule among nations, and why the idea of the Metrical
Convention had to be abandoned.

It is not without interest in this connection to remember that at the time when the American Constitution
was framed, it was admitted that even among those thirteen small states, where conditions of life were not too far
different, population alone was no criterion of the right
of representation: a slave was taken to be only three-fifths
of a human unit.

If there were great difficulties in elaborating a system
acceptable to those states, the greatest of which numbered
420,000 inhabitants—how would they compare to the difficulties when we are dealing with sixty states differing in
population from 450 millions to 300,000 inhabitants?

And the composition of the population was pretty much
the same in the thirteen American states, the standard of
education was about the same, they all spoke one language; their ideas and traditions did not show any great

difference; and they all belonged to Christian denominations. (The slave question did not at that time seem too complicated.)

No real comparison can be made between the task confronting the authors of the American Constitution and the task of those who shall try to frame the constitution of a future world organization. From every demographic point of view, the component states are widely different: in race and religion, in temperament and tradition, in education as in outlook on life, in fundamental conceptions and ideas. It would seem evident that the more complicated the system of knitting them together, the greater the difficulty of making the whole organization work. There can be no general common legislation, and the mere mentioning of the varying figures of population will demonstrate that no representative system built on human numbers alone is practicable.

Those familiar with the history of the framing of the American Constitution will know how the problem of federal taxation versus exclusive state taxation was nearly insoluble. And if it proved delicate and difficult to find a just compromise between conflicting ideas in those thirteen states one hundred sixty-five years ago, how much more complicated will be the task of getting all the states of the world to accept any World Assembly empowered to levy taxes and vote a world budget. Principles of taxation, the very conception of taxation, vary from country to country and from climate to climate. Any attempt to create a super-state or a super-government given the ordinary rights, privileges and duties of national governments, would be doomed to failure, or rather any attempt to create such a thing would prove utterly futile in the near future.

The world organization to be, like the present League of Nations, will have to depend for its finances on the contributions or quotas from States Members.

Much can be said against such a system and few, if any,
have stated the case as clearly as did Alexander Hamilton
one hundred fifty-four years ago. He wrote:

"Those who have been accustomed to contemplate the circumstances which produce and constitute national wealth,
must be satisfied that there is no common standard or barom-
eter by which the degrees of it can be ascertained. Neither the
value of lands, nor the numbers of people which have been
successively proposed as the rule of State contributions, has
any pretention to being a just representative.

"The wealth of nations depends upon an infinite variety of
causes. Situation, soil, climate, the nature of the productions,
the nature of the government, the genius of the citizens, the
degree of information they possess, the state of commerce, of
arts, of industry,—these circumstances and many more, too
complex, minute or adventitious to admit of a particular
specification, occasion differences hardly conceivable in the
relative opulence and riches of different countries. The consequence clearly is that there can be no common rule of
national wealth, and, of course, no general or stationary rule
by which the ability of a state to pay taxes can be determined."
(*The Federalist*, No. 21.)

Still we have made a good deal of progress during the
century and a half that has passed since he discussed the
problem, and various ways of international tax-assessment
have been tried. But even the rules of the Universal Postal
Union proved unsatisfactory when they were applied to
the budget of the League of Nations. It has always been a
very modest budget, some $6,000,000 a year, but still that
was more than one hundred times the budget of the Universal Postal Union, and states which had been willing to
pay 1000 Swiss francs a year to the Union resolutely refused to pay 100,000 Swiss francs to the League.

The very, very small contribution to the Postal Union
and the other unions seem to pass all parliaments without
remarks. They are non-political grants. But the contribution to the League budget was felt to be a political grant.
Items which have invariably been found in the budget

for seventy years are seldom questioned. But this was a new thing, and the standard of honor among nations and the feeling of common responsibilities have not improved since the adoption of the Postal Union. States which loudly claimed equality, and had the most exalted ideas of sovereignty, protested violently against contributing three units to the League budget when the Great Powers did not pay more than twenty-five. A special committee set up recommended that the two directing principles for fixing the contribution should be the state revenue and the population of the different countries. Both principles were quite impossible in practice.

The figures of state budgets are no basis for any comparison because the structure of the state budget varies from country to country; and not even the principles upon which state budgets are built up are identical within any group of states.

The ordinary federal budget of the United States, for instance, is incomparable with the budgets of countries where various public expenditures here left to the individual states are included in one budget. In one country the entire cost of public education is left to municipal or local initiative and taxation. In another country all taxation is to the state, and appropriations are partitioned out by the state to cities and townships. One country has a terrible burden of debt, and so is forced to have much heavier taxation than a state with no public debt; but that does not mean that the first state is much richer and should contribute a good deal more to a world organization of nations.

And as to figures of population as a yardstick of relative national wealth, no man would seriously consider it today. Only among states with similarity in conditions of life, of climate, and so on, can paying capacity be measured by figures of population—as among the Scandinavian states, among Canada and the United States and between certain states of Latin America. But, even so, those figures give no unimpeachable indications. On one occasion the delegate of one Latin American state before the Allocation Committee of the League denied that comparative figures of population could be used to indicate what should be the contribution of his own country as compared to neighboring countries, claiming that his own country still had a considerable number of man-eaters, which should be deducted from the remaining number of producing people.

The two principles, so simple on the face of it, were not sacrificed without fight. But as it was an absolute necessity for the League to have a budget, a procedure was adopted under which the League appointed a special assessment committee, the Allocation Committee (*"le comité de repartition des dépenses"*), which worked with the competent functionaries of the League to elaborate the scale of allocations. This scale has been subject to rectifications from time to time; the system has worked, and in spite of great difficulties it can safely be said to have worked well. Up to the end of 1939 the sum of the budgets of the League (not the actual expenditure, which is considerably lower) voted since 1920 totaled $120,000,-000; of this sum 93.15% has been paid, 1.64% has been consolidated and is paid off in yearly installments, 0.88% is recoverable, 4.33% has been canceled.

The actual scale of allocations shows a far greater difference among states than the classification of the Postal Union. It varies from 108 units for the United Kingdom to one unit for a number of small states. But until now no small state has ever complained of this lack of equality. On the contrary, some small states have declared that they wanted to pay less than one unit and could afford only half a unit. And there have been resignations from the League for this financial reason, in spite of the fact that one unit for several years has been less than 25,000 Swiss francs and is for 1942 20,000 francs ($4500). The payment of this sum can hardly constitute a hardship for any nation.

No state ever complained that this assessment was an infringement on its sovereignty. And various states, members of the International Labour Organization, but not of the League proper, have paid and are paying under the accepted League scale of allocations. The one outstanding exception is the United States. The rugged individualism which is characteristic of pioneer communities has, quite naturally, found an international expression in a somewhat belligerent and exalted conception of national sovereignty which (in Europe) is believed to dominate the Senate of the United States. So when the United States joined the International Labour Organization, those who very actively worked for this decision thought it unwise to state that a League Committee should decide the contribution of the United States, and an agreement was reached between the interested parties that the United States should pay as much as the greatest single contributor, i.e., the United Kingdom. Owing to this peculiar and shy modesty, the United States pays far too small a contribution, and we are faced with the paradox that Canada per one million inhabitants contributes more than three times as much to the International Labour Organization as the United States. It is highly flattering to Canada, but, perhaps, does not give an entirely exhaustive picture of the relative wealth of the two countries.

In a similar way certain states, not members of the League, but adhering to the Permanent Court of International Justice, have contributed towards defraying the expenditure of the Court after the League scale of allocation.

It is difficult to define on what principles the scale of contributions has been built up. It might be said that states have been assessed on all possible information, after a study of all the facts contained in the International Yearbook of Statistics. Figures of production, of export

and import, bank deposits, gold, state budgets, length of
railroads, merchant marine—all national assets have been
considered. Representatives of the various states have been
heard by the Allocations Committee; supplementary information has been given and the financial capacity of the
states discussed at length.*

If we take the scale of allocations of the League of Nations as a standard, and even if it is not perfect, no better
standard exists, we shall find that thirteen states have been
assessed at only one unit, 2 at 2 units, 3 at 3, 4 at 4 and 4
at 5 units. Only one state is assessed at more than 100
units, the United Kingdom. (In this class might also be
put the United States.) Next came Soviet Russia with 97
units, then France with 80 units, Germany and Japan
with 78 units, Italy with 60, India with 49, China with 42,
Spain with 41, Canada with 35, Poland with 32 units.

One group of states pays considerably more per million
inhabitants than any other group, namely: New Zealand,
Switzerland, Australia, Denmark, Norway, Sweden, Canada, Finland; this may serve as a good indication that those
countries are at the front in the march of human progress
and civilization.† (Holland and Belgium, having colonies,
cannot well be compared to the states mentioned.)

More than once it has been suggested to include among
the elements of classification certain less ponderable fac-

* This is not the place to discuss fluctuations in the scale of allocations;
only one case might be mentioned because it is of specific political interest. When the new Austria entered the Postal Union after the war, she was
put in the lowest class, paying three units. At the reclassification in 1924,
she was even worse off, and only one unit was allocated to Austria. But
helped along by the League of Nations and for years under international
financial administration, conditions in Austria rapidly improved, and her
contribution to the League of Nations was mounting—the last time in
1937, when Austria accepted an increase of 25 percent and reached the
comparatively high figure of ten units, ten times as much as Liberia, the
only member state to have been assessed with Austria at one unit in the
Postal Union in 1924.—This fact throws a peculiar light on the German
claim that the Reich had to take over Austria because she was in such
a bad economic plight.

† When the Union of South Africa is not mentioned here it is because
any comparison is made difficult by the large black population. Per
literate inhabitant South Africa is very heavily taxed.

tors, as for instance the military budgets of nations. But it was found both unfair and impracticable. If one state, owing to a privileged geographical position, considers itself outside any possible danger zone and only maintains an etiquette defense, while another state, believing itself in constant danger, and so willing to pay any price for national independence, keeps up a high standard of national military preparedness, the latter state should not be punished by having to pay a higher international tax. And if one small state does not give a cent to armaments because her neutrality is guaranteed, the fact that she is spared the burden of national defense is no reason for giving her also a financial privilege at the expense of less fortunate neighbors.

On one occasion it was suggested that the budgets devoted to the foreign service of the various countries should be taken into consideration, and states calling their envoys ambassadors should be taxed more heavily than the more modest states content with having ministers. But it was soon agreed that the amounts devoted to diplomatic and consular service give very little indication of the relative wealth of nations. And even if it may be tempting to tax national vanity, as in some states individual vanity is taxed by a special duty on titles and decorations, it was found that the moral classification of states might, perhaps, be said to go outside the sphere of competence of any Allocations Committee.

The budget of the League and the work of the Allocations Committee may seem very trivial things, and still more so the collection of contributions. But even from this hard soil of monetary and financial facts romance can spring, and a payment become a political factor of some importance.

Ethiopia had been a loyal member of the League, paying its dues regularly until the war with Italy. After the conquest of Ethiopia the country still figured on the list of member states as shown in the budget. The League as such never recognized that the Italian king had taken over the sovereignty of Ethiopia. But gradually a large number of states members of the League recognized the Italian conquest, France and England among them. Italy did not like that Ethiopia still was on the printed list of member states, and England, with Lord Halifax in the Foreign Office and France, with Flandin at Quai d'Orsay, were eager to appease Italy. So it was agreed to take action at a meeting of the Council (which anyhow would have been entirely unconstitutional) and decide to strike Ethiopia off the list of member states * on the ground that Ethiopia did not exist any longer; there was no government; there were arrears and nobody to pay. This was in 1938.

Now, there were members with greater arrears than Ethiopia, and no political action had ever been taken against defaulting states. The Chairman of the Contributions Committee, whose duty it was to make states pay, approached Haile Selassie, suggesting that an installment on the contribution of Ethiopia might be a good investment for the country, better, perhaps, than any kind of propaganda. Haile Selassie, having ascertained that an installment would be accepted, sent the treasurer of the League £500 two days before the Council meeting. So when the subject was broached on the Council, the Secretary General had to inform the spokesmen of the appeasers that the Government of Ethiopia had paid an installment and the action had to be dropped. Some French newspapers regretted it rather violently. But, maybe, a good many people are quite happy today that Ethiopia is still on the list of member states, and so is still recognized by the other members of the League. It is not necessary to take any step to re-create the formal sovereignty of Ethiopia. It was there all the time.

* The list with specifications of payments of contributions was sent to States Members of the Council every month.

Another little story will illustrate how easily the question of a contribution may become an incendiary bomb.
The Fourth Committee of the League of Nations met at
Geneva in December, 1939, to discuss and adopt the
budget of the League for 1940. At that time Germany
and Russia had occupied Poland, incorporated her territories in their own and communicated to the world that
Poland had ceased to exist. But the Polish delegate met in
the Fourth Committee, and Poland, of course, figured in
the budget for 1940. The Russians had a full delegation to
the Fourth Committee. The Swiss Government was nervous and had made clear that any discussion of the Polish
question might endanger the neutrality of Switzerland and
complicate the position of the League in Switzerland.

There was an electric tension in the Fourth Committee.
It was generally supposed that when M. Souritz, the Russian Ambassador to France, had met there with a staff of
experts and advisers it was to protest against the inclusion
of a Polish contribution in the budget for 1940. As unanimity was required for the adoption of the budget, the
Russian delegate was in a position to veto any part of it.
On the other hand, it was under discussion to exclude
Russia from the League on account of the attack on Finland. And Russia had no desire to be excluded. M. Souritz
was exceedingly nervous; he was smoking cigarettes inces-
santly and his hands were shaking when he rose to make
some remarks. He seemed to be afraid that there would
be a strong demonstration in favor of Poland and against
Russia. The Polish delegate was persuaded to keep absolutely silent. No incident of any kind occurred, and a gasp
of incredulous surprise passed through the crowded hall
when finally the Russian delegate voted for the whole
budget, including the Polish contribution. It was a paradox. Poland in Poland did no longer exist, according to
Russia; but Poland on the League continued to exist with
the Russian vote. (Incidentally, Russia, as long as she re-

mained a member of the League, was a good and interested member.)

The budget of the League thus adopted (it is mentioned here because under any form of world organization some similar procedure would have to be followed) would then under the financial regulations be circulated to all the member states in due time before the Assembly meeting in September; and it would be examined by all the various Treasury Departments. No national budget is more strictly scrutinized than the various items of (comparatively) infinitesimal League expenditure. And if public speakers knew how grudgingly states pay their contributions to any international institution, and how many states try not to pay at all, they would probably understand better one of the practical problems a strong international government would be up against, and the difficulty of making peace and payment live harmoniously together.

Every single representative in every single member state of any international organization feels that he has a right to criticize its budget and restrict its expenditure. There are certain well-known difficulties in every national Treasury Department. In an international organization they would be multiplied by the number of adhering states.

In the League of Nations, on top of the difficulties familiar to national tax authorities, was the supreme complication that the League had no power of jurisdiction of any kind. The Covenant did not provide for any step that could be taken against any defaulting member. "National honor" is a very strong phrase when mentioned in all those international treaties of arbitration in which governments have excepted matters of national honor from the questions which shall unconditionally be given a peaceful solution. But when it comes to fulfilling financial obligations, "national honor" is a most elusive conception. When states did not want to pay their contribution to the League, they did not pay. And that was that. No action could be taken; they continued to be full members with all the rights and privileges of membership. Not only did they not lose their right to vote and to veto any part of the budget; but it has been quite customary both in the committees of the League, in the International Labour Conference, and the Governing Body of the International Labour Organization to hear delegates from non-paying states ask for and vote for higher appropriations and new credits. And, no doubt, this has been one of the factors naturally leading states and statesmen to look upon the League as not too serious a business proposition.

The lesson to be drawn from the experience of twenty years is obvious. In a future world organization states automatically must lose their right to vote if they do not fulfill their financial obligations, and it must be laid down beforehand what further steps should be taken to ensure the balancing of the budget. For if such an organization shall be able to accomplish serious work, and have real power, it must have financial security.

When the rule of payments is established, we are then immediately faced by a practical problem of far-reaching and fundamental importance: *Under what system shall great states be guaranteed their legitimate influence in world affairs?* Shall they rest content to pay the piper but not have any formal right to call the tune?

More than once it has been suggested in the League of Nations that states should have as many votes in the Assembly as they pay units to the budget of the League. The suggestion never came under very serious consideration, owing to the particular constitution of the League. But if we see the necessity of an international organization of all nations either in a World Union, or a Federation of States, or in a remodeled League of Nations, the most obvious possibility is a constitution so far following the American Constitution that there must be an Upper House, a Senate, a Council, whatever it may be called, representing certain principles of sovereignty; and a Lower House of Representatives: an Assembly to which states send their delegates authorized to cast as many votes, not as indicated by figures of population only (as in the House of Representatives of the United States), but as decided in a special scale. This voting scale may be simply such a scale of allocations as adopted by the League, or it may be a function both of this scale and of certain other factors, such as the burden of keeping a special airforce or police force at the disposal of the international organization; or states may be grouped in certain classes as in the Universal Postal Union. Only under such a scheme will it be possible to get nations to agree to finance any kind of international government, and be willing to give up the principle of unanimity.

XVII: The Problem of Unanimity

In international life the embodiment of the Sovereignty idea has been the rule of unanimity in all decisions. At the third meeting of the Commission which was drafting the Covenant of the League of Nations, Lord Robert Cecil stated that "all international decisions must, by the nature of things, be unanimous." On this axiom the Covenant of the League was framed and on this axiom it failed, as any federation of states so constructed will fail until men are born perfect. And the time has come for a dispassionate study of the historically known results of the unanimity rule.

The two greatest organizations of states known in history are the United States of America and the League of Nations. In the course of eight years the American Articles of Confederation nearly killed the Union. The states were in so bad a shape that Jay could write in his letter to Washington of June 27, 1786: "I am uneasy and apprehensive, more so than during the war."

The Articles of Confederation were practically unchangeable, because any amendment had to be *adopted unanimously* by the thirteen states. The first important amendment of 1781 was accepted by twelve states, but vetoed by the smallest state in the Union, Rhode Island. The important amendment introduced in the Continental Congress in 1783 was also approved by twelve states, but rejected by the state of New York.

The only good thing that can be said for the unanimity rule has been said by John Fiske in his discussion of the Articles of Confederation:

"Such was the constitution under which the United States had begun to drift toward anarchy, even before the close of the Revolutionary War, but which could only be amended by the unanimous consent of all the thirteen states. The historian cannot but regard this difficulty of amendment as a fortunate circumstance; for in the troubles which presently arose it led the distressed people to seek some other method of relief and thus prepared the way for the Convention of 1787, which destroyed the whole vicious scheme." ("The Critical Period of American History," p. 117.)

It may be hoped that the unanimity rule as laid down in the Covenant of the League of Nations may inspire a future historian to some similar kind of comment. But much more cannot be hoped from it.

On the axiom expressed by Lord Cecil those who drafted the Covenant went much farther than the Articles of Confederation:

"Except where otherwise expressly provided in this Covenant or by the terms of the present Treaty, decisions at any meeting of the Assembly or of the Council shall require the agreement of all the members of the League represented at the meeting." (Art. 5.)

The exception relates to the appointment of the Secretary General and (later) to elections to the Council.

Viscount Cecil in his recent autobiography, "A Great Experiment," defends this article in the only possible way:

"Whether the rule is good or bad, none other was possible at Paris. The Great Powers were obsessed with the wholly unreal danger that the small nations might band together and vote them down. The smaller countries were more reasonably afraid that their stronger neighbors would easily persuade a majority to give them whatever they wished, irrespective of the protests of the weaker States." (p. 72)

No other rule had been possible in Paris, because the great majority of the men who had met to discuss political decisions did not want a League of Nations that might become a reality. They looked upon it as a strange and ugly changeling, left in the cradle of the future by the great medicine man from the west, before he went back to his primitive continent. But before Lord Robert was made Viscount Cecil he tried to defend the rule as "not bad but good"; because the Assembly, being "made up of representatives met together for the purpose of preserving the peace of the world and passionately anxious that that purpose should succeed," made of it not an obstacle to action but an incentive to agreement. ("The Way of Peace," pp. 187, 188.) As long as the going was good there seemed to be a good deal of truth in this remarkable piece of forensic sophistry; but as soon as the going became rough the spirit of the Assembly was widely different from the prognosis of Lord Cecil. There was a very strong feeling among the victors at Versailles, and perhaps particularly among some of the representatives of minor states, which had been given by the peace treaties boundaries that were contestable, that their condition for accepting "the great experiment" was that it should be handled in such a way that it would always remain an experiment.

But to such an extent was the League a natural thing, that slowly and gradually, almost imperceptibly, the amorphous experiment was hardening and taking on a definite shape. In spite of almost incredible impediments the League was becoming a reality. And part of this development was a wonderful tacit compromise that was formed, getting the League round the dangerous promontory of unanimity, when the waters were not troubled.

When the League Assembly meets, it constitutes itself into six standing Committees, on which every single state represented in the Assembly has a member. All the items on the agenda of the Assembly are divided among these

Committees; every single question coming up, every single proposal made, is referred to one of them. The Committees discuss the various questions referred to them and report on them to the Assembly. The reports are printed as League documents.

Rule 19 of the Rules of Procedure of the Assembly states:

"Except where otherwise expressly provided in the Covenant or by the terms of a Treaty, decisions of the Assembly shall be taken by a unanimous vote of the members of the League represented at the meeting."

and Rule 27 lays down:

"These rules of procedure shall apply to the proceedings of Committees of the Assembly."

But nevertheless nobody has for many years claimed that the decisions taken by the Committees should necessarily be unanimous. And more and more the practice has become an unwritten law, that when, sometimes after very heated discussions, a majority decision has been taken on a Committee, the minority resigns itself to its fate. The discussion is not renewed at the plenary meeting, and the report including its resolutions and decisions is approved unanimously, quite often with some states declaring that they have voted against the recommendations of the report in the Committee, but shall abstain from voting in the Assembly.

There is a special story to be told in connection with Rule 27 as a typical illustration of the ingenious way in which the art of interpretation has been carried to virtuosity in international matters as a result of the Unanimity Rule, a story that may serve as a warning to the potential authors of future international constitutions.

In 1924 the Netherlands Delegation, to make clear exactly what could be done on a Committee, proposed to add to Rule 27 a second paragraph worded as follows:

"Provided that decisions of the Committees shall be taken by the vote of the majority of the members of the League represented at the meeting."

A sub-committee was appointed to study the proposal, and, although the committee admitted that the amendment was merely intended to legalize the existing practice of the Committees, it still was "of the opinion that it would be preferable not to bind the Committees by a rigid rule as proposed by the Netherlands Delegation, but to allow them to continue to use the elastic procedure which has hitherto been followed." So frail was the whole structure felt to be.

The Netherlands Delegation was prevailed upon to withdraw its proposal, to prevent a discussion which might expose the whole weakness of the system of unanimity, a system which cannot but sap the vitality of any organization, politically and morally. Politically because no clear decision can be arrived at in any controversial matter on the basis of unanimity, and morally because the constant compromising between right and expediency will make any organization inefficient and inactive.

The regular procedure has been what was indicated in the story of Rule 27. A sub-committee is appointed to find a formula so vague that it does not say anything, or—to quote from a Norwegian comedy—"to find the golden middle way between just something and nothing at all." When the report of that sub-committee is referred back to the Assembly or the Council, the compromise put forward, by a slow process, is watered until nobody can object to it, because it means hardly anything or is worded so carefully that it can be interpreted in any way found desirable by any particular Government. Of course there have been honorable exceptions, but such has been the rule. And more than one highly intelligent man, active in League work and accustomed to this process, gradually has been led to believe that international statesmanship consisted in finding such formulas, and that they had an innate meaning and importance. He was tempted to forget vulgar realities, until one day he woke up to realize that safety valves of paper cannot stand much steam pressure.

The art of interpretation at last reached such heights of subtlety that every single obligation under the Covenant was dissolved and explained away. The result was, as expressed by a Polish Delegate in the League Assembly in 1938:

"The League of Nations has ceased to be an organization which can hope to take decisions having a general application."

The atmosphere was felt to be more and more unrealistic, and as the League on the so-called non-political side grew to be a great concern, it was becoming more and more unsatisfactory that any state, not even paying its contribution, could actually kill the League by blocking the whole budget, which must also be adopted by unanimity.

There was another way of getting round the principle of unanimity than by interpretation. It was found that even if unanimity was required for any *resolution* to be adopted by the League, there was nothing in the Covenant to prevent the Assembly from expressing desires by a majority vote, *vœux,* as the technical French term is. So a distinction was made between *recommendations,* which needed unanimity, and pious wishes. But an organization made impotent by the unanimity rule cannot increase its prestige by pious wishes; it can only emphasize its inefficiency.

And the constant effort to use Practice to undermine Principle and make it a hollow shell, has not been salutary to the international atmosphere.

Viscount Cecil, who has some of the fond feelings of

the parent for the unanimity rule, even in his last book makes a feeble attempt to defend it. He writes:

"I do not regard the so-called unanimity rule as a blot upon League procedure. At the worst it may have made the Council and Assembly cautious in discussing radical proposals, but that, I am inclined to think, is, in international affairs, a good thing." ("A Great Experiment," p. 72.)

This is the philosophy of the art of interpretation at its worst. Privately every Delegate to the League would be willing to admit that the League, or any League, with a unanimity rule can never be a suitable instrument for action in an emergency. And maybe some Delegates would add that this fact more than anything else has made the League politically possible.

The discussions of recent years have been most illuminating on this point. They came to a head when the United Kingdom Delegation to the League in September, 1938, proposed an amendment to Article 11, Section I, of the Covenant, which says:

"Any war or threat of war, whether immediately affecting any of the Members of the League or not, is hereby declared a matter of concern to the whole League, and the League shall take any action that may be deemed wise and effectual to safeguard the peace of nations. In case any such emergency should arise the Secretary General shall on the request of any Member of the League forthwith summon a meeting of the Council."

The amendment suggested was very moderate. The resolution proposed by the United Kingdom Delegation reads:

"The Assembly having regard to the views expressed by certain Delegations concerning the unanimity rule embodied in Article 5, paragraph I, of the Covenant in its application to paragraph I of Article 11;

Without prejudice to any question of principle concerning the scope or interpretation of the said rule or to the powers of the Council: Resolves that where a dispute is brought before the Council under paragraph I of Article 11, the Council may, by the unanimous agreement of all its members *other than the parties to the dispute:*

(1) Express an opinion or adopt a report concerning the facts of the dispute;

(2) Make recommendations as to the measures to be taken by Members of the League, other than the parties to the dispute, for the purpose of safeguarding peace."

But even the idea that the Council should be authorized to take the mild action stated under points 1 and 2 without the consent of both parties to the dispute, raised a storm in the Sixth Committee of the League and made the situation perfectly clear.

The most exalted ideas of sovereignty were found among the Central European States, created or re-created or given their new frontiers at Versailles. They manifested the most dogged opposition to changing any letter of the Covenant and to accepting the theory that the rest of the nations of the world combined should have any right to prevail upon two contesting parties to find a peaceful solution to their dispute.

When the United Kingdom Delegation had declared that "the United Kingdom Government felt that the somewhat rigid manner in which the unanimity rule had been applied to proceedings under that useful and frequently invoked provision of the Covenant, had led to serious diminution of its utility and effectiveness," M. Commène, then Foreign Minister of Roumania, stated as his Government's opinion:

"To attempt to replace unanimity by the majority rule, was to ignore the very basis of the Covenant, which provided for coöperation, not subordination, between the Members of the League."

In the same way Poland spoke against the British proposals, declaring that they "were likely to change the juridical structure of the League by limiting even to an appreciable extent the constitutional guarantees which had hitherto safeguarded the sovereign rights of the States Members of the League." And the Hungarian Delegation declared that it "appeared impossible to open a breach in the principle of unanimity."

The most hardboiled declaration made by any delegate fell from the lips of a Roumanian representative: "In no matter, in no dispute in which the interests of a country were at stake, could a solution be imposed upon that country or recommended to it without its consent."— Echoes from the discussion in the United States one hundred and sixty years ago.

In vain did the English and French Delegations try to prevail on those states. The proposal of the British Delegation was adopted by the Sixth Committee, by twenty-five votes to two, seven states abstaining from voting. But when it came up before the Assembly, the states which were against the British proposal refused to follow the tradition and abstain from voting against the majority. The report, not obtaining a unanimous vote in the Assembly, was rejected.

It is possible, it is even probable, that Roumania was afraid that Article 19 of the Covenant (see p. 35) might be invoked, and that Hungary might demand a revision of the Treaty that had given to Roumania such large sections of Magyar land.

M. Paul-Boncour, speaking for France, expressed himself in the Sixth Committee in the following terms:

"Those who were reluctant to allow the unanimity rule laid down in Article 11 to be ignored, even in the very limited cases proposed by the United Kingdom Delegation, would probably feel less apprehensive if they had the assurance that the proposal was not intended to be an indirect way of bringing into operation provisions contained in other articles—to be precise, in Article 19."

Various delegations had declared that the unanimity rule was the very basis of the Covenant, and others claimed that the sanctions were the fundamental point, but the Hungarian delegate maintained that the "authors of the Covenant had intended Article 19 to be the keystone of the edifice of peace." "It was meant to serve as a safety valve for the effective prevention of possible conflicts." And he declared that it had been disconcerting to find that "occult forces had been at work to minimize both the theoretical importance and the practical scope of that article."

These examples will serve to show how extremely difficult it has been found to harmonize conflicting conceptions of the very substance of the Covenant, and how more than difficult it was to make the League move under the unanimity rule, when a single state, let us say Roumania, could prevent all the other member states from reconsidering a treaty that had become "inapplicable . . . or might endanger the peace of the world."

Nomenclature cannot solve any real difficulty. Whether a new world organization be called a Union, a Federation or a Confederacy, it will be up against the same difficulties experienced by the League. It is only when all the vague general plans are discussed in their practical application that we can know where we stand. And it is hardly to be doubted that we may run the risk, when the war is over, of seeing a number of ambitious plans, backed by enthusiastic but inexperienced opinion, laid before a peace conference, only to be discarded because they are impractical and have not been sufficiently prepared in detail.

The many debates in League Committees also give evidence that it would have been highly desirable to have authoritative and generally accepted commentaries to the Covenant written by its fathers, a handbook as illuminating to this document as *The Federalist* to the American Constitution. But, of course, Hamilton, Jay and Madison

knew exactly what was meant by every clause in the American Constitution. Their idea was to make every principle
clear. The authors of the Covenant of the League of Nations felt it necessary to veil principles or, at best, keep
the meaning of the articles in an ambiguous chiaroscuro.

The question of sovereignty and of unanimity will face
the peace conference this time as in 1919; and there is a
possibility that small states, now as then, may believe that
the unanimity rule will give them a strong protection. In
reality that is a mistake.

More than one small state has been tempted to abstain
from voting, because it did not wish to take the responsibility of resisting alone the desire of a strong group of
powers. As an American jurist has said, "All persuasion
has an element of coercion." That is particularly true of
diplomatic persuasion. It must always be remembered that
one vote was sufficient to prevent any League decision. A
small-nation delegation would sometimes know that other
small states might be in agreement with its stand; but they
might find it more convenient to rest anonymous. A very
current form of philosophy was once expressed by an Oriental delegate to a Norwegian delegate in the following
words: "If moral courage is the only asset of a small nation, it ought to be applied with the strictest sense of
economy." This expedient but entirely false worldly wisdom is responsible for most sins of omission in international political life. Moral courage, applied in larger
doses by individuals and by nations, might have saved the
League politically and prevented the present war.

It would hardly be discreet to give any detailed account
of attempted coercion. But one example may illustrate:
Article 4 of the Covenant, the rules concerning the composition of the Council, came up in the Assembly in
1927.* Spain and Poland had expressed a desire to be rec-

* Under this Article there were four non-permanent seats on the
Council.

ognized as Great Powers and wanted permanent seats on the Council. England and France had promised them semi-permanent seats, i.e., they should be elected for three years at a time, but declared permanently reëligible. And Polish and Spanish diplomats in the various capitals had demanded—sometimes in rather categorical terms—that governments should instruct their delegations to support this idea. Norway had a seat in the special committee to report on this question. And the Norwegian delegation stated that the suggested solution did not satisfy the smaller nations. There should not be more permanent seats on the Council, but rather an increase of elected members; and it was against the idea of international democracy to create a new class-distinction between states. Warning words were spoken by diplomats in Oslo. And one day Briand came to see a member of the Norwegian Delegation. "I come to warn you as a friend," he said. "You know France and England have promised this thing. And it will be made very disagreeable for Norway if you insist on going against us." Mildly and modestly the Norwegian delegate pointed out that the League had not been mandated to Great Britain and France; they had no right to dispose of any seats on the Council, and the arrangement planned was strictly against the spirit of the League. As Norway did not give in, the original plan was dropped, and a compromise reached under which any member state of the League, when its three-year term had expired, could demand to be declared reëligible for another three years. Such a decision would require a two-thirds majority vote in favor. At the same time the number of non-permanent seats was increased from four to six (later eleven).

When the result had been achieved Briand came once more to see his Norwegian friend. "I congratulate you," he said, "that you had the courage of your opinion. I did not like to try to persuade you; but I had promised. I can only say that I am glad I did not succeed." And there was no disagreeable aftermath.

Few states which were in a more or less exposed position would care to make use of the publicity the League Assembly afforded them. It might be rather unwise to expose a more powerful neighbor. Great Powers, on the other hand, did not fear diplomatic pressure. But it can safely be said that no small state ever lost in prestige or in any other way because it was possessed of moral courage and applied it.

On the contrary, it sometimes happened that some Great Power was glad to take cover behind the moral courage of a small state. A story is related from the early days of the League, before any Foreign Minister from a Great Power came to the League Assembly. (Mr. Austen Chamberlain, in 1925, was the first.) Mr. Branting then represented Sweden on the Council. The French delegate made a proposal which caused some commotion in England. If the British Delegation voted for it, disagreeable comments were to be expected in the Commons. If it voted against it, there might be some tension between the Quai d'Orsay and Downing Street. The British representative on the Council cabled London for definite instructions and received the cryptic answer: "England expects every Swede to do his duty." And when the proposal came up Mr. Branting immediately declared that as a representative of a small nation he was bound to vote against it. The British delegate then spoke and regretted that such an interesting proposal should be killed right away; but as unanimity was required and the agenda were charged, he would not waste the time of the Council by examining a proposal which had now only an academic interest. And the debate was closed.

The history of the League also gives us rich evidence of the facility of doing good international work without any unanimity rule.

It is in discussions among diplomats and politicians that considerations of national prestige and privilege make it difficult to arrive at positive results. Where practical men meet, the chimera of Absolute Sovereignty does not wag her serpent tail. Even at Versailles, when the International Labour Organization was set up, it was not found necessary to establish any unanimity rule. Article 403 of the Peace Treaty lays down:

"Except as otherwise expressly provided in this Part of the Present Treaty, all matters shall be decided by a simple majority of the votes cast by the Delegates present."

The exceptions mentioned in Article 402 are also illuminating. This Article declares that if the Government of a member state formally objects to the inclusion of any particular item on the Agenda for the Labour Conference, still the Conference can decide by a majority of two-thirds of the votes cast *not* to exclude this item.

This great rupture with the principle of individual state sovereignty has never caused any difficulties. And it is not without interest to observe that even Viscount Cecil, with his fond preference for the unanimity rule, seems to have, in some recess of his cautious mind, a lurking suspicion that there may be other alternatives. Having mentioned in his book the procedure practised in the International Labour Organization he remarks:

"The results of the system have been very good, and I have often wondered whether some system of the same kind could not be applied to the League itself. ("The Great Experiment," p. 323.)

And in his book he pays tribute to the so-called Bruce Report (see p. 17). Constitutionally speaking, there are two new things to remark in that report, both pointing toward new developments in international affairs, and both of value for the future constructive peace-work. It is proposed in this report, which was unanimously adopted by the Assembly, that the new Central Committee set up to direct the social and economic activities of the League with very extensive power, shall consist not only of state delegates, but also of "not more than eight members appointed in a personal capacity on the grounds of their special competence and authority whose collaboration it [the Central Committee] considers would prove of special value." These eight will be coöpted by the Committee itself. And there are no national or other restrictions set for the appointment. In this way there will be established a new kind of international officers, not appointed by Governments and not representing Governments. The element of personal responsibility will be emphasized, and independent personalities of the highest qualifications called to take their quite personal share in world affairs.

Next it was resolved that "all matters shall be decided by a majority of the members present."

By unanimously adopting this report, the Assembly tacitly admitted the abandonment of the idea that "all international decisions must, by the nature of things, be unanimous."

But it was hardly necessary for the Assembly to demonstrate this fact. In the most important field of international decisions, those of the Permanent Court of Arbitration and those of the Permanent Court of International Justice, it has never been pretended that unanimity should be required. All decisions are taken by a majority vote. And even in cases when the vote has been eight to seven, no single country has maintained that the vote was not valid.

And it is of interest to note that the Permanent Court of International Justice itself in a famous advisory opinion gave a restrictive interpretation of the unanimity clause. The question at issue was the boundary between Turkey and Iraq under Article 3, paragraph 2, in the Treaty of Lausanne. According to Article 5 of the Covenant unanimity is required for any decision of the Council, "except where otherwise expressly provided." There was no such provision in this case. In spite of this the Court by analogy applied the exception in Article 15, paragraph 6:

"If a report by the Council is unanimously agreed to by the members thereof, other than the Representatives of one or more parties to the dispute, etc."

The Court stated verbatim:

"The well-known rule that no one can be judge in his own suit holds good."

So, evidently, the Court did not share the view later expressed by the Roumanian delegate quoted.

XVIII: International Loyalty

The rules laid down for the composition of the Central Committee mentioned in the previous chapter lead us on to far-reaching questions of fundamental practical importance for any international organization.

They bring up the question of the place and part of the individual as differing from the part and place of the state in international collaboration and administration; they bring up the question of international loyalty as differing from or overruling national loyalty. And they bring up the question of international civil servants and their status.

No kind of League or Union or Federation, no such world organization as has been rather sketchily envisaged as one of the cornerstones for the peace to come, can be worked without a secretariat, a staff of competent collaborators. Still less can any world government be imagined without a great administrative machinery. What are the prospects of finding the personnel to rule and administer the future set-up? We have had twenty-two years of the "great experiment." What have we learned?

In theory, in the direction of any League or Federation of independent sovereign countries, there is no room for individuals, only for States Members. At practically all international conferences, in practically every international council, committee or commission, which is not of a purely technical character, members are appointed by Governments. They represent Governments and not themselves. They are not responsible to any international body, only to the Government by which they have been appointed. Their loyalty is to the country which they represent and not to any international idea. And in any World Organization to be set up, particularly so if it should have the character of a supergovernment at the head of a tremendous international administration, the question would immediately pose itself: Whom are the men in charge serving? To whom is owed their supreme loyalty? To the whole or to a particular part of the whole? To the world community or to the country from which they are headed? To the world government as such, or to the government that has appointed them, or in whose interest and on whose bidding they took up their international career?

To mention these very obvious questions is to illustrate the complexity of the problem, and the need for utter wariness and circumspection in any attempt to create a superstate. No parallel can be drawn with any existing union of states, because in any such federation there is a unity of language and traditions, or of race or geography. But in any world combination the instinct of disintegration would be very much stronger than the instinct of adhesion; the centrifugal force would have the character of a primary power of nature, and the centripetal force would be a second-hand product of teaching and reflection.

If we should ever hope to organize a superstate, upon what base of feeling and sentiment would it be possible to build? Could we have the support of any kind of super-patriotism, of any clear loyalty to such a structure? If not, what would be the hope of the superstate weathering any kind of storm? No federation of human beings, or of states made up of human beings, can have any power of cohesion without some kind of loyalty cementing together the various states and groups and classes. If that is not realized we shall build on sand, and our house will be carried away by the first flood.

Can it be truly said that the world has been educated to a reasonable degree of international understanding and loyalty? Can we be guided in any way by precedent and experience?

The internal history of the League of Nations will give us the material we want and make clear how difficult it has been only to attain the recognition of the idea that such a thing as international loyalty could exist. When the League was being created, Sir Maurice Hankey was invited to be the first Secretary-General. He declined, perhaps because he had small belief in the possibility of building up an international body. But it "is well known that he was at that time in favor of a system based on that of the inter-allied committees during the war, and of the Peace Conference itself, under which the secretarial work for the Council, the Assembly, or other League organs should be done by the staffs of the various national delegations." (F. B. Walters: "Administrative Problems of International Organization," p. 16.) This was also the spirit of the unwilling sponsors of the League. One of the delegates at Versailles exclaimed, when the question came up of a League building: "What is the difficulty? Take any three-story house. The French can take the ground floor, the British the first floor, the Italians the second floor. We leave the attic to the Japanese, and the rest of the nations can get some ushers and walk-sweeps if they want to."

But the League of Nations merely by being called into existence proved to have an innate dynamic force stronger than suspected by any of its godfathers. And Sir Eric Drummond (now Lord Perth) who was made the first Secretary General, when Sir Maurice Hankey had declined, saw that only by organizing his staff as an international civil service could he make the League a going concern. He boldly decided to do so; and it can safely be stated that when the League sprang into life, nearly as quickly and as completely as Pallas Athena sprang from the brain of the all-wise Zeus, it was the enthusiasm for and the loyalty to an international idea that animated Sir Eric's collaborators on the Secretariat, Americans, British, Dutch, French, Norwegians and Swiss that made this process of creation possible.

Slowly and gradually, the staff of the Secretariat became even more independent of individual governments in its international character than Sir Eric had anticipated or planned. His idea had been that the international staff he had organized should be directed by top-officers, the Secretary General, a deputy secretary general and under-secretaries general (every one of them representing a Great Power), who were closely in touch with what was called their "home governments." But the Assembly of the League did not stop at that. It can be said that the smaller nations stood for the idea of a truly international administration with an international loyalty. The Great Powers were reluctant to give up any part of their diplomatic control and stuck to the tradition of national loyalty. In this tug of ideas the international conception came out victorious, and the Assembly in 1932 decided that any member of what was called "the high direction" of the League,* on his appointment, at a public meeting of the Council, should take an oath or pledge himself solemnly never to take any orders or instructions from the country of which he was a national. Every other permanent servant of the League should have to sign a declaration to the same effect (a similar reform was carried out in the Staff regulations of the International Labour Organization). At the same time the Great Power monopoly of the higher posts was broken, and it was decided that if the Secretary General was a national of one of the Great Powers (the technical term is "of a country with a permanent seat on the Council"), the deputy secretary general should

* The High Direction comprised the officers mentioned above and all the directors of the various sections of the League staff.

be a national of a country without a permanet seat on the Council. And further, that not more than two nationals of any one country could, at the same time, hold posts in the High Direction. (Of course, from the international point of view no discrimination between countries is ideal; but it was necessary to make this roundabout movement in order to break a privilege and educate Great Powers to the idea that international matters can be well handled by international functionaries and not necessarily by diplomatic representatives of national interests.)

That this experiment in education has not been entirely unsuccessful is proved by the fact that since July, 1941, the Acting Secretary General of the League has been an Irishman; his next in command is a Greek; and since August, 1941, the acting director of the International Labour Office is an Irishman; his next in command is an American. Great Britain and all the Dominions have never shown a greater loyalty to the League than during the present war. And no voice has been lifted claiming any change in the direction of the League. France (after the occupation) has fulfilled its financial obligations to the League and paid in full; and it has never been objected that there was no longer any high French official on the staff of the League. This *de facto* demonstration of international loyalty and of confidence in the international character of the League would have been unimaginable ten years ago.

But some of the leaders among the small states' delegations that had carried this reform were not fully satisfied with the results obtained. They wanted more than a declaration of loyalty to the League; they wanted a truly international staff, owing allegiance only to the international institution they are serving. When the war broke out it had been under preliminary discussion to give to all permanent functionaries on the League institutions an international status, a League citizenship making them for the time of their contract citizens of the League of Nations with a suspended citizenship in the country of their origin.

It was felt that especially in times of emergency an international organization might lose its character of a nonpartisan mediator, umpire or arbitrator if its functionaries could be mobilized for duty in their home countries or for their home government. They would, at best, have a divided loyalty; at worst they might be called upon to work directly against the interests of the international community. It was also felt, as a danger to the League, that just at the moment when the acquired experience of its functionaries would be of particular importance for the world community they could be drafted for the armies of their home governments. To meet this difficulty the League tried to obtain from various governments an undertaking that they should not mobilize such of their nationals as were serving on the League organizations. Such an undertaking was given by the Norwegian Government; and in Holland a special law was passed granting such functionaries exemption from military duties for the duration of their service with the League.

One of the objections raised against giving to the League functionaries an international status was the fact that certain great countries were not members of the League, and that a passport issued by the League would not be respected in Germany, in Italy or in Japan. This objection would be of no importance in a universal organization of states.

The present war has given ample evidence that it would have been well if the functionaries of the League had been truly international servants, even from the strictly formal point of view. And there has been a growing feeling that such a reform as indicated might be most timely.

This feeling was so pronounced in the International Labour Organization that in March, 1939, a questionnaire was sent to the States Members asking them to express their opinion on this subject.

A number of countries, like the United States, Brazil, France, gave entirely non-committal answers. But from some governments came very positive statements giving evidence that the idea of an international civil service with international loyalties was no longer strange to official minds.

The Government of Canada replied that:

"It does not contemplate the recalling for military service in the event of war of Canadian nationals belonging to the staff of the International Labour Organization."

From London came the statement that:

"His Majesty's Government has decided that any British member of the staff of the International Labour Office whom you wish to retain at his post in the event of war shall be permitted to remain."

Ireland answered in the same spirit. Lithuania answered that:

"The Ministry of National Defence has decided in the event of mobilization to exempt from active military service Lithuanian nationals serving in important posts on the Staff of the International Labour Office."

From Norway came the reply that under the new regulations (of 1939):

"Norwegian nationals being members of the staff of the International Labour Office are exempted from mobilization."

The Swiss Government, having asked for detailed information and a list of employees, with a special list of those whose services were considered indispensable, answered:

"That the officials whose names appear on your list II may remain at their posts on the staff of the International Labour Office in the event of war."

Without this growing understanding of the character of its work the International Labour Office would hardly have been able to carry on as it has done.

If it was felt of importance on the League of Nations to demand an undivided loyalty to the League from the permanent servants, it is obvious that this question would be far more vital at the moment of creating a wider world organization, with far more extensive powers, or even a world government. An international police force could hardly be built up unless the men and the officers owed their full allegiance to the international body employing them, and to nobody else. For any discussion of an international army this question would be of paramount practical importance. And a future peace conference will have to find a solution of the problem. Even if the future world organization should be only a reformed and revitalized League of Nations, it can hardly be doubted that there would be need for a reform along the lines indicated, and that a system should be worked out providing for a permanent staff of international civil servants and a staff of temporary functionaries possibly elected by their governments.

The status and the loyalties of the servants of an international administration present comparatively small problems. The situation grows far more complicated if we consider the status and the loyalties of the masters of a world organization, the representatives and delegates of the countries and governments composing that body. Even here we can draw upon the very informative experience of the League of Nations, which presented a picture of the most entangled confusion on this point, because it was found in practice absolutely impossible to decide where individual responsibility started and state responsibility stopped, where the man was a man and where he was only a label with a state name.

As mentioned previously: in practically all official, political international collaboration, all the participants represent governments and are appointed by governments. Even at the Permanent Court of International Justice the Judges are, to a certain extent, thought to represent countries (compare p. 282). There are exceptions, but they are mostly what might be termed limited exceptions. Certain very important international organs were appointed by the Council of the League of Nations, which again consists of representatives of governments. The Saar Commission (see p. 167) was such an institution, in the same way the Mandates Commission of the League of Nations. But even if the members were formally appointed by the Council of the League, their names were always suggested by the various governments, or, if they had been suggested by anybody else, the respective governments would be sounded, and only those who represented the views of their government would be appointed.

The Saar Commission is of particular interest in this connection because it demonstrates a peculiar stage in the process of political evolution. The members of that Commission when first appointed became independent of their governments, and the Commission became a legal subject. On the other hand the Mandates Commission of the League was never a legal subject. No League organ had any juridical status; the League itself, in spite of its extensive functions and powers, was a legal subject only in a very restricted sense. It could not be sued or summoned before any court of justice. For the benefit of its own functionaries it had established an administrative tribunal and authorized it to pronounce in litigations over contracts. But that was all.

A peace conference to come, when discussing the future international organization, will have to weigh very carefully what kind of legal status should be given to the Union or Federation. When the Covenant of the League was conceived there was no kind of experience to guide the authors. The League was not and could not be a finished product. Great care must be taken to give the new or reformed organization so dynamic and elastic a character that its own experience can be translated into amendments and reforms, and that it can emerge from the ambiguous chiaroscuro beloved by diplomats into the morning of clear daylight beloved by practical men.

All the same there are formal problems which can hardly be solved, and some of them of far-reaching moral importance. Under strict form there are no individuals in the Assembly or the Council of the League of Nations; there are just member states, represented by governments' delegates. Now, in human affairs, it is impossible to live under any consummate form, or any perfectly logical formula. G. K. Chesterton illustrated this when he first saw against the horizon the walls of Jerusalem, and wrote: "The walls are rules regulating our lives; the gates are the exceptions making it possible to live within the walls." In pure theory, when presidents are elected in the various bodies of the League, they are not elected as individuals but figuratively speaking as tags of state. This is strictly true in the Council of the League, where states preside according to the principle of rotation. If France is presiding and the French Foreign Minister or Permanent Delegate cannot attend, any French delegate or substitute delegate, or technical adviser can replace him, and no vice-president can take the chair as long as there is any Frenchman left. But it was felt that to preside the greater body, the Assembly, was a more complicated business and required some experience in handling meetings. So, the President of the Assembly is elected as an individual. On the other hand, the vice-presidents of the Assembly are elected impersonally: the first delegate of States so and so, which again means that if the President should be prevented from meeting at the bureau of the Assembly, he has no substitute, but any vice-president can be replaced by any member of his delegation. In the same way the presidents of the big Committees of the Assembly are elected personally and cannot be replaced by any member of their delegation, but practically on every League body a member can be replaced by any of his compatriots.

The one outstanding exception to the general rule was the Supervisory Committee of the League. The members of this most important of League Committees are elected by the Assembly of the League, personally and not nationally. It is expressly stated that they serve in their individual capacities. That means, among other things, that if a member is prevented from attending a session of the Committee, he cannot be replaced by any compatriot appointed by his government; and the Committee has ruled that no member can appoint a substitute to replace him in case of illness or unavoidable absence.

Now, with the very extensive powers given to the Supervisory Committee, its authority is limited to the financial and administrative field. It is not a policy-shaping body. But to the Central Committee "shall be entrusted the direction and supervision of the work of the committees dealing with economic and social questions." And this Committee of worldwide importance, given such power of initiative and planning, shall be authorized to coöpt eight members "in a personal capacity on the grounds of their special competence and authority, whose collaboration it considers would prove of special value."

It is, no doubt, the first time such an attempt has been made in international politics to coördinate state authority and individual authority. And it may be said in a modest way to initiate a depoliticalization of what has been called with a very wide term "technical activities" in international affairs. But as these activities embrace the handling of all social and economic questions, fiscal questions, problems of international transport and communication, of health and education, it will be seen that the political field has been stripped of most of its provinces.

When it has proved impracticable in the League to decide on any general solution of the formal problems, and has been thought preferable simply to find some way out of every difficulty arising, without trying to be logical or to stick to any hard and fast rules, it may be taken as a proof that there was no general solution. Those who were mainly responsible for the conduct of League affairs always had a tendency to be not only absolutely correct, but even very formalistic; laxity of form had always a factual background. And any political realist had to admit that the essential thing was to find a modus that made it possible to do the work and that an attempt to create a formal congruence between partial solutions arrived at, might endanger the whole structure of the League.

Abraham Lincoln once said of the American Constitution that it was like an old overcoat; if you tried to button it in front, it would burst in the back. At a given moment any written constitution, any covenant, will be like that. A living organism is never static; to bind it too closely to any formula will mean either a crippling or an explosion.

If this applies to the questions discussed in this chapter, it certainly has an even greater application to the complicated problems of responsibility which any world organization to come will have to face.

XIX: International Responsi-
bility

Mr. Clarence Streit in his important work *Union Now* has defined very clearly the difference between a league as he sees it and a union. A league is a government of governments, for governments and by governments. Its laws can only be broken by a people acting through its government and enforced only by the league coercing the people as a unit. Its laws are made by the peoples acting through their governments or the delegates of their governments as units of equal voting power, regardless of the number of individuals in each state. And a league is made for the purpose of securing the freedom, rights, independence, sovereignty of each of the states in it taken as units equally. A union governs each individual in its territory directly; its laws can be broken only by individuals and can be enforced only by coercing and punishing individuals. They are made by the individuals in it through their chosen representatives, each state's voting power being ordinarily in close proportion to its population. A union is made for the purpose of securing the freedom, rights, independence and sovereignty of the individuals in it taken as units equally. To secure the sovereignty of the state a league sacrifices the rights of men to justice and to equal voting power whereas a union sacrifices the sovereignty of the state to secure the rights of men.

To any person who believes that a just and durable

peace can be won only when all states, big and small, agree to live in an international democracy, Mr. Streit's observations are pertinent and of weight. But even if his definition holds true when applied to the League of Nations, it would not necessarily be true of any league. On the League of Nations itself there was a growing tendency to introduce the personal and individual element, as we have seen in the institution of the Central Committee (see p. 238). The mandates system was created primarily for securing the rights of individuals in the mandated territories; and the minority procedure openly aimed at protecting individuals and their freedom. Still, in the main Mr. Streit's objections to the League of the Covenant are valid.

It has been set out in previous chapters how a World Assembly might be constituted to meet the objections of common sense to any league built on the pious fiction that all states are equal and equally sovereign. In the Washington declaration and its promise to guarantee religious freedom and human rights to every individual in every country a long step is taken toward sacrificing the sovereignty of the state to secure the rights of men (compare CHAPTER XXI). But only by synchronizing the efforts to give security to individuals directly and the need for giving security to individuals indirectly, by way of the communities they have instituted, only by applying among states the principles of law and regulation which are adopted for the lives of individuals, can we hope to construct the difficult but possible way to international democracy. (Cf. Mount Vernon Speech, p. 22.)

Constitutionally, there is no great difficulty in establishing such an order that, within the framework of a world organization which is not a union, laws can apply to individuals directly and be enforced on individuals. It is even necessary. Only by emphasizing the element of personal responsibility can we make any world order work.

A keystone to the whole structure of democratic government is the principle that power and responsibility should be intimately united and not separated. They are the obverse and the reverse of the whole coinage of democracy. And from the constitutional point of view this marks a crucial difference, perhaps the most vital distinction, between dictatorship and democracy. Under a dictatorship, power and responsibility are disconnected, and the very idea that he might be held responsible and have to answer for his actions, is not only abhorrent to the dictator, but is the most abominable heresy to the doctrine of the leader-principle.

In the national democratic state, the application of the system of political responsibility is comparatively simple and regulated by law and constitution. Not so in any wider confederacy of countries. There are no precedents; the very complicated problems involved have never been fully discussed, and theories of international law can give us but little help as no rules exist, and no experience has been accumulated in this difficult matter.

The only international organization where the question of responsibility might have been discussed is the League of Nations. But the Covenant of the League does not mention any kind of responsibility for delegates to the League, or officers of the League. The word appears only once in the Covenant and has no connection with either the Assembly or the Council. Article 22 mentions the nations which can "best undertake the responsibility for the tutelage of peoples in the mandated territories."

It is mentioned in the Covenant that the League shall have a Secretary General. But it is not stated to whom, or for what, he shall be responsible. The word occurs once in the Rules of Procedure of the Assembly. Rule 9 lays down that "the Secretary General shall be responsible for the organization of the Secretariat of the Assembly and of the secretariat of any committees set up by the Assembly."

No other kind of responsibility seems to have been envisaged.

We are bound to believe that this is no oversight, but that the feeling prevailed that it would be so inflammable a problem that any attempt to include the idea of responsibility in any article, paragraph or rule might have prevented the League from coming into existence. And the delicate and difficult question has never been raised in the League itself. On the contrary, it may be maintained that the framework of the League rested on the presumption that there would never be any discussion of responsibility, either for states, or for individuals. And the absence of this corollary and corrective to the democratic system of government tended to make the debates in the League Assembly and on the Council more anemic and less realistic than profitable for progressive peace. No delegate could be called before any court of justice; the Council, the Assembly, the various committees could not be impeached; they could never be questioned by any board of electors; possibly they might be taken to task in their own country, but never as citizens of a universal community or as officers of a worldwide organization.

It was the established rule of the League that all budgetary power rested with the Assembly; the budget was discussed in and passed by the Assembly. But it happened once that the Council without any budgetary authorization or any credit voted spent a considerable amount of money to enlarge and embellish the Council chamber. This gave rise to a conflict with the Supervisory Committee. But there was no provision for any such case. Even if millions had been spent nobody would have been responsible in a legal sense. The guilty gentlemen on the Council could not be made to refund the League. The member states whom they represented would probably declare that they were in no way responsible for any internal action in League affairs taken by their representatives. The Secretary General, even if he was morally responsible, could not be sued—and as he was part of the Covenant he could not be dismissed; and it would take international unanimity to amend him.

No member of the League staff could be made legally responsible for any sin of omission or commission against the League. He could be dismissed; he could lose certain acquired rights. There was an internal administrative tribunal to protect his privileges, and he could be brought before no other court of justice even for theft or embezzlement. The League was an extraterritorial body in Switzerland; Swiss law did not apply in any League matter.

Non-responsibility as a principle can never be considered perfect. And even if no great sins were committed of such a kind that they ought to have been punishable, an article establishing personal responsibility in League matters was sadly lacking.

Maybe the value of any proviso of this kind would have been more formal than real. But form—the cohesive interpretation of the forces binding nation to nation—is in itself a reality, as people sometimes are too willing to forget. And, no doubt, some indications that delegates were speaking and acting under some specific international rule of responsibility would have been of a certain moral and constitutional importance.

As an outstanding case can be mentioned the attitude of the Japanese representatives in matters of drug control. Not only were they not coöperative; they were concealing facts, they were lying, they gave assurances which were never seriously meant. Premeditated and wilful violation of conventions, laws and treaties was the Japanese policy, and there were no means of holding responsible the delegate of the Japanese government. Every year he gave the Advisory Committee of Opium to understand that the Japanese government would take effective measures to deal with the situation, and every year the situation became worse and worse.

"Japan engaged in illicit opium traffic as an instrument of national policy for a decade before Pearl Harbor" (Secretary Morgenthau, Jan. 26, 1942). Commissioner of Narcotics, Harry J. Anslinger, reported to the Secretary:

"Many shipments from narcotic factories licensed by the Japanese government have been smuggled into the United States. For instance, year after year from 1920 to 1935 large quantities of the Fujitsuri brand of cocaine illicitly entered the United States, Canada, China and India. In reply to our demands that the traffic be suppressed we got only bland expressions and futile answers.

"Japanese penalties (an open scandal) were two months' imprisonment, usually suspended, and a 100 yen fine, for an offense which in this country would carry 5 to 10 years' imprisonment, or capital punishment in China. One shipment seized in Seattle from four Japanese totaled a million shots of morphine. It came from a government licensed factory, the Japanese Pharmaceutical Establishment at Osaka. We also seized a large shipment of morphine concealed in soy beans which arrived in the United States on the same ship with Prince Chichibu, the Emperor's brother.

"We have experienced Pearl Harbors many times in the past in the nature of dangerous drugs from Japan which were meant to poison the blood of the American people."

Nobody was ever responsible. The Emperor's brother was not indicted; the diplomats shrugged; the delegates to Geneva smiled blandly. And it was allowed to be that way; for there were no rules of responsibility; there was a fear of sinning against etiquette by speaking openly.

But there was a lack of responsibility in another and more immediate sense. Delegations were not even responsible as spokesmen for their nations, i.e., they were not plenipotentiary representatives of their governments. Few things have been more detrimental to the authority of the League than the fact that even Great Powers looked upon the delegates in the Assembly, the decisions taken and the resolutions adopted in any matter, except internal League questions, as of mere academic interest and of hardly more serious consequence than a resolution adopted by a well-intentioned mass meeting in Albert Hall or Madison Square Garden.

Recommendations of a far-reaching character more than once were adopted unanimously by the League of Nations Assembly, and under general applause from nearly every country. And they were never acted upon. Or even worse: in due time, when they came under consideration by the governments and parliaments, even the cabinet ministers and representatives who had been the initiators and warmest supporters of the recommendations, turned their back upon them and without a word of protest—sometimes with their own active assistance—saw them passed over to the archives of the Circumlocution Office to be put on files *ad calendas græcas*. Such was the fate of the Geneva Protocol of 1924.

On October 2, 1924, by the unanimous vote of forty-eight states the Assembly of the League decided to "recommend to the earnest attention of all the members of the League the acceptance of the said draft Protocol." Ten states, France among them, affixed their signatures to the Protocol on the same day. The Protocol was the well-considered result of five years of hard work. It was an attempt to prohibit all forms of aggressive war; to provide for the pacific settlement of all disputes, other than those over domestic questions and the peace treaties, either through the Permanent Court, the Council of the League, or a committee of arbitrators; to provide an automatic method for determination of an aggressor; and to extend and make definite the obligation to apply sanctions. By thus strengthening the principles of compulsory submission of disputes to peaceful settlement and of united action against the aggressor, it sought to remove the necessity for large armaments and thus lead to a general program of armament reduction.

The debate preceding the adoption of the Protocol was one of the greatest in the history of the League, and it was applauded by the entire world. But without the ratification of Great Britain the Protocol was doomed. And the Baldwin Government, which succeeded the MacDonald Government in November, 1924, promptly stated that Britain could not adhere to the Protocol. The most ambitious effort in the history of the League thus came to naught.

Under a new system it will be essential that such things should not happen. The delegates to a World Assembly, howsoever that Assembly be constituted; the representatives on an International Council, whatever name may be given to that body—must be authorized to act and not only to talk for their governments; they must be given responsibility and authority to make binding decisions.

We are here at a very crucial point, facing one of the major difficulties of the coming peace conference and a permanent danger to the efforts to create a world order based on a dynamic peace.

An essential problem for any kind of international political collaboration will be to lay out the best possible, and most acceptable, line of demarcation between national authority and international authority in the regulation of world affairs, and in the adoption of treaties, conventions and arrangements. A constant stumbling-block in international life has been that principles of ratification vary from country to country; no two constitutions have exactly the same rules regulating this intricate boundary zone between executive rights and privileges of parliament. And a number of very disagreeable contentions between states have arisen out of this difficulty. One of the best known is the five-year conflict between the United States and France (1831-1836) concerning the ratification of the convention for payment in satisfaction of the spoliation claims of American subjects for damage done by France to their ships and other property during the revolutionary wars. Diplomatic relations were broken off and reprisals threatened.

The prospect of all nations agreeing to a peace treaty is also related to the question of ratifications. A look at the constitutional practice in the allied countries at war will make clear that the greatest difficulty to the stabilization of peace conditions when the Conference once has arrived at positive results will be in the United States Senate.

In Belgium the power resided in the King to make treaties. The two Chambers should be acquainted with these treaties as soon as the interest and the safety of the state permitted. But certain categories of treaties, especially those "liable to place a financial burden either upon the State or upon individuals" had to be voted by both Chambers. Under the Belgian Constitution the Chambers were not empowered to modify or amend the treaties referred to them.

In Great Britain there is no Act of Parliament or any other regulation binding the government, which has a very wide discretion in these matters. But the practice is that every treaty which is signed in respect of the United Kingdom and which is subject to ratification shall lie before Parliament for twenty-one days before it is ratified. Under this practice an opportunity is given to Parliament to raise questions concerning the treaty before its ratification. Resolutions expressing the desire that all treaties should be laid before Parliament for its approval before being finally concluded, have been defeated in the House of Commons at various times.

Under the Chinese Constitution of 1931 only the President of the Republic has the right to ratify treaties. But a declaration of war and the opening of negotiations for peace shall be decided at the meetings of the Executive Yuan.

In the Netherlands the Sovereign ratifies all treaties; but no treaty shall be ratified without having been approved by the States General.

In the Constitution of Norway it is laid down that "treaties concerning matters of special importance, and, in all cases, treaties which necessitate legislative measures or a decision of Parliament are not binding unless they are approved by Parliament." Such approval is given with simple majority.

In Poland the President of the Republic concludes treaties and conventions with foreign states and acquaints the Diet thereof. But commercial and customs treaties, agreements which impose permanent financial burdens on the Polish State, which contain legal provisions imposing obligations on citizens or which introduce changes in the frontiers of the state, and alliances, cannot be concluded without the consent of the Diet. The Diet cannot modify or amend treaties, and even if the Diet has given its consent, the President is under no obligation to ratify.

In the Soviet Union peace treaties require ratification by the Presidium of the Central Executive Committee.

Different from the rules of all other countries are the regulations governing ratification of treaties in the United States, the only country where under the Constitution (Art. II) a two-thirds' majority of a Senate is necessary for ratification, where treaties and conventions are not voted *en bloc,* but where texts can be modified or amended; where there is practically no limit set for interference and alterations, and where years may go by before a treaty, signed by the government, is given final consideration. The convention of 1929 about safety of life at sea, although it laid very definite international duties upon the government of the United States, was not ratified until 1936 (see p. 210).

It would certainly be futile to discuss any alteration in the American system; it is there; and although it constitutes a potential danger to any world settlement, and may be a grave handicap for any Secretary of State with an intimate insight and keen interest in international relations, this American Constitution is a ponderable political fact. Presumably the system will not be changed to suit any international organization. Those desirous of an intelligent world order and believing that it is possible to obtain a just and durable peace will have to calculate with the powers that be and not with the powers that might have been.

No doubt most authorities on foreign relations agree with Viscount Bryce's statement in "The American Commonwealth" (New Edition, London, 1917, Vol. I, pp. 109-110):

"This gives great power to a vexatious minority, and increases the danger, evidenced by several incidents in the history of the Union, that the Senate or a faction in it may deal with foreign policy in a narrow, sectional, electioneering spirit. When the interest of any group of States is, or is supposed to be, against the making of a given treaty, that treaty may be defeated by the senators from those States. They tell the other senators of their own party that the prospects of the party in the district of the country whence they come will be improved if the treaty is rejected and a bold aggressive line is taken in further negotiations. Some of these senators, who care more for the party than for justice or the common interests of the country, rally to the cry, and all the more gladly if their party is opposed to the President in power, because in defeating the treaty they humiliate his administration. Thus the treaty may be rejected, and the settlement of the question at issue indefinitely postponed. It may be thought that a party acting in this vexatious way will suffer in public esteem. This happens in extreme cases; but the public are usually so indifferent to foreign affairs, and so little skilled in judging of them, that offences of the kind described may be committed with practical impunity. It is harder to fix responsibility on a body of senators than on the executive; and whereas the executive has usually an interest in settling diplomatic troubles, whose continuance it finds annoying, the Senate has no such interest, but is willing to keep them open so long as some political advantage can be sucked out of them. The habit of using foreign policy for electioneering purposes is not confined to America. It has been seen in England, and in France, and even in monarchical Germany. But in America the treaty-confirming power of the Senate opens a particularly easy and tempting door to such practices."

Bryce's book was written before the last war and before the events of 1919-1920 had given such a tragic and world important confirmation of the passage quoted, to be in the future referred to by every writer on international law as the outstanding example of the non-existence of any feeling of responsibility among a group of men, whose action or non-action affected the entire future history of nations.

During the debate in the Senate and the Presidential elections of 1919 nobody advocated that Amercia should withdraw from the League of Nations and its attempted organized international coöperation. "Reservations" were mentioned, but not repudiation. An elaborate world system had been set up, largely on official American initiative. And what happened? It cannot be more graphically described than in the words of Arthur Sweetser (*The Annals of the American Academy of Political and Social Science*, Philadelphia, July, 1941: "America Seen from Abroad"):

"Towards the end of the campaign, two weeks indeed before the election, thirty-one of the most eminent members of the opposition party appealed to the voters to vote for their candidate as the most effective way to meet the League issue. That appeal was signed by one man who later became the first post-war Secretary of State, another who became Secretary of Commerce and President, another who became successively Secretary of State and of War, and still another who became Secretary of the Interior. These foremost members of the Republican party assumed the responsibility of declaring to their fellow countrymen:

" 'The question, accordingly, is not between a league or no league, but is whether certain provisions in the proposed League agreement shall be accepted unchanged or shall be changed.

" 'The contest is not about the principle of a league of nations, but is about the method of most effectively applying that principle to preserve peace.

" 'We have reached the conclusion that the true course to bring America into an effective league to preserve peace [is not to insist on Article X but to call frankly on the other nations to agree to changes]. The Republican party is bound by every consideration of good faith to pursue such a course until the declared objective is attained.'

"Something very extraordinary happened at that time, however, which was to cast a shadow over the next epoch of history. Whether it was a complete failure of government or an extraordinary irresponsibility of leadership is for history to say. President Harding, before the triumphal bonfire in Marion, declared that the League of Nations was now dead.

"This was a shattering statement indeed. The other nations had not anticipated anything even comparable to it. They had, as I have said, foreseen change but not repudiation. They waited in vain for any protest from the thirty-one leaders who had urged President Harding's election on the League issue, a strange silence seemed to have fallen on many tongues.

". . . The United States, instead of entering, supporting, and giving leadership to an agency which it had itself created and required the other nations to accept, suddenly turned around when they had become committed to it and withdrew into complete isolation on the other side of the ocean. The bottom dropped out, so to speak, of the spiritual side of the peace settlement.

"The other nations waited for a repudiation or at least an alternative from Washington, where some of the thirty-one eminent leaders were now in high office, but none came. The promises made in the political campaign were not fulfilled; no project, proposal, or suggestion was ever received abroad to meet any difficulties with which the United States might feel it was faced. Instead, the United States signed separate treaties with the ex-enemies, assuring itself all the benefits and few of the obligations of the original treaties. It was a hard bargain, indeed, which Americans should deeply ponder when they assess responsibilities."

It would prove a certain staleness of mind to believe that a similar thing is bound to happen again; but it would be most unwise to take it for granted that the Senate of the United States would easily consent to the ratification of a peace treaty providing for a world organization of countries including the United States, and with a Covenant which would have to contain articles which in various respects would bind all member states in the future. On the contrary, it would be the duty of the Senate to exercise its privilege and discuss fully and in detail any such provisions and their repercussions on the political system of the United States. And if the Covenant should demand that the delegations to the World Assembly should have the authority to oblige their countries without any other act of ratification, ample time should be given for an open discussion of this problem among leaders of public opinion in America. And the necessary rules should be elaborated which would make such a thing possible under the American system.

For the universal ratification of the Peace Treaty, including the Covenant of a world organization, it may prove necessary to lay this document before the Senate of the United States before it is ratified by any other country, because no other parliamentary body will have the right or power to modify or amend the treaties; and it would cause delay, irritation and interminable international discussions if all the rest of the countries should first ratify a treaty and then, as a consequence of American amendments, have to go over all its articles again, modify and amend and have the altered treaty sent to their parliaments for a new act of ratification.

For American participation in the peace conference and for the appointment of the American delegations to a World Assembly it will probably be necessary to accept the principles followed by every democratic country (except until this war the United Kingdom). The delegations to the League of Nations were non-partisan delegations, or rather they were all-partisan and numbered prominent representatives of all political parties, from the opposition as well as from the supporters of the Government. And delegations were appointed under the consideration that the Foreign Relations Committees of the various parliaments always should be fully conversant with the problems under discussion, and in reality should be consulted before any decisions were made. It was very strongly felt, especially among the smaller states, that questions of foreign policy are national issues and should not be made party issues. And, on the other hand, the leaders of political parties admitted the wisdom of the old lawyer's maxim that the art of living consists in acquiring the right kind of accomplices, which holds particularly true where stability in the direction of foreign affairs is involved. Only if all groups and parties are made active in decisions concerning foreign politics, only when they are all fully informed, when they are all given a share in national responsibility, can full loyalty be exacted from them.

This general principle of responsibility has even more importance in international life; and when it comes to appointing delegates to an international organization intended to wield real power, it can safely be said that delegates without sufficient authority from their governments will never feel that national and individual responsibility which can alone make international political life as serious as—or more serious than—national political life.

Of course, this would change the character of the representative body as it has been known for twenty years in the League of Nations, and would necessitate far more serious preparation of all the questions put on the agenda. A good deal of work and the main burden of responsibility would be shifted over from the Secretariat of the world organization to the Delegations; and every Delegation would have to keep in close contact with its home government. The sessions of the Assembly would probably last longer than did the sessions of the Assembly of the League of Nations, but on the other hand it would not be unnatural if delegations could be made less numerous and a number of minor items referred to smaller committees which might be given an extended power to make recommendations that would be referred directly to the governments without passing through the ordinary Assembly routine.

There will be little difficulty in formulating the rules of procedure needed or such elastic forms of representation as can ensure positive results.

But not only the forms of representation will have to be altered, also the character of representation. In a famous speech by Elihu Root he declared, "We need the substitution of a judicial sense of responsibility for diplomatic sense of responsibility." In a very particular degree this holds true of national representation in any kind of world organization.

Sir Nevile *Henderson* who, as ambassador to Berlin, held the most important political post under the Foreign Office, writes in his book "Failure of a Mission" (p. VIII):

"The first commandment of a diplomatist is faithfully to interpret the views of his own government to the government to which he is accredited; and the second is like unto it: namely, to explain no less accurately the views and standpoint of the government of the country in which he is stationed to the government of his own country."

Whether we find this definition satisfactory and exhaustive or not, we have to take it for granted that this was the traditional idea to which young British diplomats were brought up. Maybe that is why so many have failed when it was necessary to be something more than the transmitter of the views of others.

Wendell Willkie in an article in *The New York Times Magazine* (February 15, 1942) remarks: "In our American language the complicated League Covenant and the diplomats in striped trousers never seemed like the real thing."

And although diplomats in shirtsleeves seem less real to Europeans than diplomats in striped trousers, Wendell Willkie is right. He is right because the old-time diplomat, like another royal remnant from predatory times, never lost his stripes.

Some two hundred years ago a well-known British Ambassador defined a diplomat as "a man who lies abroad for his country." He was discredited by his government for having coined that phrase and in vain he tried to be equivocal and point out that "lie" is an ambiguous word in English. His government did not like one definition better than the other. The man is forgotten, but his words stuck.

Now, there is a great difference between a diplomat representing his country and a cabinet minister, or a prominent member of the national parliament, representing his country. The diplomat is a civil servant appointed by his government, pledged to full allegiance and loyalty. He is acting under orders like an officer at the front. He can remonstrate with his government; he can tell them what, in his opinion, they ought to do. But in the last instance he cannot disobey. If the difference of opinion between him and his government is of extreme gravity, he can resign. But it must be borne in mind that under certain conditions a diplomat has no more right to resign than an officer when the battle is raging. Resignation may mean desertion or treason. The diplomat's *raison d'être* is to be the silent and discreet instrument of a policy laid out by others. He has no right to voice publicly any private opinions. And, in most countries, it has been considered his duty not to stop at lying, if the alleged interests of his country should require even more striped action. The criminal record of diplomatic and consular services will be dealt with below. But the blame is not on the individual only.

It has taken an unconscionably long time to civilize national life. The civilization of international life has hardly begun. Nations still live under the presumption that acts which, perpetrated in private civic life by any individual would send him to jail, are patriotic or heroic acts when they are committed for their government in the name of their country.

It is this ever-widening gap between the individual code of ethics and the national code of ethics which underlies the adoration of Sovereignty. The individual is not authorized to decide whether or not his rights have been violated, whether or not he will react by private punishment against another individual responsible (according to him) for the violation of law. Such decisions have since the beginning of social civilization been entrusted to a judge, a special organ, different from and independent of the parties in conflict. And the individual who claims the right to decide for himself, whether and how he will punish his alleged enemies, is considered an asocial type, an abnormal person, suffering from megalomania or some kind of paranoia. And if he acts according to his ideas, he will soon find himself in a lunatic asylum, in jail, or in the electric chair.

But nations claim the privilege of deciding whether or not their rights have been violated, whether or not they will react by private punishment against another nation responsible (according to them) for the violation of law. The essence of sovereignty as popularly understood is the right for every nation to be judge in its own case. As this is contrary to generally accepted moral ideas, a peculiar sophistry has been developed to support the idea that it is perfectly legitimate for any state to take the law into its own hands. To justify this thesis it has been necessary to decree that there were also two different sets of moral laws for individuals, one when they are acting in their private capacity and another when they are acting for the State. This philosophy was brought to a triumphant climax with the Japanese attack on Pearl Harbor. But we have to admit that the difference in conception has been more in degree than in kind.

The diplomat is trained to the idea that loyalty—loyalty to his country and loyalty to his government (or perhaps rather to the Foreign Service)—goes before anything else. So far no line has been drawn to make clear where loyalty ends and individual responsibility begins. The diplomat cannot expose his government, except in his memoirs, and very often he must be prepared to be made the scapegoat for mistakes and miscalculations of which he has not been the author, but only the Hendersonian transmitter. If he feels that the laws of right and wrong are absolute and should not be adapted to the pattern of any particular national policy, he can never make any such statement, being only the servant of a government.

A parliamentarian, on the other hand, whether he be a member of the cabinet or not, is no civil servant. His *raison d'être* is that he has a private opinion and is able and willing—sometimes more willing than able—to state it with a good deal of publicity. He can represent his country only when he has discussed with his government the line of action it will take and has agreed to it. He is one of the authors of his own instructions. If he does not agree in the policy pursued, his duty is to make that clear. If he fails to do so, if he silently consents to follow instructions contrary to his conviction, not only does he become an accomplice to the acts he condemns, but he evinces a lack of moral responsibility that should disqualify him for public life. It seems hard for people to admit that this should apply to international activities. Some of us may have seen or heard delegates to the League of Nations, for instance, supporting a view in public and deploring it privately, acting under the delusion that loyalty to a government means more than loyalty to a moral principle.

"Those who would treat politics and morality apart will never understand the one or the other," declared old Lord Morley,* one of the most dispassionate and level-headed philosophers and statesmen Great Britain ever had.

It is essential that it should be accepted in international life as in national life that such is the case, and that the man who would act for his government as he should never dream of acting for himself, is a danger to his country and to the international community; because he understands neither politics nor morality; and in his spiritual confusion obscures the outlines of truth and reality.

And until nations demand that the same principles of moral responsibility shall govern international life as are enforced in national life, no new world order will prove successful.

It will be objected to the application of absolute honesty in international political discussions that those who represent their countries may find themselves in the position of lawyers engaged to defend certain interests. Their duty is to the client and not to the other party. In case of litigation, and within certain limits, that may be so. But then there is a court of law to pronounce sentence on right and wrong. And if two parties are discussing a contract, any lawyer knows that the withholding of material facts will invalidate the contract; he knows that any deceptive or misleading information given will prepare a case for the other party. He may not instinctively like to be honest, but he knows from his own experience and

* John Morley, first Viscount Morley (1838-1923), as an author is best known for his three volumes of biography of his friend Gladstone; was in Parliament from 1883 to his death, Secretary for Ireland in Gladstone's and Roseberry's cabinets; Secretary of State for India in the Campbell-Bannerman cabinet, advocated the Boer point of view in the 1890s and resigned as a cabinet minister when England went to war in 1914. His memoirs in two volumes form an important source of knowledge of recent British history.

from the experience of others and from his study of the law that in big business it does not pay to be dishonest. It may be tempting to experiment with your ability to get away with it; but the risk is too great. In the background is always the court of law and certain principles of justice to which every civilized state professes to adhere.

Nobody would demand that any delegate representing his country should follow quixotic ideas, or pretend that he would be justified in doing less for the interests of his client than an honorable lawyer should do. But the counsel engaged for the management of the case is responsible under the code of ethics of his profession, under the rules of the Bar and under the laws and regulations of his country. To violate any of them would incapacitate him for his career, might lead to his dismissal from the Bar and might land him in the penitentiary.

But the delegate who represents his country internationally knows that he is acting under no accepted code of ethics; he knows that he cannot be summoned before any court of justice. To use a time-honored phrase of ill repute, he is "responsible only to God and his own conscience." This may eventually lead him into Purgatory or Hell or, at best, to some lonesome Limbo. But from the constitutional point of view, it places the delegate virtually in the same position as the dictator. Here again there is power without any corresponding corrective of responsibility.

The question then seems to be: Can there be created such a system of international law and regulations, can there be enforced such a code of ethics, supported by courts of justice, that the standards of international responsibility can be elevated?

In order to answer that question it is necessary to know the existing courts of international justice, to study their experience and examine what has been done for further development in this direction.

For the establishment of law instead of violence, for the substitution of right for might, it is of vital importance to build up courts of justice, empowered to decide in international conflicts, and in questions which left undecided might lead to international conflicts, empowered also to act so as to prevent such provocations as might lead to international disturbance.

These problems may be less controversial and less spectacular than some of the more exciting political questions, but they certainly are more fundamental, and probably might be more easy to solve in such a way that the cause of dynamic peace would be furthered by it. For this reason the question of international courts will be dealt with at some length.

XX: Permanent International Courts

The Constitution of the World Assembly that will meet as the supreme organ of peaceful international coöperation and of international control, will take care of the greater number of problems to be dealt with financially and politically. But this body can no more than any national house of representatives have the competence, the power and the responsibility of the judiciary. The whole system of international courts of law must be extended and reinforced.

When discussing international courts of justice we are again covering ground on which has been accumulated a vast store of experience during the last forty years. We know what has been accomplished; we know what has been lacking, and we know that we need something more than we have had, what might be termed a new order of international law and justice, and of law enforcement.

Irrespective of the present war, the need already existed for a kind of international court of justice, different from those we have had since 1899, or, *de facto*, since 1902.

The International Peace Conference, held at the Hague in 1899, adopted a Convention for the Peaceful Adjustment of International Differences, which was ratified by the twenty-six powers that had been in conference. The only state that openly spoke against peaceful adjustment of international differences was Germany; but public opinion all over the world was so strongly, nearly passionately in favor of the creation of an international tribunal that Germany at last decided not to be left out.

The Interparliamentary Union in 1894 had adopted a declaration in favor of a permanent court of arbitration, and, especially in the United States of America, there was a never-lagging interest. In 1896 a declaration similar to that of the Interparliamentary Union was adopted unanimously by the annual Mohonk Conference on international arbitration, and by the New York State Bar Association, the latter presenting to the President of the United States a memorial setting forth a permanent tribunal as the essential feature of any general scheme of arbitration.

As a tangible symbol of this American interest in the cause of international peace Andrew Carnegie, on April 25, 1903, donated the sum of $1,500,000 for the erection of a Temple of Peace, comprising a comprehensive library of international law and a courthouse which could be used as a meeting place for the Permanent Court of Arbitration. And in this building the Court has met ever since its inauguration.

The Convention provides for a Court of Arbitration, defines its jurisdiction, the principles which are to guide it, the manner in which its members should be elected and the rules governing its procedure.

There are no judges permanently attached to the Permanent Court of Arbitration at the Hague. Its status is well described by Dr. Manley O. Hudson:

"In a strict sense the Permanent Court of Arbitration is not a *permanent Court* and not even a court. It is rather a panel out of which tribunals may be constituted from time to time." ("The World Court," p. 2.)

Forty-nine states are contracting parties to one or both of the Hague Conventions. And every state adhering to

them has the right to appoint not more than four persons
"of recognized competence in questions of international
law, enjoying the highest moral reputation" as members
of this "permanent court." The members never meet. The
affairs of the Court are directed by an Administrative
Council, composed of the diplomatic representatives at
the Hague of states parties to the conventions, under the
presidency of the Dutch minister of foreign affairs, and by
a secretary general who is really permanent and has his
office in the Peace Palace at the Hague.

The members of the Permanent Court of Arbitration
are not necessarily judges. They need not even be lawyers;
some of them are; others are diplomats, parliamentarians,
former cabinet ministers.

When two states agree to go to the Court of Arbitration
at the Hague they also agree upon the number of judges
to be called in to constitute the particular court of arbitration. There may be one, three or five judges; and the
states in question can draw upon those committees of four
each from forty-nine states.

As a rule, when two states about to litigate their case
have appointed their judges, the judges so appointed will
elect among the multitude of their colleagues on the
"court" the president of their particular tribunal. If they
cannot agree, it is usually stipulated either in the existing
treaty of arbitration between the two states, or in the exchange of notes previous to the decision to take the case
to the court of arbitration at the Hague, who shall elect
the president of that particular court, if the appointed
judges cannot agree on the election. Quite often the privilege will be incumbent on the President or the Chief
Justice of the Supreme Court of the United States.

No state can be forced to accept the competence or the
authority of the Permanent Court of Arbitration in any
single case. Most states have clauses in their recent treaties,
binding them to a procedure of arbitration in case of liti-

gation. But, as a rule, there is an exemption made for any conflict touching the "national honor and vital interests" of the contracting parties. And there is hardly a question of litigation between states which cannot be interpreted as touching upon the vital interests or national honor of the countries involved; and the Permanent Court of Arbitration at the Hague has no competence to discuss or decide in litigations between individuals or between individuals and states. In consequence of this, states not seldom have had to identify themselves with private individual interests, or have had to find a formula under which encroachments on the rights of individuals are declared a national concern.

This system in itself is not of a kind to make relations between states more cordial or intimate. And sometimes a government may be reluctantly forced by public opinion to adopt a case which, under more elastic rules of procedure, and if there had existed international courts with jurisdiction in litigations between private interests and states, would hardly have been considered a legitimate national concern.

Such questions very often are exactly of a nature to whip up popular sentiment and those waves of national emotion which are the worst enemies of dispassionate legal discussion and judicial decision.

To take an instance: A ship is arrested for trying to smuggle liquor into a certain country and is taken into one of the ports of that country. Under a violent quarrel with the police officers the first mate of the ship and part owner of its cargo is seriously hurt. The press of his native country is swept by sensational indignation at this outrage. First of all the ship was arrested in waters where the other state had no uncontested jurisdiction; and then come violent protests against the brutality and corruption of the police of that state, and the government of the home country of the ship is passionately demanded to make a national cause of this incident, to take it before the Permanent Court of Arbitration at the Hague, to claim the highest possible damages, to expose to the whole world the methods practised by the other state and so on.

There will be an ensuing exchange of notes of rising asperity. The government accused of violation of international law or treaties or conventions probably will refuse to take the difference to the Hague; and for years such a case which cannot be taken automatically before an international court of justice may poison, or at least inflame, relations between two friendly states and cause the governments no end of work and worry.

Such, or similar, cases well known to the Department of State in this country and in many another country could be enumerated.

A typical affair of this kind is the famous Hannevig case between Norway and the United States. When, in 1917, the United States entered World War I, a number of Norwegian shipbuilding contracts were requisitioned. And just compensation was promised. Norwegian shipowners appealed to the Norwegian Government which made their case its own. In 1919 a compromise was accepted for one group of contracts and $34,000,000 was paid in compensation. After long negotiations the United States Government consented to take the remaining claims before the Permanent Court of Arbitration at the Hague, and in 1922 the United States Government was sentenced to pay to the Norwegian Government, representing a group of Norwegian shipowners, a sum of $12,239,852.

But the United States Government had made an exemption for one of the Norwegian claimants, Christoffer Hannevig, and refused to take his case to the Hague. His case did not only concern requisition of shipbuilding contracts, but also of shipyards and property in the United States, and so presented an aspect different from the case of the rest of the shipowners. Hannevig had bought the Pusey &

Jones shipyards and started shipbuilding on a grand scale; and it was felt that he was deprived of the fruits of his initiative and enterprise.

In Norway there was gradually built up a strong opinion for Mr. Hannevig, a popular feeling that great injustice had been done to him and that he was entitled to a fair compensation. The Government was prevailed upon to take up his case; he claimed a sum of $42,000,000 plus interest since 1917. It became a political issue in Norway; a special mission was sent to the United States to negotiate, and two Norwegian accredited ministers had to resign from their posts as a result of the turmoil about the Hannevig case. It was brought up before the Norwegian Parliament, which decided by an overwhelming majority to authorize the government to go all the way with Mr. Hannevig. Ten thousands of pages of learned legal opinion have been written, hundreds of notes have been exchanged. Every kind of argument and precedent has been brought forward, and very fully discussed. The American Government claimed that Mr. Hannevig had not exhausted all local remedies, but at last, in 1938, the Norwegian Government and the United States Government agreed on a procedure. The Norwegian Government, through its counsels, should give a complete presentation of its claim. The United States Government should then, in a similar way (within a time limit of six months), state its objections to the claim; the Norwegian Government should then, within four months, file a brief, to which the American Government could file a counter brief. If the two Governments could not agree on a solution after this exchange of views and arguments, each party should appoint a special arbitrator; and if the two arbitrators could not agree, they should appoint an umpire.

The first documents had been prepared when World War II broke out; and the United States Government de-

manded an adjournment until the war was over. In this
way Mr. Hannevig, who is now in the United States, can
celebrate his silver wedding to the famous case, which
would never seriously have troubled the two governments,
if there had existed a tribunal competent to pass judgment,
or enforce arbitration in litigations between states and individuals.

The Permanent Court of Arbitration, since first a dispute was referred to it in 1902, has decided in twenty-three
arbitrations, some of them taken before special arbitral
tribunals coming under the resort of the Court.

As the United States of America had taken a keen interest in the establishment of the Court, so its government
took the step needed to make of the Court a reality. The
first difference to be referred to a tribunal of the Permanent Court of Arbitration was the *Pious Fund Case* between the United States and Mexico in 1902. This action
was taken by the United States Government to prevent
the Convention for the establishment of the Permanent
Court of Arbitration from becoming a dead letter.*

The second difference brought to the Hague was the
complications between Venezuela and the United States,
and various European countries in 1903. This attitude of
the United States Government was in the line of the
finest traditions in American foreign policy. The treaty
concluded by John Jay in 1794 was the first important gen-

---

* The Pious Fund difference had been rankling in Mexican and American minds ever since the Mexican war. In 1842 Mexico had seized certain
religious funds in California belonging to the Roman Catholic Church
(which had been disestablished some years previously) and had promised
to pay the bishops yearly. But Mexico had not paid; and when the
United States took over California this claim was one of the assets of the
new territory. After sixty years of futile quarreling the United States
proposed to go before the new court of International Arbitration with
the case, and Mexico agreed. As no country had previously seen fit to
appeal to the new instrument of arbitration, its opponents hoped to see
it never brought to life. This was prevented by the United States Government, which, incidentally, won its case. Mexico was sentenced to pay a
yearly contribution of $43,050 to the Roman Catholic bishops of Cali-
fornia.

eral treaty of arbitration and a model for a century of peaceful efforts.

There is only a very weak connection between the Permanent Court of Arbitration at the Hague and the Permanent Court of International Justice set up by the League of Nations in accordance with the Versailles Treaty and under a statute annexed to a protocol of signature, signed by fifty-seven states.

The Permanent Court of International Justice is what the name signifies: a real court of justice. There are fifteen members. They are all elected—for a period of nine years—by the Council and by the Assembly of the League of Nations. To be elected, a candidate must obtain the absolute majority of votes, both in the Council and in the Assembly; and balloting goes on simultaneously in both bodies until the vacancies have been filled. The candidates eligible are nominated by the national groups of judges of the Permanent Court of Arbitration, and only those so nominated can come under consideration.* That is the one connecting link between the two organizations.

The idea of absolute national sovereignty so baleful for all international coöperation has limited the jurisdiction of the Permanent Court of International Justice—as it limited the sphere of action of the Permanent Court of Arbitration. The principle of compulsory international jurisdiction was not generally accepted just as the principle of obligatory arbitration had not been accepted. The same limited competence was given to the court in both cases.† What was called the optional clause in Article 36 of the Statute ‡ was not approved for a long time by any

---

* States not represented on the Permanent Court of Arbitration have the right to constitute corresponding "national groups" for the purpose of this nomination.

† "The jurisdiction of the Court comprises all cases which the parties refer to it."

‡ "The Members of the League of Nations and the States mentioned in the Annex to the Covenant may, either when signing or ratifying the Protocol to which the present Statute is adjoined, or at a later moment, declare that they recognize as compulsory ipso facto and without special

Great Powers—only by the smaller states. The greatest
country adhering to the Permanent Court of Justice without being a member of the League of Nations, Brazil, in
1921 made its acceptance of the optional clause dependent
on the ratification of the clause by two Great Powers with
a permanent seat on the Council of the League. But not
until 1930 did the United Kingdom ratify the Clause and
then with so many reservations that the character of the
acceptance was rather dubious. France, Italy and Germany
followed with their reservations. Japan never ratified the
Clause.

In a future world order compulsory jurisdiction of International Courts of Justice must be universally accepted.

The conception of absolute national sovereignty also in-
fects the Statute of the Permanent Court of Justice in another way. The judges, in spite of the oath they have taken
to serve only the Court,* are still regarded not as judges
only, but as representatives of nations. And the Statute
prescribes that if a state has a case before the Permanent
Court of International Justice and is unrepresented on the
bench, the government of the state in question has the
right to appoint one of its nationals to serve as judge
ad hoc.

The reversed procedure would more correspond to judicial practice in most states. If the question of the nation-

agreement, in relation to any other Member or State accepting the same
obligation, the jurisdiction of the Court in all or any of the classes of
legal disputes concerning:

   (a) the interpretation of a treaty;
   (b) any question of international law;
   (c) the existence of any fact which, if established, would constitute a
        breach of an international obligation;
   (d) the nature or extent of the reparation to be made for the breach
        of an international obligation.

The declaration referred to above may be made unconditionally or on
condition of reciprocity on the part of several or certain Members or
States, or for a certain time."

* Article 20: "Every member of the Court shall, before taking up his
duties, make a solemn declaration in open court that he will exercise
his powers impartially and conscientiously."

ality of the judges should be raised at all, in itself an asper-
sion on the impartiality of the court, it should be on the
supposition that a judge whose home country had a case
before the court should be disqualified.* The practice has
been taken over from the Permanent Court of Arbitration.
But for the application of the principles of law and justice
there is a difference in kind and essence between the two
forms of court. And the poor judges *ad hoc,* what is their
duty? To administer justice or to serve the supposed interests of their country? They can never have an enviable
task. And if they should pronounce against the alleged
interests of their country their homecoming would hardly
be triumphant—an indication that the system is not sound.

The same anxiety lest the principle of sovereignty
should be encroached upon, the same lack of confidence
between states, the mutual distrust has also been reflected
whenever there has been a vacancy to fill. Under the strict
application of Article 2 of the Statute, judges shall be
"elected regardless of their nationality from among persons of high moral character, who possess the qualifications
required in their respective countries for appointment to
the highest judicial offices, or are jurisconsults of recognized competence in international law." But with rare exceptions the members of the Permanent Court of International Justice have never served as judges before. They are
diplomats or professors of law. And some of them have
been exactly the men whose previous career makes it extremely doubtful whether they ought to have been eligible
to the Court. This, of course, is no reflection on the individual judge, but a criticism of those who nominated and
elected him.

Formally it has not strengthened the Court that among
the judges are the former legal advisers of the British Foreign Office and the French Ministère des Affaires Etran-

* This was also the recommendation of the "Union Juridique Internationale," founded in 1919 to promote International Law.

gères. No doubt, those members of the Court are excellently qualified. But the men who for long years have been jurisconsults to the two leading Great Powers in questions of foreign policy will not be generally admitted to have the full impartiality demanded of judges. On many questions that can be expected to come before the Permanent Court of International Justice they will, at one time or another, officially or unofficially, have expressed an opinion. They are not of an unimpeachable neutrality. And surely the famous word about the virtue of Cæsar's wife applies to a body like the Permanent Court of International Justice more than to most human institutions.

Article 17 of the Statute declares:

"No member may participate in the decision of any case in which he has previously taken an active part as agent, counsel or advocate for one of the contending parties, or as a member of a national or international Court, or of commission of inquiry, or in any other capacity."

But the parties appearing before the Court have no right of recusation. It is left to the discretion of the individual judge whether he will consider himself as disqualified or not; "If, for some special reason, a member of the Court considers that he should not take part in the decision of a particular case, he shall so inform the President." (Art. 24.)

As the right of national representation has been established in the Statute, there is nothing to encourage any judge to consider himself disqualified, unless he has been officially active in the dealing of the particular question under the provisions of Article 17.

The judges in question are most highly respected. But if all the Great Powers should be represented on the Court in a similar way nobody would pretend that that would serve the purpose of the Court. And there is no denying that there has been a general feeling in many quarters that when a man for years has been *advocatus diaboli* he may not *a priori* be considered the best and most impartial judge available.

On the other hand an important current of public opinion has maintained that under present world conditions the Permanent Court of International Justice cannot overlook established political facts; if not, it might be deemed very admirable, but its decisions might be so much in the abstract that they would be of little practical importance.

Only in one case has it been claimed that the decision of the Court was of a political character. The division of votes when the proposed customs union between Germany and Austria was declared incompatible with treaty obligations, no doubt, seemed to indicate that judges were influenced by national opinion. But the full publicity as to how the Court reaches its conclusions, including publicity for the arguments which it rejects, is the best guarantee for unbiased decisions. And gradually governments have become more and more willing to make full use of the growing authority of the Court.

The most numerous cases taken to the Court are those involving questions of sovereignty or treaty rights. One of the most interesting conflicts decided was a dispute between Switzerland and France. Under the peace settlement after the Napoleonic wars certain adjacent districts in France were to be maintained as free trade areas in order to give the canton of Geneva an adequate economic hinterland. France obtained the insertion in the Treaty of Versailles of a clause declaring this arrangement to be no longer in accordance with existing circumstances. Switzerland, not being a party to the Versailles Treaty, protested; France took the law in her own hands and advanced her customs barriers to the political frontier, but subsequently consented to go to the Court; and the Court decided in favor of Switzerland.

Two advisory opinions of the Court prevented the reopening of frontier decisions of the Conference of Ambassadors. And on the whole it must be admitted that the Court has been of great use to the international commonwealth. It may even be said that the Court has moved to a higher position than some governments have realized.

The very way in which candidacies for the Court are canvassed by them proves that they are far from realizing the full dignity and potential importance of the Court. Although, formally, the judges are nominated by the national groups constituting the Hague Court of Arbitration, the candidacies are taken up by a number of national governments. They announce in the various capitals through the usual diplomatic channels that they are "candidates" for the Permanent Court of International Justice. They ask to be supported; they are willing to make a deal; they sometimes cannot even abstain from discreetly veiled threats in case the governments to which their diplomats are accredited should not be willing to promise to give "their candidate" its vote.

But even if some of the transactions behind the curtains are rather undignified, and sometimes shady, the Court itself has a splendid record. It may not have contributed to the creation of new international law to the extent hoped for by many enthusiasts. But it has won a name for dignity and fairness, for general competence, for honorable conduct and handling of delicate affairs, for scrupulous integrity which could not be finer. And surely it is in itself an evidence of the need for an international court of justice, an evidence that it was established in the fulness of time that this great and imposing experiment proved so successful in spite of all misgivings and all difficulties.

Since 1923 the Court has passed judgment in thirty-one cases of litigation between states and has given twenty-seven advisory opinions and seven "orders" which have, more or less, the character of judgments.

The following states have applied to the Permanent Court of International Justice: Belgium, Brazil, Great

Britain, Bulgaria, China, Czechoslovakia, Denmark, France, Germany, Greece, Hungary, Italy, Japan, Lithuania, Netherlands, Norway, Poland, Sweden, Switzerland, Turkey, Jugoslavia.

No judgment and no order of the Court has been disputed or contested; the question of execution has never come up, as all parties involved have accepted the decisions.

No doubt the international good-will created by the Court and built up by all the decisions and the whole practice of the Court is of a most particular future value. And it should be the interest of every civilized state to make its contribution to carry the Court over this period of danger and distress, because the prestige and authority, the impartiality and unbroken tradition of the Court will be more needed when the war is over than it has ever been.

It will be seen from the summary here given that whereas the Permanent Court of Arbitration was set up primarily on a diplomatic basis, the Permanent Court of International Justice was intended to be a strictly judicial body. In the long-standing struggle between the advocates of the principle of law and justice against the advocates of momentary expediency and moral elasticity, the former had gained a most important victory. All the States signatories to the Statute of the Court of Justice had in reality accepted the thesis expressed by Mr. Elihu Root in his address delivered before the First National Peace Congress at New York in 1907:

"What we need for the further development of arbitration is the substitution of judicial action for diplomatic action, the substitution of judicial sense of responsibility for diplomatic sense of responsibility."

This development led from a Court of Arbitration to a permanent Court of International Justice. But, as indicated above, it has been difficult for a good many states to give up their time-honored conception that questions of foreign policy should be dealt with by diplomats and not by judges or parliamentarians, and that any matter in controversy between states should be negotiated in privacy and secrecy and not discussed openly and decided in a Court of Justice. And in the nomination of the judges and the system of election the older school has taken its last stand.

A number of judges have been appointed directly from the diplomatic career and some of them have later been elected presidents of the Court. They have served with distinction and they have forgotten the ways of their past career or remembered them only as a warning.

At the supplementary election in September, 1935, the Council and the Assembly of the League of Nations had a regrettable relapse to diplomatic methods. It was the last successful fight of the old foreign-office school. Mr. Adatci, the highly respected Japanese member of the Court, had died. And at the request of the trade-union of Great Powers the elective bodies set aside Article 2 of the Statute of the Court—"a body of independent judges elected regardless of their nationality"—and agreed to elect a Japanese candidate in spite of the fact that Japan had left the League and that the attitude of Japan in the Manchurian conflict had given evidence of a national conception of international politics entirely foreign to the conception of law upon which the Permanent Court of International Justice had been built. It was a political action in favor of an aggressor state, taken by England and France in that futile belief which gradually led to the present war, that if only aggressor states were given all that they demanded and a little more, they would be appeased and behave and be good children ever after. The candidate put up by Japan and supported by the Great Powers was elected.

In the quite authoritative article on the Court published

in the first report from the American Commission to Study the Organization of Peace, suggestions are made for amending the statutory rules of election to the Permanent Court of International Justice. One is that the election of the judges shall be left to the Assembly of the League of Nations only, and that the provision that the Council shall also act as an electoral body ought not to be retained. Those who have assisted at the elections and have studied methods of election will not agree with the writer. And if the Council has ceased to be the mouthpiece of the Great Powers, the more reason to continue the previous practice, which may sometimes serve as a safeguard against too casual decisions.

Next, the writer maintains that it would be better if one-third of the Court was elected every three years instead of allowing the nine-year term of all the judges to expire simultaneously. No doubt he is right; and in the Convention for the creation of an International Criminal Court (see below) this conception has been carried out (a similar amendment was accepted in the League for the election of the Supervisory Committee).

The writer furthermore declares that the judges are too old and that there ought to be an age limit. Here again he is probably right.

The most far-reaching amendment suggested by him relates not to the elections, but to Article 38 which lays down that the Court shall apply: (1) International Conventions, (2) International custom as evidence of general practice accepted as law, (3) the general principles of law recognized by civilized nations.

It is advocated as sufficient to state that the Court shall apply "international law and equity." This is a highly controversial question and in many countries such an amendment would be felt to throw the doors wide open to arbitrary decisions, political interplay and expedient discrimination.

As a general consideration it may be stated that the present moment is hardly opportune for discussing any minor amendments to the statute, and that it would be unwise to affect its stability even at the Peace Conference, which, in itself, will have no authority to amend the statute. The Permanent Court of International Justice is one of the few things that remain unscathed by the world conflagration and whose authority is not seriously contested anywhere; on the other hand it may be said that owing to the international situation the Court is suffering from anemia today and should be very tenderly treated.

In the article on the Court mentioned above, the official American attitude to the Court is described as follows:

"The record of the United States is so black in this connection that American groups should be very slow in criticizing the great progress made by other states in building the World Court. The United States had not contributed a cent of the $10,000,000 expended on the Court in the eighteen years, though the Court is always open to it, and a national of the United States has always been one of the judges (Moore, Hughes, Kellogg, Hudson). At conferences the United States has prevented other states from agreeing to give jurisdiction to the Court. It seems difficult to foresee any useful contribution which the paralyzed Government of the United States can make in this connection."

The United States, not adhering to the Court, could hardly be expected to contribute to its expenses; and it is not the fault of the United States that the Assembly and the Council have always elected an American member of the Court. In principle this election has hardly been in conformity with Article 2 of the statute quoted above. For with all due tribute paid to the excellence of the American judges, no man would deny that they were elected on account of their nationality, and that they would have been elected even if they had been less excellent or entirely unknown, because it was the fond belief of the Great

Powers leading the League that if only the right obsequious subservience was shown in every domain states would be cajoled to behave and become loyal members of the League. And, on the other hand, it was felt that the refusal of the Senate to accept American adherence to the Permanent Court of International Justice was such an incredible break away from the finest traditions in American history, that some day, automatically, the reaction had to come.

But this political subservience has always stopped outside the doors of the courtroom. If such had not been the case, the world politic would not have wanted to hear the opinion of the Court.

The Permanent Court of International Justice, like the Permanent Court of Arbitration, is competent to decide only in litigations between States and not in litigations between individuals, or between individuals and states.

The situation is then actually this today, that individuals or groups which have suffered what might be termed an international injustice are completely without any right of redress and have nowhere to turn. And paradoxically, it so has happened that the very institution organized by all the world to protect the underprivilged and look after international justice, equity and collaboration, the League of Nations, had already been confronted by this difficulty and been absolutely helpless.

The cases may not be very important, but nevertheless, this strange interlude illustrates a state of affairs which cannot satisfy anybody, and factual examples are more striking than imaginary constructions.

One of the institutions set up by the Versailles Treaty was the International Saar Commission, the local government in charge of that rich country until the plebiscite of 1935 which resulted in Germany's reincorporating the Saar. Under the International Saar Commission were working a number of international civil servants and functionaries, judges, etc. To all these had been given certain guarantees for their future, such as pension rights and prospects of indemnities. And it was laid down in the Saar Convention that if the plebiscite went in favor of France, France would take over the obligations to pension the functionaries no more needed; if the Saar went to Germany, Germany would indemnify the men in question.

Among the functionaries were certain Germans and Austrians who had been serving the International Saar Commission with loyalty and competence, and who had refused to take orders from the Nazi propaganda machine previous to the plebiscite. The Saar Commission in due time disappeared; Germany took over all its obligations and offered to give to the functionaries in question—who, at the time, had preferred to take their abode in Switzerland or in France—positions, the rank and remuneration of which corresponded to their positions in the Saar.

Two of the functionaries proceeded to Germany and were promptly interned in concentration camps. The four who were left refused to go to Germany and demanded the pension to which they were entitled. Germany refused to pay and claimed that they had been given the opportunity of being appointed to honorable and well-paid positions in Germany, had refused and so had nothing more to demand.

Then commenced the long *via dolorosa* of those functionaries. They tried to sue the German state. But where? They had nothing to claim under German law; the courts of justice in the Saar had disappeared, the Saar Commission under which they had served was no longer existent; the original Saar Commission in its turn had been appointed by the Original Council of the League, which was even more non-existent and never had any legal personality.

The Saar functionaries asked to be allowed to take their case before the administrative tribunal set up by the League of Nations to decide in all matters of controversy

between the League and any of the functionaries of the
Secretariat, of the International Labour Office and of the
Permanent Court of International Justice. But the administrative organization of the Saar district had no connection with the League; the functionaries had not been appointed by the League and clearly the League had no responsibility for the Saar Commission, and the Administrative Tribunal no competence.

The former Saar functionaries then turned to the Permanent Court of International Justice and were dismissed.
The Permanent Court is competent to deal only with
litigations between states, not between states and individuals, and still less between individuals and the shadows
and ghosts of Great Power conferences.

In the meanwhile the functionaries and their families
were starving. They turned to the Supervisory Committee
of the League of Nations, asking for a pension in the name
of equity. But there is no account for gifts in the budget
of the League, and the Supervisory Committee is not empowered to give grants *ex gratia* out of the scanty contributions from the member states.

The functionaries in question had ceased to exist as
legal subjects. They had lost their German citizenship;
Austria later ceased to exist as a state. But these unfortunate men could not obtain a Nansen passport, because,
under the international conventions, the Nansen Office
had no competence to deal with German refugees. And
the High Commissioner for Refugees had no power to
deal with them because technically they were not refugees.

The Supervisory Committee of the League, deeply re-
gretting the misfortunes of these men and their families,
suggested to the Council of the League of Nations to give
them some aid out of the funds for unforeseen expenditure
always at the disposal of the Council; and the Council
voted them an *ex gratia* donation of 10,000 Swiss francs
each. But two of the functionaries refused to accept this

gift. They were not begging for alms; they were seeking justice. They succeeded in stirring up a good deal of feeling, and the Council of the League of Nations, at its last meeting, in December, 1939, most unwisely decided to act temperamentally and accept the role of arbiter in the case of these two men. They have taken a lawyer, the Secretary General has engaged a prominent law-firm; if the lawyers don't agree the Council has consented to ask an opinion from the Permanent Court of International Justice on the procedure to be followed. And more money has already been spent than the original claim of the two men.

The League of Nations some years ago made extensive contracts for the construction of the new League building, popularly called *le Palais des Nations.* Some of them were long-time contracts. They were all concluded in the terms of Swiss francs, although a number of the contracting firms were French, German or Italian. While the building was under construction the Swiss franc was devalued, and the general contractors demanded an indemnity from the League, claiming that they had to pay a number of their subcontractors in currencies that were not devaluated.

There were other points of difference. There was the question of delay, charged by the contractors to the fault of the architects or of such committees of the League which had to give their approbation to minor alterations in the plans, and so on.

The League of Nations cannot be sued under Swiss law; and the Secretary General refused to accept, without prejudice to any principle, the competence of the courts of Canton de Genève in this particular case. The questions at litigation could not be taken to the Permanent Court of International Justice, because that Court can deal only with controversies between states and not between states and individuals. Whether the League would be defined as falling under the category of "states" is in itself an open question.

In other words: before the war international justice, where private interests were concerned, was homeless, a waif on the plains of arid formality, general distrust and lack of efficient international coöperation.

Even in this quite important field of international activity it is necessary to draw lessons from the experience of the last decades, the negative experience as well as the positive experience.

In the annual report of the Permanent Court of International Justice for 1939, it is stated: "It often happens that private individuals apply to the Court with the object of laying before it matters at issue between them and some government. These are generally claims for compensation for dispossession and arise as a rule from the fact that the applicants have lost their original national status and have not acquired another and, for this reason, have met with refusal on the part of the courts to which they have applied."

Some practical examples have been mentioned above to illustrate how the very existence of great international organizations will give rise to new questions that can only be answered by some competent international court of justice.

Further we have the cases of the stateless and of minorities; and after the present war those cases may be expected to multiply.

The Report of the Permanent Court of International Justice emphasizes the monetary aspect of the question. But there is also a constitutional and a humanitarian side, as was felt when *L'Institut de Droit International* at its New York Session in 1929 adopted a resolution in favor of the international rights of man. And, certainly, in the light of what has happened in the decade following the meeting in New York, the time has come for considering what can be done to protect these rights.

XXI: The International Rights of Man

The adoption of the Declaration of the International Rights of Man was proclaimed as a great event. It was considered important that this declaration should have been made on American soil, and on the anniversary of the second discovery of the New World (12th of October, 1929). The preamble refers to the American Constitution, to the Fourteenth Amendment to the Constitution,* and to the unanimous interpretation of that Amendment given by the Supreme Court of the United States, that by the terms of this Amendment it is applicable within the jurisdiction of the United States "to every person without distinction of race, color or nationality, and that the equal protection of the laws is a guarantee of the protection of equal laws."

The Declaration itself has six articles and was adopted in the following form:

"(1) It is the duty of every State to recognize the equal right of every individual to life, liberty and property, and to accord to all within its territory the full and entire protection of this right, without distinction as to nationality, sex, race, language, or religion.

"(2) It is the duty of every State to recognize the right of every individual to the free practice, both public and

---

* "No state shall make or enforce any law which shall abridge the privileges or immunities of citizens of the United States, nor shall any state deprive any person of life, liberty or property without due process of law, nor deny to any person within its jurisdiction the equal protection of the laws."

private, of every faith, religion, or belief, provided that the said practice shall not be incompatible with public order and good morals.

"(3) It is the duty of every State to recognize the right of every individual both to the free use of the language of his choice and to the teaching of such language.

"(4) No motive based, directly or indirectly, on distinctions of sex, race, language, or religion empowers States to refuse to any of their nationals private and public rights, especially admission to establishments of public instruction, and the exercise of the different economic activities and of professions and industries.

"(5) The equality herein contemplated is not to be nominal, but effective. It excludes all discrimination, direct or indirect.

"(6) Except for motives based upon its general legislation, no State shall have the right to withdraw its nationality from those whom, for reasons of sex, race, language, or religion, it should not deprive of the guarantees contemplated in the preceding articles."

The president of L'Institut de Droit International, the great American jurist, Dr. James Brown Scott, in a speech delivered at Havana one month after the adoption of the six points, made this statement: "The Declaration of the International Rights of Man is a stage in a long development that leads from inequality to the most perfect equality. It is a solemn manifestation of a new spirit in a new world."

In the same way the editor of the *American Journal of International Law* shortly after the adoption of the Declaration wrote in his editorial comment:

"It aims not merely to assure to individuals their *international* rights, but it aims also to impose on all nations a standard of conduct towards all men, *including their own nationals.* It thus repudiates the classic doctrine that states alone are subjects of international law. Such a revolutionary document, while open to criticism in terminology and to the objection that it has no juridical value, cannot fail, however, to exert an influence on the evolution of international law. It marks a new era which is more concerned with the interests and rights of sovereign individuals than with the rights of sovereign states." *

Unfortunately this new era has not yet started, and it is doubtful how many of those who voted the resolution in 1929 like to remember it today. But among the delegates to the New York convention were some of the most prominent jurists of the world and a number of the judges at the Permanent Court of International Justice at the Hague. And nothing could illustrate more crudely and cruelly the retrograde movement in world morals and in the region of human conscience than the very mentioning of the International Rights of Man. The Declaration was thought to be a statement of non-controversial principles and accepted rules of international conduct and law. And in the years gone by since 1929 the six articles have not only been violated more flagrantly than in any other period since the Reformation; but they have been renounced and repudiated and refuted in word and in action by a number of states believed in 1929 to belong to the civilized nations, and no single state has taken any action to defend or uphold those principles.

In centuries gone by states could afford to hold feelings of obligation and responsibility; there was within narrow limits a sentiment of solidarity among states belonging to the same sphere of religious or moral ideas. Christian states sometimes took action when Christians were persecuted and slaughtered. Mohammedan states went to war when Islam was attacked. But democracies have been unwilling to take any action, when every principle of democracy has been trampled underfoot, and every right of democracy been ridiculed and made a farce. And the problem of a dynamic peace is the problem of active democratic solidarity. If democracies cannot learn to act on long sight and not only on short term, if they cannot develop a will-

* The italics by the author of the article.

ingness to sacrifice narrow self-interests for common democratic principles, democracies will face hard times. And democratic solidarity in international individual life is expressed in the Declaration of the International Rights of Man.

It can be said that the principles of the Declaration of the International Rights of Man are embodied in the Atlantic Charter. They are even more clearly formulated in the joint agreement of the twenty-six nations when they declare that "complete victory over their enemies is essential to defend life, liberty, independence and religious freedom, and to preserve human rights in their own lands as well as in other lands."

But even a joint Declaration from a number of governments (not ratified by the corresponding number of parliaments) has no legal power. Something more is needed. Only if the declaration is embodied in an international convention, binding all the countries in question to give the principles declared effect in their national legislation, can religious freedom and human rights be safeguarded. And it will be necessary that states should go even further and be pledged to give each other mutual assistance whenever these principles are in danger. If we desire, with the editor of the *American Journal of International Law,* to open a new era which is more concerned with the interests and rights of sovereign individuals than with the rights of sovereign states, there is one obvious way to proceed. We have to repudiate, openly and officially, the old doctrine that states alone are subjects of international law, and on the basis of the promises of the Atlantic Charter and the Washington Declaration adopt an International Bill of Rights. A little over two hundred and fifty years have passed since the Lords and the Commoners of Great Britain wrote the first national Bill of Rights; it certainly could not be premature to make international law what is national law in every democratic country.

In order to give the International Bill of Rights universal application, it would be desirable to establish an international penal code for the protection of religious freedom and human rights, and to incorporate the enforcement of such a code in the provisions for an International Criminal Court discussed below.

Sixty-five years ago we seemed more close to such a possibility than we are today, and it is of interest to compare the words of the Washington Declaration with the documents from the Berlin Congress of 1878. Today it is necessary for great states to be engaged in the most terrific war in the history of mankind in order to defend principles which in 1878 nobody dared to assault. When Serbia in that year asked to be recognized as a state, the Berlin protocol tells the following story:

"Lord Salisbury (Great Britain) recognizes the independence of Serbia, but is of opinion that it would be desirable to stipulate in the Principality the great principle of religious liberty.

"Mr. Waddington (France) believes that it is important to take advantage of this solemn opportunity to cause the principles of religious liberty to be affirmed by the representatives of Europe. His Excellency adds that Serbia, who claims to enter the European family on the same basis as other states, must previously recognize the principles which are the basis of social organization in all states of Europe and accept them as a necessary condition of the favor which she asks for.

"Prince Bismarck, associating himself with the French proposal, declares that the assent of Germany is always assured to any motion favorable to religious liberty.

"Count de Launay said that, in the name of Italy, he desires to adhere to the principle of religious liberty, which forms one of the essential bases of the institutions of his country, and that he associates himself with the declarations made on this subject by Germany, France, and Great Britain.

"Count Andrassy (Austria-Hungary) expresses himself to the same effect, and the Ottoman plenipotentiaries raise no objection.

"Prince Bismarck, after having summed up the results of

the vote, declares that Germany admits the independence of Serbia, but on condition that religious liberty will be recognized in the Principality. His Serene Highness adds that the drafting committee, when they formulate this decision, will affirm the connection established by the Conference between the proclamation of Serbian independence and the recognition of religious liberty."

This spirit of religious liberalism had evaporated before World War I; Clemenceau and his collaborators did not grasp the importance of immaterial forces in human life; but in the joint declaration of the twenty-six nations we find once more a spark of that holy fire of human solidarity which has lighted the way of civilization. But no indication is given as to the means and methods by which the individual rights of man shall be preserved.

No peace can be just and durable unless the principles which inspired the Congress in New York are respected, and states are willing to live up to the duties proclaimed in the Declaration. But today there is no authority whatsoever with a jurisdiction to supervise the application of the six points. And it will be essential in the post-war world to establish such an authority.

Under the Versailles Treaty the Council of the League of Nations, within the framework of the Treaty, was authorized to protect minorities, which meant in practice to be responsible for the application of Articles 3 and 4 of the Declaration—but not everywhere: minorities within the borders of the victorious Great Powers were not given such protection.

When Clemenceau transmitted to Paderewski the treaty for the protection of minorities which Poland was required to sign simultaneously with the Treaty of Peace with Germany on June 28, 1919, he stated in a letter of June 24:

"This treaty does not constitute any fresh departure. It has for long been the established procedure of the public law of Europe that when a state is created, or even when large accessions of territory are made to an established state, the joint and formal recognition by the great powers should be accompanied by the requirement that such state should, in the form of a binding international convention, undertake to comply with certain principles of government. This principle, for which there are numerous other precedents, received the most explicit sanction when, at the last great assembly of European Powers—the Congress of Berlin—the sovereignty and independence of Serbia, Montenegro, and Roumania were recognized." *

The letter is of a particular interest because, quite naïvely, it is based on the idea that only new states should be requested to comply with certain principles of government. Within the domains of the Great Powers what has been established shall not be touched. So even Clemenceau believed that a lasting peace can be static and that the Principal Allied and Associated Powers "can be exempt from dynamic changes."

And, no doubt, we shall find when this war is over that the greatest obstacle to the establishment of a just and durable peace will be this idea that a number of states, called Great Powers, should have the undisputed right to demand that other states should comply with certain principles of government; but no other states and no organization of states should have any right to demand similar things from the Great Powers.

No stable world-organization could exist that would not, formally and constitutionally, give to great countries the greater share in world decisions, in world administration, in world responsibility. But, on the other hand, no world organization could exist for any length of time on the idea that there are two sets of principles of government, one to be made applicable to Great Powers and the other to smaller states, two conceptions of right, two conceptions of justice.

The progress of national democracy has been marked

* See George A. Finch in the *American Journal of International Law*, 1941, p. 662 ff.

by a constant fight of vested privileges. And the progress of international democracy which has modestly begun will be marked by a similar fight against state privileges, still harder to combat because they are not even based on acquired rights but merely on acquired pride and acquired prejudice—prejudice of nationality, prejudice of race.

And, maybe, it will be found on the day of peace-making that the hardest thing for individuals and for nations to give up is prejudice. We can give up gasoline and tires; we can reduce our consumption of sugar and practically anything else, but not to be allowed to use more prejudice than allotted to us on an international ration-card will be incredibly hard. But we have to get accustomed to the idea if we want to establish an International Bill of Rights.

The minority clauses of the Versailles Treaties proved good. But they ceased to be a political reality when they were used as a ladder in an attempt to scale the wall of Great Power prerogatives.

During twenty years the minority section of the League of Nations accumulated a vast experience in dealing with these delicate and combustible matters; we have ample proof that the League machinery set up for dealing with minority problems was sufficient to solve a great number of difficulties as long as the prestige of the League gave authority to the decisions taken. And as long as the minority clauses were honestly applied they gave a limited protection to individual human rights.

But ample proof was also given of the danger of granting too wide privileges to minorities without defining clearly and strictly what shall constitute a minority in any state. And it is hard to deny that without clear definitions and the necessary correctives at hand an uncritical application of Articles 3 and 4 of the New York Declaration may lead to endangering peace and creating artificial dissatisfaction.

The Assembly of the League of Nations in 1922 laid
down some general principles on the subject of minorities.
In the first of a series of resolutions the Assembly recognized that unnecessary appeal to an outside authority by
a minority for the redress of its grievances, real or imaginary, would only intensify the ill-will existing between it
and the state to which it belonged. It therefore expressed
the judgment that, while the Council should have full
power in cases of grave infraction of the treaty agreements,
good relations could best be promoted by "benevolent
and informal communications" between the minority and
the government concerned.

Another resolution recognized the injustices that might
result were minorities to agitate without adequate cause
against the treaty-bound states. The Assembly declared
that while it was the "primary right of the minorities to be
protected from oppression," it was also their duty to "co-
operate as loyal fellow citizens with the nations to which
they belong." And only if it is borne in mind that even
minorities are citizens, and have duties and are under
certain moral obligations to the majority and to the state
in which they live, can the right kind of fellowship be obtained.

It is of interest in this connection to mention that as
long as Germany remained a member of the League the
German Government always claimed to be especially interested in the protection of minorities; and although minority questions appertained to the League Council and not
to the Assembly, every year the German Delegation requested the reference of the Council's report on minority
problems to the Sixth Committee of the Assembly. Today
all the world can appreciate what kind of interest Germany takes in minorities; and in retrospect it is clear for
what purpose Germany wanted to pose as a protector of
minorities. But it is worth remembering that, in spite of
this attitude, until Nazism took power in 1933, there were

no complaints from the minorities of the German language in Czechoslovakia. The difficulties that led up to Munich all originated and were planned in Germany after 1933.

And the whole problem of minorities was made more complicated by the attitude of Poland after the withdrawal of Germany from the League. At the Assembly of 1934, in plain violation of its international obligations, Poland declared that, pending the introduction of a general and uniform system for the protection of minorities, the Polish Government would be compelled to refuse all coöperation with the international organizations in the matter of the supervision of the application by Poland of the system of minority protection.

But the Great Powers, Britain, France and Italy, while more than willing to recognize the International Rights of Man in other countries, were entirely unwilling to establish any order which would make possible any international interference within their own territories. And, of course, the great colonial powers realized that nations, races, continents, do not live on the same level of civilization, hardly in the same epoch of evolution, and that the same principles cannot be applied everywhere, or given the same kind of application, without unfortunate results.

So, in the very interests of peace, while it is necessary to establish an international authority with power to supervise the application of principles of liberty, it is equally important to institute the restraining and controlling rules without which small groups, by abusing the privileges of democracy, might make liberty intolerable and the orderly conduct of state affairs next to impossible.

Under the present system applied by the League of Nations, petitions from minorities are gone into by the minority-section of the Secretariat, and if it proves impossible for the Secretary General to find a solution to the difference between the government of the state in question and the petitioning minority, petitions are referred to the Council. And the Council has no real means of compulsion. What is needed is, to use once more the excellent words of Elihu Root, "the substitution of judicial action for diplomatic action, the substitution of judicial sense of responsibility for diplomatic sense of responsibility," meaning that if no solution can be arrived at by using the ordinary League machinery of conversations, the difference must be referred to an International Court of Justice.

As the duties of this Court will be widely different from the duties of the existing Permanent Court of International Justice, which can deal only with litigations between states, so the whole setup of the Court must be different, and the Court must be safeguarded against having to decide in matters trivial or brought before the Court only to sow dissension or mischief. A procedure might be envisaged under which some kind of organ of the new world organization might strain out the insignificant cases, or whereby the Permanent Court of International Justice might decide whether a case should be considered by this new international tribunal or simply dismissed.

The result of the work of the committee of jurists who drafted the convention against crimes of terrorism was excellent. Although the purpose of the new tribunal would be something different and less technical than that of an international criminal court, it might be wise to have a committee of expert lawyers to draft the rules of procedure to be followed.

The Court, more or less established for the protection of the international rights of man, should also have to decide in such cases as referred to in the last annual report of the Permanent Court of International Justice (see p. 295). But here also it will be necessary to establish certain guarantees against abuse. It might be considered to extend the jurisdiction of the Permanent Court of Arbitration and empower it to decide, or at least to recommend, decisions in matters at issue between states and individuals.

It might be advisable to lay down that the condition for being allowed to bring a matter of confiscation or dispossession before any new international court of justice should be that the financial interests involved had to exceed a certain minimum, or that the questions of principle involved were of a particular interest. Various modalities could be imagined, and even in this question it might be wise to obtain an opinion from the Permanent Court of International Justice.

The question will naturally arise: Should there be any appeal from such an international court of justice?

The authors of the convention for the establishment of an International Criminal Court decided that, in their case, there should be no right of appeal.

"Against convictions pronounced by the Court, no proceedings other than an application for revision shall be allowable." (Article 43, 1.)

And if an International Tribunal is set up, under all the guarantees provided for in the Statute of the Permanent Court of International Justice, or in the Convention for the Creation of an International Criminal Court, that Tribunal should represent the highest international authority in such a way that the question of any higher instance could never arise.

But another problem of an entirely different character would certainly have to be met: The problem of execution of any judgment passed against a state, or an individual.

Naturally, the question of an international police force will pose itself.

The authors of the Convention for the Creation of an International Criminal Court have met the problem in a different way. And it is of a considerable interest for any discussion of the establishment of a world order that will ensure peace to study this Convention and its various provisions.

XXII: The International Criminal Court

In the previous chapters reference has been made to the Convention for the Creation of an International Criminal Court.

The murder of King Alexander of Yugoslavia and M. Barthou, the French Minister of Foreign Affairs, at Marseilles, on October 9, 1934, precipitated into action the jurisconsults who had been vaguely discussing the possibility of establishing such a court.

The Council of the League of Nations on December 10th of the same year adopted a resolution, stating that, in the opinion of the Council, "the rules of international law concerning the repression of terrorist activity are not at present sufficiently precise to guarantee efficiently international coöperation in this matter," and it decided to set up a Committee of experts to "study this question with a view to drawing up a preliminary draft of an international convention to assure the repression of conspiracies or crimes committed with a political and terrorist purpose."

The repercussions of the murder and the reactions to it among Central European nations proved what a very real danger to peace such an act of political terrorism constituted. And after exhaustive studies and long preliminaries, delegates of thirty-one states meeting at Geneva in 1937 adopted a convention for the prevention and punishment of acts of terrorism and a convention for an international criminal court.*

The terms of the first-named convention placed the following crimes under the jurisdiction of the Permanent International Criminal Court:

(1) Any wilful act causing death or grievous bodily harm to:

    (a) Heads of States, persons exercising the prerogatives of the Head of the State, their hereditary or designated successors;

    (b) The wives or husbands of the above-mentioned persons;

    (c) Persons charged with public functions or holding public positions when the act is directed against them in their public capacity.

(2) Wilful destruction of, or damage to, public property or property devoted to a public purpose belonging to or subject to the authority of another High Contracting Party.

(3) Any wilful act calculated to endanger the lives of members of the public.

(4) Any attempt to commit an offence falling within the foregoing provisions of the present article.

(5) The manufacture, obtaining, possession, or supplying of arms, ammunition, explosives or harmful substances with a view to the commission in any country whatsoever of an offence falling within the present article.

Next, each High Contracting Party agreed to make the following acts criminal offences when they were committed on his own territory with a view to an act of terrorism falling within the article just quoted, and directed against another High Contracting Party, whatever the country in which the act of terrorism was to be carried out:

(1) Conspiracy to commit any such act; (2) Any incitement to any such act, if successful; (3) Direct public incitement to any act mentioned under heads 1, 2 or 3 of foregoing article,

* By acts of terrorism, the Convention means "criminal acts directed against a State and intended or calculated to create a state of terror in the minds of particular persons or a group of persons or the general public."

whether the incitement be successful or not; (4) Wilful participation in any such act; (5) Assistance, knowingly given, toward the commission of any such act.

The mere enumeration is sufficient to show how wide a competence the International Criminal Court might have had, and how far-reaching an importance in international relations its very creation would have carried. But although the Convention was signed by the representatives of all the participating states on November 16, 1937, it was never ratified by the various governments. Acts of terrorism were spreading on a scale hitherto unknown in history, as the openly professed policy of certain Great Powers, and the ordinary political machinery was left far behind. Still the constitution of the permanent International Criminal Court, as proposed, is of particular interest and gives us an indication of the path we ought to follow in the future. At the same time the Convention embodies some of the experience acquired through the practice of the Permanent Court of International Justice, marking a step in the direction suggested by Mr. Elihu Root in 1917.

The judges shall be chosen among jurists who are "acknowledged authorities on criminal law and who are or have been members of courts of criminal jurisdiction, or possess the qualifications required for such appointments in their own country." A comparison with Article 2 of the Statute of the Permanent Court of International Justice (see p. 283) will show the far stronger stress laid upon legal experience and judicial training.

And the conception of national sovereignty has been happily removed from the Convention in spite of the fact that national passions and questions of sovereignty may be particularly strongly appealed to under the application of its provisions. Article 22 simply states:

"If the Court has to apply, in accordance with Article 21, the law of a State of which no sitting judge is a national, the court may invite a jurist who is an acknowledged authority on such law to sit with it in a consultative capacity as a legal assessor."

When this article is compared to the corresponding rules in force at the Permanent Court of International Justice (see p. 282), the development away from the old-time idea of absolute national sovereignty is very striking. No judges *ad hoc* can be called in to sit on the International Criminal Court and act as half diplomatic agents of their governments. But the Court itself can invite an expert of the criminal law to be applied in the particular case to assist as an assessor.

There are other interesting points of difference. In the case of the International Criminal Court the nominating power is in the hands of the responsible governments; each of them can nominate not more than two candidates. And the Permanent Court of Justice shall be requested to choose five judges and five deputy judges from the persons so nominated. The Court itself will determine its rules of election.

The judges of the Permanent Court of International Justice are elected for nine years and the terms of all fifteen expire at the same time. The judges of the Criminal Court should hold office for ten years and every two years one regular and one deputy judge should retire. As will be seen, the modifications correspond to the suggestions made by the American writer quoted before (see p. 289). In every respect the innovations have been improvements.

The Convention for the Creation of an International Criminal Court has a proviso concerning execution of judgments which will be dealt with below and which is of a very particular interest. Doubly so, when compared to the Statute of the Permanent Court of International Justice, where nothing is said about the execution of its judgments.

The jurisdiction of the Permanent Court is defined in Article 36, and the signatories to the Protocol have recognized as compulsory *ipso facto* this jurisdiction in all or any of the classes of legal disputes concerning:

(a) The interpretation of a treaty,
(b) Any question of international law,
(c) The existence of any fact which, if established, would constitute a breach of an international obligation,
(d) The nature or extent of the reparation to be made for the breach of an international obligation.

So far no state has disputed the judgments passed by the Court, and the problem of execution has never been brought to an issue. But, of course, execution where individuals are concerned is materially different from execution where only states are involved, and offers us entirely new problems.

Even if the judgments of the Permanent Court of International Justice have not, so far, been contested, it does not mean that the problem of execution may not rise at any moment. Especially if the Court—or Courts—be given a wider competence and a greater power, the question of execution may become acute; and it will be necessary to have provided for this exigency beforehand.

When in 1848, revolution threatened old-time Prussia, General Wrangel marched some of his troops down to the revolutionary diet, sat down on the steps, lighted his pipe and sent into the building a corporal and two privates with orders to the revolutionaries to clear out within five minutes. A deputation was sent out to the general and their spokesman declared: "We are here empowered by the revolutionary will of the People; we can only be dispersed by violent brutal force."

"*Ist schon da*" (Is already here), grinned the general. The revolutionaries dispersed and the revolution was over.

The art of government, national and international, consists to a very large extent of being able to declare in any emergency *"Ist schon da!"* If the armed forces are on the spot at the right moment there will be no revolution and no fight. But if the force is not there, and nobody knows whether there will be any force, things will happen.

What possibility would there be of law enforcement in a country where the laws did not mention punishment, but where, when a murder had been committed, the parliament would have to meet to discuss what punishment, if any, should be applicable to murder, and where a good many members might be inclined to reason: "Let us have no hard and fast rules. It is always dangerous to establish a precedent. Some day I might be tempted to commit a murder."

But in the international world that is what actually takes place, as demonstrated in the Assembly of the League of Nations more than once.

Any form of sanction, to be effective as an instrument to prevent international disorder, should be clearly defined in advance and not left to public discussion after the fact.

The establishment of an international army or an international police force has sometimes been warmly advocated. But for the question of execution of judgments of the Permanent Court of International Justice it should not be necessary and certainly not desirable to resort to military coercion. If in any individual state the execution of judgments can be effected only by the officers of justice having recourse to the forces of army and navy, it may be taken as a convincing evidence that all is not well in that state; and the body politic in ill health. In the same way in the international world: If judgments can be executed only by the way of military coercion, this would not be the mark of strength, but the mark of moral impotence and political inflammation. On the other hand, if every single state adhering to the system of Permanent Courts of Justice had bound itself by the Protocol to uphold the authority of the Court without any reservation, and the complete boycott of the recalcitrant state would be a fore-known fact, and it was clearly understood beforehand that any attempt of armed resistance by the offender would be met by a complete and indisputable system of sanctions, there would be no attempt to obstruct the execution of any judgment.

In the same way: If new courts of international justice should be established with competence to pronounce judg-ment in litigations between states and individuals or, under certain conditions, between individuals of different nationalities, all the states adhering to the network of in-ternational law would have to bind themselves to put at the disposal of the International Court for the execution of its judgments their entire system of law enforcement.

Such a solution of the problem would be far simpler and cheaper than the creation of any new instrument for the enaction of judgments; it would probably be far more efficient; and it would certainly prevent the multiple pos-sibilities of friction which always will occur wherever a new federal police authority is superimposed on an exist-ing local force, and which will naturally tend to be even more bitter when an international authority should be superimposed on the national law-enforcement body. This solution has already in principle been accepted by a great number of states.

In the Convention for the Creation of the International Criminal Court all rules for the execution of judgments have been carefully elaborated and clearly show that those experienced jurists who prepared the convention found such a system as has been roughly sketched above, practical and not in any way utopian.

Having stated that the Court shall decide whether any object is to be confiscated or be restored to its owner, and that the Court may sentence the persons committed to it, to pay damages, Article 39 of the Convention goes on:

"(3) The High Contracting Parties in whose territory objects to be restored or property belonging to convicted persons is situated shall be bound to take all measures provided by their own laws to ensure the execution of the sentences of the court.

"(4) The provisions of the preceding paragraph shall also apply to cases in which pecuniary penalties imposed by the court or costs of proceedings have to be recovered."

Then follow Articles 40 and 41:

"(1) Sentences involving loss of liberty shall be executed by a High Contracting Party chosen with his consent by the Court. Such consent may not be refused by the State which committed the convicted person to the court for trial. The sentences shall always be executed by the State which committed the convicted person to the Court if this State expresses the wish to do so.

"(2) The Court shall determine the way in which any fines shall be dealt with.

and:

"If sentence of death has been pronounced, the State designated by the Court to execute the sentence shall be entitled to substitute therefor the most severe penalty provided by its national law which involves loss of liberty."

The whole principle of execution is perfectly clear and well defined to serve as a model for the establishment of such other Courts of International Justice as have here been discussed.

It will be remarked how the whole system envisaged is built up in such a way as to maneuver safely round the dangerous promontories of national sovereignty. No new code of penal law is inflicted upon any nation; all the contracting parties retain their right to use their own penal code. In this way the most complicated question in this whole domain does not arise: the question of international legislation as opposed to or imposed upon national legislation.

In any known federation the question of lawmaking has been the great stumbling block. In every single state forming part of a federation there has been a strong opposition to the idea that federal laws should overrule the individual state laws adopted by the local popular government. The wider and broader the federation, the more pronounced this jealousy will be.

The convention so carefully prepared by a number of jurists of national and international experience demonstrates that the difficulties here mentioned sometimes are more of a spooky nature than of a concrete substance.

It will be asked: But will states observe their international obligations? They have not done so heretofore.

The answer is that if we do not believe in the possibility of states' honoring their contractual obligations, we had better stop every attempt to create any kind of order in this world. In spite of all, the vast majority of international conventions, treaties and agreements are scrupulously kept. The exceptions are cruel, outstanding, devastating and revolting. Our task and our duty is to make their recurrence impossible.

And one of the obvious things to do will be to establish the International Bill of Rights and adopt an International Penal Code which would neither be opposed to nor imposed upon national legislation, but simply make internationally binding certain articles which are already on the statute books of civilized states.

The kind of criminal court needed is not exactly the kind envisaged in the Geneva Convention, but the careful work of study and preparation should be utilized and supplemented.

For the enforcement of an international penal code it will be necessary not only to give governments the right to prosecute, but also to institute a supervisory body to which individual and official violations of the international bill of rights can be reported and that should have the right to investigate and to indict.

Closely related and affiliated to this task of supervision would be the task of supervising systems of education (compare p. 109). No protection of human rights would be possible if schools were allowed to teach that the very conception of human rights is a dangerous fallacy.

The machinery set up to prevent illicit traffic in drugs is of interest in this connection. The international trade is strictly supervised, nationally and internationally, through the Permanent Central Opium Board, and special police coöperation for the prevention of illicit traffic has been organized and an international clearing-house created for this purpose—the Opium Advisory Committee and its secretariat. And under the 1936 convention central police offices have been created for the supervision and coördination of all operations necessary to prevent and punish illicit traffic and other contraventions of drug laws.

These things are mentioned, not because they constitute a direct parallel, but because it is important to realize that we are not entirely on new ground when we discuss law-enforcement on the international plane.

XXIII: Distinguished Crooks

The enumeration given in the previous chapter of crimes which ought to lead to indictments before an International Criminal Court does not give a full picture of international criminality of recent years. The preaching and the practices of totalitarian states have made necessary the creation of a new criminal code among nations to protect them against dangers and menaces which hardly existed fifteen years ago. Three categories of crime particularly and three groups of potential criminals will have to be included.

Under the first category should come such crimes as were dealt with in Articles 228-230 of the Versailles Treaty, only those articles were completely unilateral, and it might be wiser, for the future, to make the application of the penal laws general and not only a privilege for the victors.

The Articles in question run as follows:

Article 228

"The German Government recognizes the right of the Allied and Associated Powers to bring before military tribunals persons accused of having committed acts in violation of the laws and customs of war. Such persons shall, if found guilty, be sentenced to punishments laid down by law. This provision will apply notwithstanding any proceedings or prosecution before a tribunal in Germany or in the territory of her allies.

"The German Government shall hand over to the Allied and Associated Powers, or to such one of them as shall so request, all persons accused of having committed an act in violation of the laws and customs of war, who are specified either by name or by the rank, office or employment which they held under the German authorities.

Article 229

"Persons guilty of criminal acts against the nationals of one of the Allied and Associated Powers will be brought before the military tribunals of that Power.

"Persons guilty of criminal acts against the nationals of more than one of the Allied and Associated Powers will be brought before military tribunals composed of members of the military tribunals of the Powers concerned.

"In every case the accused will be entitled to name his own counsel.

Article 230

"The German Government undertakes to furnish all documents and information of every kind, the production of which may be considered necessary to ensure the full knowledge of the incriminating acts, the discovery of offenders and the just appreciation of responsibility."

It will be necessary this time to give to the corresponding articles a somewhat different formulation. The majority of crimes committed by invading nations since September, 1939, have not been committed in actual warfare, but have been perpetrated in cold blood, when the fighting was over.

In some countries the principal criminals have been German civil servants, Gestapo functionaries, the governors, reichs-commissioners and administrators sent into the occupied countries to strike them with terror. In other countries, in Russia, in Jugoslavia, in occupied France, the military commanders seem to be the principal criminals. Maybe even worse have been the thousands of petty tyrants, sadistic henchmen, brutal believers in bullying force, who followed them and who have been sucking life and blood out of the conquered nations and torturing them in a way unparalleled in human history.

Careful investigation will be necessary in every case.

The International Penal Code discussed below cannot be made applicable. The United Nations cannot start by making an international law retroactive. But neither can they be prevented by impotent formalism from administering to the demands of justice.

Most writers on international law have agreed that soldiers in uniform and under command cannot be held individually responsible when they are obeying orders. But most writers on international law have been philosophizing without knowing totalitarian warfare, which in itself is a denunciation of all international law; and, at best, they are commentators, not legislators. Soldiers in uniform committing ordinary crimes, or the most extraordinary crimes, cannot be acquitted merely because they are obeying orders. To accept such a theory would be to make a farce of the sufferings of millions. The slaying of hostages is a crime; to wipe out any Lidice is a crime. How far the plea of an individual that he was acting under orders can be taken as an extenuating circumstance must be left to the judges to decide.

Under what criminal law the guilty should be punished will have to be decided by the victorious powers, whether under the law of the home country of the soldiers and policemen, Germans, Hungarians, Italians, Roumanians—or under the laws of the country where the crime was committed—Belgium, Czechoslovakia, Norway, Poland and so on. Whole populations have been wiped out because they obeyed the orders of their legal governments. It is unthinkable that those who killed them should go unpunished for any purely technical reason. If in due time, when the Allied Powers will be occupying more and more German, Italian and Roumanian land, similar crimes should be committed by any of their officers or administrators, those found guilty will receive their punishment.

Articles 228 and 229 of the Versailles Treaty were hardly applied at all. The articles in question in the preliminary peace treaty to come must be formulated in such a way and with such legal assistance that they can be made really and immediately applicable. There is no hope of improving political morals and public mind in the post-war world if hundreds of the most sinister international criminals should be allowed to continue their careers without being brought to justice, and the outraged instincts of justice and righteousness among the oppressed millions would be dangerously inflamed. The problem of reconciliation after the war is often discussed on the understanding that it will be of great importance to reconcile the Germans after an Allied victory. It is a peculiar misunderstanding. The main object of reconciliation will be to administer peace in such a way that the tortured nations can be reconciled. It is not the criminal who needs tenderness but his victims.

That is why the governments of Belgium, of Czechoslovakia, of Luxembourg, of the Netherlands, of Norway, of Poland, of Yugoslavia, of Greece, and the Free French National Committee on January 13, 1942, signed the following declaration:

"Whereas, Germany since the beginning of the present conflict, which arose out of her policy of aggression, has instituted in occupied countries a regime of terror characterized in particular by imprisonments, mass expulsions, execution of hostages and massacres,

"And whereas, these acts of violence being similarly perpetrated by allies and associates of the Reich and in certain countries by accomplices of the occupying power,

"And whereas, international solidarity is necessary in order to avoid repression of these acts of violence simply by acts of vengeance on the part of the general public and in order to satisfy the sense of justice of the civilized world,

"Recalling that international law and, in particular, the convention signed at The Hague in 1907 regarding laws and customs of land warfare do not permit belligerents in occupied countries to perpetrate acts of violence against civilians, to bring into disrepute laws in force or to overthrow national institutions:

"(1) [The countries mentioned] affirm that acts of violence thus perpetrated against civilian populations are at variance with accepted ideas concerning acts of war and political offenses as these are understood by civilized nations;

"(2) Take note of the declaration made in this respect on Oct. 25, 1941, by the President of the United States of America and the British Prime Minister;

"(3) Place among their principal war aims punishment through the channel of organized justice of those guilty and responsible for these crimes, whether they have ordered them, perpetrated them or in any way participated in them;

"(4) Determine in the spirit of international solidarity to see to it that (a) those guilty and responsible, whatever their nationality, are sought for, handed over to justice and judged; (b) that sentences pronounced are carried out."

Russian leaders have previously given out statements to the same effect; and even if so far no similar statement has been made by the United States, the United Kingdom and the Dominions, it can hardly be imagined that these countries whose peoples have not suffered in the same way and whose real war sacrifices are so much smaller should not also and wholeheartedly include among the war aims that "those guilty and responsible, whatever their nationality, are sought for, handed over to justice and judged."

But the courts to deal with these criminals of war and aggression will belong to the period of transition. They will not be permanent courts, but accomplish their work of moral and humanitarian sanitation in the years between the provisional peace, or armistice, and the meeting of the congress to draft the final peace.

Under the next category should come crimes against the laws and constitution, or against the security and legitimate interests of a country, committed by diplomatic and consular representatives of another country, whether they reside in the country or not.*

Political developments, during the last few years, have made clear that no nation with a regard for its own security and peace can accept any longer the idea of the absolute immunity of diplomats and consuls. Their persons, their baggage, diplomatic pouches and so on were considered sacrosanct under the supposition that they were living up to their privileges, that they were of a class representing the majesty of sovereign states, vested with an august dignity that could never be disturbed and against the conceptions of which they could never act.

It is no longer possible to keep up the legend of the dignified diplomat, whose privileged position was felt by himself and by his country as an honorary obligation. The very idea has been exploded by political practice in the twentieth century. German philosophers, with their proclamation of atavistic tribal instincts as the highest law in national and international life, carefully prepared that grand-scale relapse to barbarism which has been consummated under unscrupulous dictators. But here again it is necessary to bear in mind that Nazism has not created anything new. Hand in hand with the old-time diplomat worked the intelligence officer and the spy. Only, officially, in civilized countries the former knew nothing of the latter.

Colonel Repington in his "Vestigia" relates the following incident from the days (in 1895) when he was head of the British Intelligence work in Paris:

---

* Quite often operations by one state against another are directed not by the embassy in the victimized country, but by the embassy in a neighboring country. Thus German espionage in Norway, to a large extent, was directed from the German legation in Stockholm; as, no doubt, a good deal both of German and Japanese intrigue, espionage and sabotage in U. S. A. have been directed from the German and Japanese embassy in Mexico or from German or Japanese legations and consulates in various Central American states. In this way investigation is made more difficult and complicated.

"One of my agents belonged to a Latin race. He turned up at my headquarters one day and after making his report, began to hum and haw and finally said that he had a proposal to make to me. I told him to fire ahead. He then said that he belonged to a secret society whose speciality was to get rid of inconvenient people, and that if I had any political or personal enemies, his society would guarantee to dispose of them at the rate of fifty louis a head. It was rather sudden, as the girl says in the play, and I replied that the proposal was most enticing, but that so many names came into my mind that I felt that I was in danger of being recklessly extravagant. Would he give me time to think it over and make the selection? He kindly consented, and I took the earliest opportunity of ridding myself of this enterprising but bloodthirsty individual. In our time we have replaced the good old system of private assassination by that of the Press."

Now, take as a correlate to Colonel Repington's story the so-called Rautenfels episode from the last war. One day in the early months of 1918 the police in Oslo, Norway, reported to the government that they had found on the top floor of a certain house in the East-end of the city, a number of big and tremendously heavy chests, sealed with the official seals of the German Empire. The police felt sure that the chests contained bombs and time-machines to be used for the sinking of Norwegian vessels going to England. So many of them had disappeared in a mysterious way. The chests were taken to the Foreign Office and the German chargé d'affaires was sent for—the minister was absent. The chargé d'affaires, Prince Zu Wied, declared that the chests were so heavy because they were packed with German propaganda literature, and stated that it would be a violation of international law and most dangerous for Norway to break the official seal of the German Empire. Nevertheless the seal was broken and most of the chests found to contain bombs and time-machines intended for Norwegian ships. Some of them contained chewing tobacco seasoned with carborundum so that one clot of spittle in the engine of a ship or the machinery of some factory might be sufficient to destroy its vital parts. Other chests contained still more ingenious devices, and one loaves of sugar infested with anthrax bacilli, kind gifts to be presented to the horses carrying on the traffic from the North of Norway across the border to the nearest Russian (Finnish) railway station. A few lumps of sugar would have been sufficient to start an epidemic among the horses. Rautenfels was the courier of the German Legation, what in England would have been termed a King's Messenger. Prinz zu Wied today is German minister to Sweden.

Take another typical instance: In World War I Franz von Papen was military attaché to the German Embassy in Washington. He was found to be an active organizer of espionage and sabotage in the United States; and for his conduct "unbecoming of an officer and a gentleman" he was expelled. Was that in any way counted against him? On the contrary. He was constantly promoted; he was made Chancellor of the Reich, and when in 1932 he negotiated in Lausanne with the representatives of Great Britain and France for the cancellation of the German reparations, it never did occur to the Governments of those countries that all was not well with the world, when they agreed to negotiate with a man whose conceptions of honor were widely different from their own—to use a polite expression. Among international diplomats he was not discredited at all. Nobody protested when Germany appointed him to look after the German interests in the Saar in the years before the plebiscite. And when he was made German Ambassador to Ankara there were no difficulties with his *agrément,* although no self-respecting government could like the idea of having as the representative of the most aggressive Great Power a man officially branded as an unscrupulous conspirator.

In the same way Sweden accepted without a demur as official representative of Germany a man who but for his diplomatic immunity would have been serving time in a penitentiary.

Sometimes one cannot help feeling that in the uppermost strata of polite international society it is not considered quite *comme il faut*, not quite the thing to remember disagreeable facts. Still, some few individuals have not been quite able to forget two ominous words from the last great war: *spurlos versenkt*—sunk without a trace. Count v. Luxdorff, the then German ambassador to Buenos Aires, the predecessor of Freiherr von Thermann, on the occasion of three Argentine freighters leaving Buenos Aires with a cargo of foodstuffs destined for France, cabled his government that it would be advisable that those freighters should be *spurlos versenkt*, sent to the bottom without a trace left and with no survivors who might tell a tale. Two of his messages with this identical recommendation were intercepted and decoded in Washington, and led to the expulsion from U. S. A. of the German naval attaché, Captain Boy-Ed. But no man can tell the number of merchant ships that have disappeared as a result of such diplomatic advice in the last war and in this war.

Germany was not the only country whose diplomats were ready to act as Colonel Repington did not want his agents to act.

During the last World War the famous Irish patriot and notorious British traitor (he was both), Sir Roger Casement, came to Oslo accompanied by his valet, Adler Christensen, who was born in Norway. The valet was approached by the British minister to Oslo, Sir Mansfeldt de Cardonnel Findlay. They discussed in the legation how and for what price to do away with Casement; Sir Mansfeldt then wrote Mr. Christensen a letter on the stationery of the legation and offered him £5,000 and impunity for bringing Sir Roger Casement alive or dead to the grounds of the British legation; he was also given a key to the gate of one of the entrances to the legation garden.

Mr. Christensen, maybe in full understanding with Sir Roger, or just being the kind of man he was, sold the original letter to Germany, price unknown, and it was facsimiled in the leading newspapers in Berlin. Sir Mansfeldt Findlay did not make any useless attempts of denying the authenticity of the letter, but claimed that he had acted for the best of his country.

It may be said that all these things related happened in the midst of a cruel war and that in a war ordinary peacetime conceptions of what can and what cannot be done have to be temporarily forgotten. But none of these things happened on the battlefront or in self-defense. They happened in neutral countries, and if we should accept the theory that the end justifies the means we should be in the midst of that Nazism, that mental disturbance which we are fighting.

Maybe it should be added that when Sir Mansfeldt was mentioned for diplomatic promotion after the war it was given to understand from the country in question that there might be difficulties with *agrément*. So it was said. Oslo was his last post.

In the diplomatic career, as in various other careers, what was fatal was not to commit certain acts, but to be found out.

It might be added that the consuls of certain countries try to follow in the steps of their diplomats. Commissioner Anslinger in his report to Secretary Morgenthau states: "Japanese consulates have acted as centers for the distribution of drugs."

The incidents here quoted are indicative of a species of diplomatic accomplishment that has been perfected by the gestapos of totalitarian states until every single consulate, legation and embassy was a school of intrigue, of espionage, of crime. It has been found out, too late, in the invaded countries; and it appears that even in the minds of the men used as diplomatic agents by totalitarian states not only every distinction between right and wrong has disappeared, but also, what probably seems of more fundamental importance to the traditional career diplomat, the distinction between the things that can be done and such things as cannot be done. In other words, it does not matter very much any longer whether you are found out or not. When conventions are dropped, it indicates that the code of ethics which they embodied is no longer in force—and no longer to be feared.

The German air attaché of the legation in Norway, like other accredited German diplomatic and consular servants, was actively participating in the treacherous attack on Norway. Still driving his privileged car with the diplomatic license plate * he was heading a motorized German force, trying to capture the King and Government. The complete moral (and diplomatic) confusion of his mind was demonstrated in his exclamation when he was hit by a Norwegian bullet: "Why, this is murder."

That any German diplomat may be expected to act in a similar way is gradually being found out in all the Latin American countries.

It is glaringly evident that under any kind of peaceful and civilized world order such things cannot continue. There is also this difference between the procedure in the days of Colonel Repington and the practices of modern totalitarian states, that Colonel Repington took the earliest opportunity of ridding himself of the bloodthirsty individual. A totalitarian colonel of today would have clasped him to his bosom and promoted him rapidly. Formerly the agent, the intelligence servant, the spy were looked upon as belonging to the night side of life. Any diplomat would officially wash his hands of them; he would disown

---

* In Geneva where they have some experience of diplomatic privileges the magical letters C. D. (Corps Diplomatic) or D. C. (Diplomatic Corps) are popularly interpreted as "Dangerous Chauffeur." But in the Near East where the experience is still more sinister, they are translated as "Distinguished Crook." (In French: "Canaille Distingué.")

them; if suddenly their actions came to light he would demand that they should be recalled or disappear. Today the diplomats are subordinated to the bloodthirsty agents; if anything goes wrong with the criminal action planned and initiated, the agent, the intelligence servant, the spy will demand that the diplomat shall be recalled, or be liquidated; if von Neurath, who once was a gentleman, will not be an accomplice to the assassinations and large-scale crimes planned in Czechoslovakia, von Neurath will have to disappear—the man of crime will officially replace the man of culture.

In states which are not under full German occupation or protection, the substitution of the Gestapo agent for the diplomatic dummy will not be an open performance, and an official façade will still be kept up; men of manners and of means will be used to screen the activities of the international gangsters and to charm the ladies and lions of the smart sets; but these social stools and diplomatic decoys will no longer be under any illusion as to the character of their activity.

To protect states, but also to protect the legitimate diplomatic agents, it is necessary to establish rules for the international game which cannot be broken with impunity.

The present system under which the petty officers of international crime are sent to jail, and the tools and instruments are punished, whereas the instigators and organizers of espionage, of sabotage, of kidnapping and liquidation remain unassailed and privileged, is revolting to any keen sense of justice and contrary to the principles of any penal law. That the murderer should be protected as soon as he gets into the sacred grounds of an embassy; that material evidence should be beyond the arm of the law, if it is smuggled into the sanctum of any consulate, that secret societies, engaged in subversive activities, working for the overthrow of the government of the country where they have found an asylum and a home, planning offenses and crimes against the laws of their land of adoption, should be allowed to keep their records, their rolls of membership, their booty outside the jurisdiction of the state of which they are citizens when they place them in the office of some emissary of evil, who has a diplomatic or consular status, should no longer be acceptable to any government.

On the other hand it would not be in conformity with principles for international relations, and it would not be safe for the idea of coöperative peace, if the ordinary courts of law of the country in question should be drawn into any such conflict. An international court of justice must have authority and take action, when any state files a complaint of this character.

Of course, democratic states never openly expected their diplomats or consuls to be thieves or gangsters, although at certain moments they may have expected them to have little hesitation in acquiring documents that had been stolen. But most states have accepted as a principle of action in foreign relations the old slogan: "Right or wrong, my country." Few indeed are the statesmen who have dared to declare in any important conflict that the laws of right and wrong are absolute and cannot be adapted to the pattern of any particular national policy. And the statesman who stands forth and declares that his country is in the wrong has rarely been popular and has often been called a traitor. If the system of international courts of justice were extended and an impartial, objective, supreme international authority established, the whole outlook would be different.

Even more important to the rule of international law than the prosecution of such crimes as here mentioned will be the right and duty to prosecute any violation of that international bill of rights which should embody the Atlantic Charter and the Washington Declaration.

If any principle is solemnly proclaimed by the government of any country, the application of the principle will be enforced through the law system of the state. If an international convention establishes or forbids any principle of action, the necessary legal provisions must be included in the statute book to make the convention more than a dead letter. Similarly the international bill of rights must be given legal power in all countries by way of national legislation. Or, it may be found convenient, and even necessary, to establish an international penal code, accepted by all states as part of the complex of peace treaties. And in this penal code will be dealt with any violation of the principle of religious freedom and human rights "in their own and in other countries."

It seems probable that an international body of supervision must be instituted to make the international penal code a reality. And, owing to the particular character of this international legislation and the fact that violations of it are likely to be committed primarily by, or with the connivance of, governments or governmental agencies, there must be established an international as well as a national right of indictment and prosecution of the crimes in question before an international criminal court.

The question of how to constitute such a court of law as here envisaged may be safely left to expert jurists, who will draft the necessary convention, asking, maybe, also to hear the opinion of the Permanent Court of International Justice and building largely on the work already done by the committee which drafted the Convention for the Creation of an International Criminal Court. There may be some difference of opinion on various technical points, but there will hardly today be any violent or very serious opposition to the idea of instituting such a court. It will be pretty generally admitted that for the establishment of law instead of violence, for the substitution of right for might, it is of vital importance to build up such a court of justice, empowered to decide in all matters of violation of the international bill of rights, or of abuse of international privileges, empowered even to indict members of national cabinets if they directly or indirectly instigate international violence or invite disregard of the international penal code.

The supervisory body mentioned must also be empowered to call attention to such provocations as might lead to international disturbance and suggest the means to prevent their continuance.

The problems here mentioned may be less spectacular than some of the more exciting political questions, and may be considered side-issues; but they certainly are of a very considerable importance and can be solved without great difficulties in such a way that the cause of dynamic peace would be strengthened thereby. But there is still another field of international activity where a court of justice is needed, or, perhaps, rather a panel out of which a tribunal may be constituted; but where it will be far more difficult to arrive at a consensus.

The question must be decided whether it is possible to enforce such a code of ethics in international relations that nations will have to accept in principle the right of international impeachment of statesmen, diplomats, negotiators who have betrayed the common interests of peace and been unworthy of the confidence shown them, and the responsibility entrusted to them nationally or internationally.

This leads us to the great problem of international law enforcement, the question of an international army or/and an international police force.

XXIV: International Law Enforcement

The question of international courts of justice has ordinarily been linked with the question of an international police force. The Convention for the Creation of an International Criminal Court points to another solution to the problem of execution. The rules laid down in the Convention, even if introduced in the conventions for all international courts, will not in themselves be sufficient to guarantee the rule of justice. But, on the other hand, it is obvious that the institution of an international police force and still more the creation of an international army would raise far-reaching and complicated problems. However, if such forms of world organization could be found as would make superfluous any particular armed body for international law enforcement, it is hardly necessary to discuss how an international army or police force should be organized, whether it should be constituted by national units or be made one unified force of enlisted men, or drafted men, how the staff of officers should be recruited, at whose command the armed force should be placed, under what guarantees it should be put into action. Nor will it serve any purpose to examine whether the existence of such a supreme army (or even an armed international police force) would not in itself constitute a danger to a demilitarized commonwealth of nations and bring within reach of the commanders of the new Prætorian Guard that very world dictatorship which this war has been fought to prevent and to make impossible.

It is a peculiar and widespread misconception that a strong police force is an indication of national strength and of good government. The better organized any state is, the less use for a strong police organization. It is only where criminality is high, where gangsters are at large, where the government has no moral authority, that law enforcement becomes a problem. Despots and dictators need a highly organized police force, democracies do not. The most elaborate police system of modern times has been perfected in Nazi Germany.

If the international commonwealth of nations is well organized, there will be very little need for coercion. Under an intelligent world order in a community of nations where governments do behave, where conventions are kept and obligations are honored, it will not be necessary to resort to punitive measures. But the knowledge that they are there is part of the intelligent world order. And not only must they be on the statute book, but every nation must know what they amount to, how they are applied, and that they will be automatically applied if any country should try to break law and order.

In the international domain such punitive measures are called *sanctions*. And their application or non-application has played an important part in the history of the League of Nations.

No doubt, the authors of the Covenant of the League, when they drafted the text, fondly believed that nations would be duly impressed when they knew that Article 16 was there, and that there would be little danger of spoiling them by sparing the birch; for the rod was so magnificent. And no arrangements were at any time made to facilitate the application of Article 16 or making it a live reality.

Article 16 lays down:

"(1) Should any Member of the League resort to war in disregard of its covenants under Articles XII, XIII, or XV, it shall *ipso facto* be deemed to have committed an act of war against all other Members of the League, which hereby undertake immediately to subject it to the severance of all trade and financial relations, the prohibition of all intercourse between their nations and the nations of the Covenant-breaking State, and the prevention of all financial, commercial, or personal intercourse between the nationals of the Covenant-breaking State and the nationals of any other State, whether a member of the League or not.

"(2) It shall be the duty of the Council in such case to recommend to the several Governments concerned what effective military, naval, or air forces the Members of the League shall severally contribute to the armed forces to be used to protect the covenants of the League.

"(3) The Members of the League agree, further, that they will mutually support one another in the financial and economic measures which are taken under this Article, in order to minimize the loss and inconvenience resulting from the above measures, and that they will mutually support one another in resisting any special measures aimed at one of their number by the Covenant-breaking State, and that they will take the necessary steps to afford passage through their territory to the forces of any of the Members of the League which are coöperating to protect the covenants of the League.

"(4) Any Member of the League which has violated any covenant of the League may be declared to be no longer a Member of the League by a vote of the Council concurred in by the representatives of all the other Members of the League represented thereon."

The text of Section 1 is very clear and very strong. But it always remained a dead letter; there was no section of the League Secretariat instructed to study exactly how Article 16 should be applied, and what practical steps member states should take to fulfil their obligations under the article, or how the actions taken by the various nations should be coördinated.

In 1921 the Assembly adopted certain resolutions as an interpretation of Article 16 and urged the states that were bound by the Covenant to take necessary legislative steps to be able to apply sanctions, if and when the time should come. But the matter was dropped, and no attempt was made at any time to work out scientifically sanctionist plans. No experts and technicians had studied the problem of applying sanctions and no details of a sanctions mobilization had been prepared. The idea of sanctions was not only that they should be punitive measures, but, first of all, that they should prevent international crime, just as any police force has the primary duty to keep order and prevent individual crime. And crime is prevented because the potential criminal knows that automatically the whole law-enforcement machinery will be set in motion if a transgression should be committed. But in the international field no law-enforcement machinery had been worked out. It had to be improvised. The mere fact that there was no sanctions section at the League was a temptation to ambitious and unscrupulous statesmen. Great Britain had consistently pursued an avowedly antagonistic policy in regard to sanctions. The well-defined policy of the Great Powers was that professed by Sir John Simon, then Foreign Secretary of the United Kingdom, in the House of Commons on February 6, 1934: "It is not the Anglo-Saxon habit to make defined engagements for undefined circumstances." The statement is typical of an attitude often taken by cagey lawyers in business transactions. It may be a sound and protective private policy, but in public matters and in international life this attitude will create uncertainty, duplicity, distrust and confusion and will lead to recriminations, accusations and, finally, to the results manifest in the world today.

Sanctions as a preventive measure had never been established, and sanctions as a punitive measure were not applied against Japan in 1933. The first time Article 16 of the Covenant was brought into play was against Italy in 1935. And the action taken by the League then, although it failed to stop Italian aggression, is of extreme value for the future. It is the first time in human history that a concerted and organized attempt has been made to stop violence by peaceful means, and it is the first time the League stepped boldly out of a somewhat anemic political existence to prove what it was by some of its creators intended to be. The courageous attempt made clear the weakness, not of the sanctions principle, but of the League system, and taught those willing to learn what was needed to make the application of sanctions a very strong weapon in international life.

The action of the League of Nations did not carry out all the provisions of the Covenant. The only steps taken were:

(1) An embargo upon the export of munitions and arms to Italy; and
(2) The imposition of certain financial and economic restrictions upon her commerce and trade.

But the mutual obligations of Article 16 provided for something more:

(1) The imposition of an embargo upon the export of coal, steel and oil to Italy.
(2) The severance of all intercourse with the aggressor nation (the diplomatic sanction).
(3) Recommendation by the Council to the coöperating States Members regarding military assistance to the victim of the aggression, and
(4) The permissive sanction of expulsion from membership of the League.

The support given to the action taken was impressive, and the work done at Geneva, without any adequate machinery, to give effect to the limited sanctions decided upon was admirable. On the 11th of October, 1935, the so-called Coördination Committee was appointed to prepare the decisions and coördinate the application of the various types of sanctions. On October 19th its report was adopted by the Assembly and circulated to the governments of League countries. By November 2nd, fifty-seven member states had accepted the arms embargo. By December 12th it was in force in fifty countries; the financial measures were on that date in force in forty-seven countries, the pro-hibition of importation of Italian goods in force in forty-three countries and the embargo on "key" exports to Italy in force in forty-five countries. The figures increased dur-ing the following month. The only states that did not coöperate were the three allies of Italy—Albania, Austria and Hungary—and a few Latin-American states.

The world was looking at Geneva with a new feeling of respect, some politicians with apprehension. Governments were impressed. Ambassador Dodd states in his Diary:

"For two months the German Foreign Office people have been amazingly silent, gently intimating now and then that Germany might apply sanctions if the United States continued its policy in that direction."

When considering the initial surprising success of the League action, it must be borne in mind that the Coördi-nation Committee of the League had to choose the meas-ures on which there was unanimous consent; that every sovereign member state had to take its own decision, and that most states in spite of the Assembly resolutions of 1921 had failed to take the necessary legislative steps which would enable them to enforce, at short notice, any measures of economic pressure which might be decided upon. Consequently, the coöperating governments needed some time to straighten out difficulties of a constitutional character.

In spite of all these impediments, fifty states marched in

step to stop an aggressor, for the first time in human history. And the effect of the very modest sanctions applied showed great results quicker than anticipated. Some figures will indicate what this meant. In the United Kingdom imports from Italy totaled $1,942,400 in January, 1935, and only $70,400 in January, 1936. In March the amount of imports had been reduced to $8,800 as compared to $2,113,700 in March, 1935. Jugoslavia had cut down imports from Italy from $481,400 in March, 1935, to $800 in March, 1936. France was most reluctant to carry out sanctions. Still imports from Italy dropped from $1,-654,000 in February, 1935, to $82,700 in February, 1936.*

But sinister forces were passionately at work to prevent the action against Italy from succeeding. To a certain group of politicians, the leader of whom was M. Laval, nothing was more abhorrent than the idea that the League of Nations, through open and honest action, in partial fulfilment of the obligations of the Covenant, should become a real factor in the great political game. To others, the imperialistic ambassadors of the old type, it seemed extremely dangerous to establish a precedent to the effect that a Great Power could be thwarted and defeated by the concerted, peaceful action of a mobocracy of nations. What would become of Great Power prestige and privileges if Italy should be stopped now? The next time representatives of fifty nations might take it into their heads to stop Great Britain or to stop France, if those powers found reason to police backward nations, or extend their empires to protect their own interests and some tribes of aborigines? So the League was torpedoed and the solidarity and the hopes of fifty nations betrayed by M. Pierre Laval and Sir Samuel Hoare. On December 13, 1935, their proposals for giving satisfaction to Italy were communicated to the

* The figures are taken from Laura Puffer Morgan's valuable essay: "Armaments and Measures of Enforcement" in "World Organization," published by the American Council on Foreign Affairs.

members of the Council by Great Britain and France. A request from Ethiopia that the Assembly of the League should be convened was not granted. With Great Britain and France backing out, the action of the League was paralyzed. On June 2, 1936, the Argentine Government requested that the Assembly be summoned, and it met on June 30th. A long communication from the Italian Government was read by the president (M. von Zeeland). The Italian Government expressed its solemn intention to "provide peace, justice and security" for the Ethiopians, a task which it viewed "as a sacred mission of civilization" and proposed to carry out "according to the principles of the Covenant."

The Emperor of Ethiopia then spoke and wound up his address with the following words:

"I ask the fifty-two nations who have given the Ethiopian people a promise to help them in their resistance to the aggressor: What are they willing to do for Ethiopia—what measures do they intend to take? Representatives of the world . . . what answer am I to take back to my people?"

His warnings were repeated by most delegations, except those from the Great Powers. Some of the speeches will tend to make it clear why no small state can leave its fate to the will, foresight or leadership of Great Britain, or any group of Great Powers alone, when we come to the question of winning the peace.

Mr. te Water, then High Commissioner of South Africa in London, declared:

"Fifty nations, led by three of the most powerful nations in the world, are about to declare their powerlessness to protect the weakest in our midst from destruction. I am to declare that this surrender, if it is agreed upon by the nations, cannot be interpreted as impotence to safeguard that trust, but as a simple denial of their ability to bear the sacrifices necessary for the fulfilment of that obligation. . . . We had succeeded in reducing the disunity of the nations to a single variable—the sanction front of fifty nations; a compression of the disorder of the world into a single manageable group. . . . But now? The hand is being thrown in. . . . What will be the end? Where are the Great Powers leading us, who have not the faith to persevere? . . . Did the fifty nations, when they solemnly bound themselves to collective action under the Covenant of the League, make the successful resistance of Ethiopia a condition precedent to the fulfilment of their collective obligation? These questions my government has not evaded or found difficult of reply."

Still more pointed was De Valera, speaking for Ireland; and, no doubt, what happened in Geneva in 1936 greatly influenced Ireland in 1939. Her leading man said:

"Over fifty nations, we banded ourselevs together for collective security. Over fifty nations, we have now to confess publicly that we must abandon the victim to his fate. For the sake of a nation in Africa, apparently no one is ready to risk a war that would be transferred to Europe. . . . The peace of Europe depends, as everybody knows, on the will of the Great Powers. If the Great Powers of Europe would only meet now in that Peace Conference which will have to be held after Europe has once more been drenched in blood; if they would be prepared to make now, in advance, only a tithe of the sacrifice each of them will have to make should the war be begun, the terrible menace which threatens us today could be warded off."

And Miss Hesselgren, speaking for Sweden, pointed to the coming world war and how the Great Powers invited it by their unwillingness to act:

"However, can we, after this, expect that any small nation can have any hope for the future? You may say, as has been said here, that everything must be done so as not to let loose war on Europe, that for this aim it is meet that one country should die for all the others. Yes; but are you sure that you are not letting it loose just by giving in to the aggressor now? Every small country must, after this, ask itself when its time will come, and ask this with no hope in the League. You are all thinking of this possibility. It has run like a red thread through every speech. Everyone has seen the looming shadow of such an event. What are you going to do? How are you going to prevent its coming? Surely it must be by going to the very root of the evil. Try to find the very sources of unrest. Try to take every dispute in hand at once and effectively, and do not let month after month go by in futile discussion."

But sanctions were called off. Without Great Britain and France the League could not act. And all those initiated knew that sanctions had been called off because they threatened to be successful, not because they had failed. "There is reason to believe that, if the sanctions in force had been maintained another month, Mussolini's regime would have collapsed. A correspondent of the *London Times* in a series of articles in the summer of 1936 came to the conclusion that sanctions were lifted just in the nick of time to save Mussolini." (Puffer Morgan, p. 155.) "The suggestion may plausibly be made that the sanctions were abrogated, not because they were ineffective, but because they were too effective." (*ibid.*)

That is the great lesson for the future. We know after 1935-36 what a terrible weapon sanctions constitute. We know that an automatic and immediate application of sanctions, carefully prepared and coördinated, would ruin any country. In the case of Italy nations honored only a fraction of their obligations under the Covenant. If they had fulfilled their duty, the world would not have been at war today.

The system of sanctions could be extended far beyond the framework of the League experience. Article 24 of the Covenant laid down:

"There shall be placed under the direction of the League the international bureaus already established by general treaties, if the parties to such treaties consent."

No attempt was ever made by the League to establish any direction over the Telegraphic Union, the Universal Postal Union, all the bureaus for the protection of trademarks, patent rights, literary and artistic rights and so on. The mere knowledge that an act of aggression would automatically lead to complete postal and telegraphic isolation, and the loss of all international protection for trademarks, patent rights, literary and artistic rights, etc., would make any country hesitate to commit an aggression or violate a convention.

Hand in hand with compulsory arbitration or adjudication of every international conflict the carefully prepared sanctions system would compel appearance before the appropriate Court or Tribunal, afford protection against injury, uphold the law and, if necessary, be used to enforce the verdicts, orders or advisory opinions of these institutions.

To meet the full purpose of policing measures it might also be useful to establish that Equity Tribunal so warmly advocated by Lord Davies.* Whether it will be not only useful, but necessary, will depend on the constitution of the future world organization. Political disputes will not always lend themselves to solution by arbitration or by adjudication. A demand for a revision of existing treaties or of the accepted international law or penal code might automatically be submitted to an Equity Tribunal, whether the parties to the dispute consent or not. The Tribunal may report to the Assembly, or to the Council of the world organization, and this report, if it be accepted by a qualified majority of that body, becomes the settlement which both parties must accept. A panel from which the members of such a tribunal should be drawn must be established beforehand; and they must be what the Geneva Protocol of 1924 described as "persons who, by their nationality, their personal character and their experience, appear to furnish the highest guarantees of competence and impartiality."

Sanctions such as are suggested here can be wholly ef-

* "Nearing the Abyss," Constable & Co., London, 1936.

fective only if it is known that they will be supported, if this should prove necessary, by the ultimate sanction, which is blockade.

This will bring us very close to the old American idea embodied in the joint resolution adopted by the Senate and the House of Representatives on June 20, 1910:

"That a commission of five members be appointed by the President of the United States to consider the expediency of utilizing existing international agencies for the purpose of limiting the armaments of the nations of the world by international agreement, and of constituting the combined navies of the world an international force for the preservation of universal peace."

Only the combined military machines of all organized nations can constitute that international force needed to preserve a universal peace. And the knowledge that, the occasion arising, such a force will be available, will do more to prevent any acts of international violence than any police force could do.

XXV: Fictitious and Factual Problems

As we are moving through the period of transition and creating more and more agencies for allied—and international—coöperation, and utilizing existent agencies of study and research, it probably will be found that certain problems which have been widely and passionately discussed are hardly problems at all. On the other hand, new questions may arise, and we may be faced with problems in other directions than we had imagined.

The German propaganda machine has been so successful in many countries because the operators realized how easily honest people are taken in; particularly in the Anglo-Saxon countries with their pronounced sympathy for the under-dog, a sympathy neither respected nor understood in Germany where for more than two centuries the nation has been educated to kick the under-dog.

Americans and many prominent Englishmen were led to believe that there was a difference in kind between a group of nations called "the haves" and another group called the "have-nots"; and some good and honest Americans with the kind sentimentality of pioneers were eager to distribute the property or the colonies belonging not to themselves but to other nations, among the "have nots." Germany had no colonies until the Kaiser started to acquire some. There was a good historical reason for it. Ger-

many never desired colonies; Bismarck was entirely unwilling to start an overseas empire. He remarked in 1871:

> "For us German colonies would be exactly like the silks
> and sables of the Polish nobleman who has no shirt to wear
> under them."

The Portuguese, the Spaniards, the English, the French
and the Dutch for centuries had that spirit of adventure,
that longing for the unknown, that spirit of discovery and
exploration which took them all the world round. The
Germans never had that spirit. They liked to stay at home.
And the Prussians preferred acquiring the land of their
neighbors to venturing overseas. When the British and the
French were staking their lives in India and in North
America, Prussia partitioned Poland. When the English
were fighting the Burmese and the French the Kabyls,
Prussia attacked Denmark. It was less expensive and was
thought more profitable. Some nations tried to extend
their territories in extra-European countries. Prussia concentrated on waging war in Europe; Germany was the
creation of the Prussian tradition; and Bismarck always
liked European soil better than African or Polynesian soil.
This was also the original idea of Hitler. Referring to the
problem of Lebensraum he states in *"Mein Kampf"*:

> "It is not to colonial acquisition that we must look for a
> solution of this question but exclusively to the acquisition of
> territory for settlement which will increase the area of the
> Motherland.
> "We finally part with the colonial and trade policy of the
> period before the war and pass over to the land policy of
> the future. . . .
> "I freely acknowledge that, even in the period before the
> war, I should have held it to have been better if Germany,
> renouncing her absurd colonial policy, her commercial fleet
> and navy, had set herself against Russia in alliance with Eng-
> land, and so gone over from a weak world-policy to a deter-
> mined European policy of acquiring continental territory. . . .

"Take every care that the strength of our people has its foundations not in colonies but in the land of its home in Europe. . . ."

But since 1936 the pro-colonial elements in the Nazi Party, led by General von Epp, have succeeded in reasserting Germany's colonial demands.

The Germans who emigrated, until the 1880's, had mainly one desire: to get out of Germany. It was an escape. The oldest German settlers in the United States, the Pennsylvania Dutch, going back to 1683, came to find a religious freedom which did not exist in the various states in Germany. Of course, their descendants are entirely American. In the latter half of the eighteenth century German princes made money by kidnapping young men and selling them to the English army for use in America. Especially the princely house of Hesse had an extensive traffic in men; and those who came to America this way and their offspring did not want to create German colonies. Those who escaped after the abortive revolutions in 1830 and 1848 certainly had no such desire.

It was not colonies but America that was the land of promise. During the last fifty years more than eighteen million immigrants came to the United States, with only some 500,000 from the whole of Europe going to the colonies. And any objective investigation of facts will make clear that colonies have no real importance as an outlet for overflow populations. In the whole German colonial empire before the last great war the entire German population was less than 24,000 people, all German functionaries and administrators with their families included. The number of German bona fide settlers was slightly under 200. And the figures for the Italian colonial empire were similar.

The bulk of trade between Germany and her colonies was less than one percent of German trade.

The total part of all colonies (Belgian, British, Dutch, French, Italian, Portuguese, Spanish) in world trade is only about twelve percent. Not more than three percent of the total present production of all commercially important raw materials come from the colonies and only three raw materials are found predominantly in colonial territories, viz., rubber, palm oil and copra. Of the so-called six basic industrial commodities—coal, iron, petroleum, cotton, rubber, copper—only one is of colonial origin; and there is some reason to believe that when this war is over, natural rubber will no longer be a basic industrial commodity.

The Committee appointed by the League of Nations for the Study of the Problem of Raw Materials published its report in September, 1937. The frequently repeated statement that some countries are at a great disadvantage because they do not control the supplies of raw materials they need for sustenance and in their factories is discussed in this report. It has been charged that many obstacles exist which prevent countries which lack colonies from getting these materials. The Report declares that:

"The Committee has not been able to find any substantial evidence of such impediments." (p. 14) "The foregoing analysis shows that the solution of the present difficulties in regard to the payment of raw materials is in a large part bound up with the solution of wider economic problems which requires concerted action to restore free circulation of capital, goods and labour." (p. 27) And "The only general and permanent solution of the problem of commercial access to raw materials is to be found in a restoration of international exchanges on the widest basis."

So, the problem we have to face is not any conflict between the "haves" and the "have nots." The real problem is not a political one but a highly complicated financial and monetary one. And the real difficulty was not that it was impossible for certain countries to obtain raw materials. The difficulty was that business in every country was too willing and eager to sell raw materials to any prospective buyer who could pay, even if it was obvious to any person who wanted to see, that the buyer was intent on using those raw materials for the manufacture of arms and munitions to be used against the country that permitted him to buy.

It is of considerable interest to note in this connection what Mr. Hoover and Mr. Gibson state in their book concerning the propaganda about "have" and "have not" nations:

"All this agitation has tended to create an illusion in the world that raw materials have a direct relation to lasting peace and an acceptance of the idea that a great problem exists somewhere in this connection. We believe the importance of the problem is entirely overestimated from an international point of view.

"The economic fact is that there have always been and are ample raw material supplies available to any nation during peace if they will produce the goods to exchange for them. Too often, nations have consumed materials and labor in making arms and munitions that otherwise could be converted into goods that could be exchanged for raw materials. That there are ample supplies is indicated by the fact that the energies of many governments have been devoted to restricting production of rubber, wheat, sugar, coffee, cotton, nitrate, potash, tin, oil, coal, and fats and fibers in order to hold a living price for the producers of these commodities."

Nobody will deny that on this point the authors speak with authority. And as to colonies, the issue presents itself in three aspects well put by Dr. Benjamin Gerig in an excellent essay:

"First, is population pressure really a problem in certain countries of Europe and Asia, say Germany, Italy, and Japan? Second, are there really vast undeveloped spaces in colonial areas where large numbers of these people could settle without displacing too many natives? And, third, under what conditions could such a transfer of populations be made, taking account of both the national and international interests involved?" ("Colonial aspects of the Postwar Settlement." Second Report, p. 195.)

Mr. Gerig then continues:

"On the first point, population pressure, it can probably be shown rationally that although Japan has doubled her population since 1875, and although that of Europe has trebled since 1800, the full use of technological methods in an orderly world of peaceful industry and trade would make the problem in reality nonexistent. But in a world of nightmarish insecurity, of trade and migration barriers, a dense population may, and does, develop a psychological condition where lebensraum and demands for expansion are as real and as unmanageable as claustrophobia."

In other words: The problem of colonies is a psychological problem and not a political problem. Its origin is mental disturbance, and this disease cannot be cured by permitting the patients to follow their manias.

But the question of population pressure, as put by Mr. Gerig, raises an entirely new problem—in its widest aspect it might be called the problem of international birth-control. Certain governments have tried for military reasons to increase their natality. They want more recruits and so they put a premium on childbirth. That has been the case in Germany and in Italy; people are ordered to multiply. Artificially the leaders of these countries strive to create an overflow population to substantiate their imperialistic demands for colonies and territories. Shall this give them a legitimate claim on nations which have not been willing to follow such a policy? The question is fundamental and will become still more important. For as a matter of fact, the colonial empires of the world are not fitted for white men, and overflow populations are entirely unwilling to be directed to the wastes, the tropical forests, the swamps and the deserts.

Mr. Gerig remarks:

"Let us admit that it must seem unfair to the Italian up on his stony terraced hillside that so much good land in the United States is lying idle."

If, with Mr. Gerig, we make this admission, the problem is brought nearer home to many of those who have expressed their willingness to distribute the colonies of the "haves" among the clamoring "have nots." And they may be more ready to understand Mr. Gerig's statement:

"Transfer of colonial territory today is not a solution although it might have been a partial solution earlier."

The overflow populations, as far as they exist, want to migrate to the United States of America, to Canada, to Argentina. The problem of regulation of populations is a complex international problem, intimately connected with the problem of the refugee populations, of the populations transferred by force to districts that are foreign to them, and to a certain extent also with the Jewish question. But the problems cannot be solved through international regulation alone; they will render necessary a new coördination of national law and international law; and they will bring up another question. When a country claims to be overpopulated and demands a right to send emigrants overseas, who shall decide to what extent such a claim is justified? For instance: In Germany not even the Hitler regime has dared to break up the large feudal estates of Eastern Prussia. Large numbers of people could be settled there. Who shall have the right to tell nations what policy to pursue at home before they can expand abroad?

The world planning needed for a rational and intelligent solution of the population problem cannot be accomplished in the transitional period after this war. It cannot be accomplished in one generation; and it may be a consolation to know that we shall leave problems enough to make international politics highly interesting to our descendants.

More and more people have come to realize that when certain nations have been demanding colonies it is mainly for military reasons, to acquire bases for attacks on other countries, and for considerations of political prestige.

To give countries needed facilities for exports and imports colonies are not necessary. No countries had a higher standard of living than the Scandinavian countries and Switzerland. And no countries had a more intensive foreign trade; exports and imports per capita were higher, considerably higher in Denmark, Norway, Switzerland and Sweden than in any other countries in the world. This trade was entirely independent of colonies. And these countries never complained that they could not get all the raw materials they desired.

The United States never sought to acquire colonies. It may be said that no country had less need for colonies. But that is not the full answer. The main reason was psychological. It has been expressed by Secretary Hull in the following terms:

"It has been our purpose in the past—and will remain our purpose in the future—to use the full measure of our influence to support attainment of freedom by all peoples who, by their own acts, show themselves worthy of it and ready for it."

No government, except the Axis governments, would openly profess today that any power has any legitimate "right" to colonies, or to dominate less advanced nations. There seems to be a general consensus that the mandates system should be extended and that some kind of international colonial commission should be established with powers to exercise direct administration in certain specified territories. And, if on examination, it should be proved that emigration from certain countries is legitimate and logical, care should be taken to direct this emigration to suitable territories. So far very little has been done to survey scientifically the possibilities of immigration in Africa and parts of South America. Any directed immigration presents great problems and can be administered only by men and women with a keen sense of responsibility. And even in this field the experience of the League and of the Nansen Office of Refugees will be not only of service, but indispensable.

It has been said, on good foundation, that what is needed for the development of certain areas in Africa and South America is money more than men. And it has been suggested that there should be created an international development fund which might be administered jointly by an international bank and an international colonial commission.

The questions of immigration laws, of race discrimination, of trade barriers, of the exaggerated ideas of minority privileges, of international currency and trade problems, are interlocked in such a way that large-scale and sweeping measures are hardly possible. But we may hope that the victorious nations will realize what was only partially realized at Versailles, that the colonies, under administration of an international commission, and the mandated territories should not be under the sovereignty of any individual mandatory power, but that sovereignty should be recognized as residing potentially in the territory itself until such time as it is considered capable of standing on its own feet and becoming a full member of the organized commonwealth of nations. And, maybe, it will be found that certain tropical territories should not be opened to exploitation at all but reserved as "international parks" for the protection of the tribes living there and alone capable of living there permanently.

XXVI: What No Peace Conference Can Do

There is some danger, both politically and psychologically, in discussing the coming peace as if every problem worrying thoughtful individuals and harassed nations could be solved, and a nostrum found to cure all social difficulties and economic diseases. It is essential to understand that no peace conference can create a new heaven and a new earth. Human beings will be very much the same after this war as before this war. Some lessons may be learnt, but it is more to be hoped than to be seriously expected that nations on the whole will be far more tolerant, more broad-minded, less prejudiced when the last battle of this war is fought. If we demand everything from a peace conference, we shall certainly get nothing; and it is of no small importance to realize that although a good many problems are universal, there is no universal solution. Particularly in the social field conditions vary to such an extent from one part of the world to another that it would be most unwise to imagine that the same set of blueprints could be used in every country.

In the Joint Declaration by Democratic Socialists of Several Nationalities it is stated:

"The social and economic changes which we Socialists desire must be won by the people of each country, and will depend on conditions and on the maturity of the population, as well as on the growing strength and solidarity of the international Socialist and Labour movement."

The remarks hold true without the limitations imposed by the socialist narrowness. The changes that all people desire depend on conditions and on the maturity of the population; and they depend to a large extent upon social education and public intelligence. That freedom from want which is one of the great points of the Atlantic Charter is not so much a social question as an economic question and a question of organization and of distribution. As mentioned in a previous chapter, the International Labour Organization has set up a machinery for discussing exactly these problems and is collaborating with a number of governments in an effort to formulate concrete plans. The work is well under way and undertaken in that spirit of unbiased research and of scientific modesty which is so much needed.

On the whole, it will easily be found that the full or a reasonably satisfactory partial solution of political questions is not impossible, not even overwhelmingly difficult; but the solution of economic problems, far vaster in scope, infinitely more complicated, will be possible, if at all, only through concentrated and coördinated efforts over a long period of time.

Fortunately the evolution of the human race and of all human institutions is so dynamic a process that no solution of great problems can ever be final. And as we rapidly pass from one epoch of industrial development to another, as we slowly move from one phase of spiritual and intellectual groping for truth into another, new questions will always arise, and every generation will be in need of its maximum of mental and physical energy.

Our ambition, if we want to win the peace, must not be to solve every problem, because then no problem will be solved, but to realize that the best we can hope to accomplish will be to build up a permanent and elastic machinery for dealing with problems and to help find the necessary processes to prevent economic epidemics, to palliate depressions, to facilitate the ordinary course of trade and distribution of goods, and to stabilize currencies.

The international economic problems, fortunately, or unfortunately, are not new; they are all well known. Nations and governments indulged in the luxury of economic warfare, not because they did not know better, but because they were entirely unwilling to do better, and also, because no single leading politician was strong enough or had sufficient moral courage to break through the barrage set up by pressure groups, by economic lay preachers, by the superstitious narrowness and by the short-sighted self-interests of farm and other blocs. We have all the experience needed to guide us, and should know, perfectly well, that no general formula exists that can lead us into a promised land of prosperity.

A good many people clamor for more and more government control and tell us that after the war governments must take over more and more of the industries, the communications, the entire world production and distribution. They forget or overlook that most of the difficulties in international economic life in recent years were due to government interference and not to lack of government control, and that private interests, even at their worst, did not directly work for war; whereas certain government interests did, assiduously and successfully. Managed economy, state control of currency, clearing arrangements were all used most directly, not only to prepare for war, but to create an atmosphere of war. And where private interests seemed to be most aggressive, they were usually directed by governments.

Professor Eugene Staley remarks in his "War and the Private Investor" (New York, 1935):

"Despite widespread beliefs and convincing theories to the contrary, private foreign investments are found much more frequently as tools of diplomacy than as instigators of diplomatic action in those cases of international friction over foreign investments which may be classified as dangerous (that is, more than mere altercations, but likely to lead toward war, especially to a big war between major powers). The foreign policy of which private investments have become the tools in these cases may have been determined wholly or in part by "economic" factors. That can be debated pro or con; it is not debated here. What does not seem to be arguable, however, on the basis of careful observation of these phenomena in the real world, is that with respect to the immediate relation of private investments to diplomacy the private investments figure most frequently (not exclusively) in cases of dangerous international friction as servants, rather than as masters."

If Staley's remarks hold true as a general experience, and it can hardly be denied that they do, his implication has gathered a tremendous momentum in the years since he published his book. In totalitarian countries business and government, production and government, exports and imports and government were one and the same thing. I. G. Farben Industrie and all its subsidiaries—whether in aniline dyes, in the production of synthetic gasoline or in the manufacture of medicaments—were part and parcel of the German mobilization for war.

Next: it is necessary to bear in mind that if political and social conditions vary from one country to another, economic capacities vary still more. What is an excellent solution of a problem in one country may be disastrous in another country because the problem presents itself in an entirely different way, and, even if the symptoms appear identical, an accurate diagnosis may prove their origins to be entirely different.

It has been quite common in recent years to praise the Scandinavian way of life and of government, "the middle way"—and rightly so. But it would be preposterous to claim that a solution of problems which was natural in small countries, where there is no great financial concentration of interests, where control is easy, the prospect of

acquiring large fortunes very restricted, and where geographical conditions and historical traditions had dictated
a certain line of action, would be equally natural in tremendous and to a large extent undeveloped countries as
the United States and Russia. Each country has to work
out its own salvation. But direction, coöperation and decisive help can be given.

It may seem a little unkind amidst all the universal
enthusiasm to remind people of the fact that most of the
things mentioned in the Atlantic Charter were embodied
in the Covenant of the League of Nations.

Points 4 and 5 of the Charter declare:

"They will endeavor, with due respect for their existing
obligations, to further the enjoyment by all States, great or
small, victor or vanquished, of access, on equal terms, to the
trade and to the raw materials of the world which are needed
for their economic prosperity;

They desire to bring about the fullest collaboration between
all nations in the economic field with the object of securing,
for all, improved labour standards, economic adjustment and
social security.

•Article 23 of the Covenant of the League stated:

"Subject to and in accordance with the provisions of international conventions existing or hereafter to be agreed upon,
the Members of the League:

(a) will endeavour to secure and maintain fair and humane
conditions of labour for men, women and children,
both in their own countries and in all countries to
which their commercial and industrial relations extend, and for that purpose will establish and maintain
the necessary international organizations;

(e) will make provision to secure and maintain freedom of
communications and of transit and equitable treatment for the commerce of all Members of the League.
In this connection, the special necessities of the re-
gions devastated during the war of 1914-1918 shall be
borne in mind."

It will be seen that the difference is not remarkable. Without discussing the purport of the reservation "with due respect for their existing obligations," we may hope that it does not mean more than the clearer and more definite words of the preamble to Article 23: "Subject to and in accordance with the provisions of international conventions existing or hereafter to be agreed upon." The International Labour Organization has been the fulfilment of 23a, and as to e, it will be admitted that the text is more positive than the Atlantic Charter, which expresses a desire. The Covenant promised to "make provision to secure . . . "

Now, what then came out of the League efforts? What guidance can we find in League experience in this field?

During the 1920's the League framed a number of international conventions designed to facilitate economic and financial relations between states. They cover a wide range of subjects, such as the simplification of customs formalities, the general adoption of arbitration clauses to be inserted in commercial agreements, measures to repress the counterfeiting of currency, and regulations to be applied to bills of exchange. But it became more and more evident that conventions intended for general acceptance had to be framed in very general terms. Important provisions in regard to which general agreement could not be secured, had either to be omitted or were subject to reservations and exceptions. The agreements reached could never be more than the greatest common measure of principles and tendencies which the contracting parties were prepared to accept, and their stipulations were frequently determined by the requirements and conditions of the states which were least advanced in their national economies, or most reluctant to sacrifice any iota of what they considered to be their national interests in the attempt to reach a general solution. And even in this field what has above been called the lack of responsible representation on the League made itself felt. Countries which had approved and signed such conventions sometimes failed to ratify them.

In the light of this experience the League in later years confined itself to convene conferences of a limited number of states specially concerned in some particular problem with a view to obtain immediate practical results, instead of a universal agreement. As an example might be mentioned the London conference of 1933 between representatives of the principal wheat-exporting and wheat-importing countries with a view to securing their coöperation in the marketing of this commodity.

It also became the work of the League to draft conventions which were not intended to be signed at Geneva and ratified by governments, but to be accepted by them as models or standards in negotiating and framing such agreements as they might feel it necessary to make on their own responsibility with other countries.

As an example of this procedure might be mentioned the work of the Economic Intelligence Organization of the League in dealing with the question of double taxation.* It furnished governments with a series of instruments which could be adapted to the needs of each individual case.

The League took up this work in 1921, and between that year and 1929 when the depression set in, some twenty-five bilateral conventions relating to this problem were concluded; between 1929 and 1935 some sixty new conventions dealing with double taxation were concluded; and between that year and the outbreak of World War II a further twenty conventions have been concluded based on the model conventions drawn up by the League Committee—a surprising achievement during a period when

* For details see "Towards a Better Economic World" (Geneva, 1939, Information Section) and "Prevention of International Double Taxation and Fiscal Evasion," by Mitchell B. Carroll (League of Nations, Geneva, 1939).

the world was suffering from the most serious economic
depression in history.

The history of the very important work of the League
in regard to world economic problems gives us most valuable indications as to the methods that must be pursued
if we want to win the economic peace. World conventions
will have a strictly limited application; the movement that
produced results was a movement from the general to the
particular, from universal to limited conferences, from
preparing the way for multilateral conventions to preparing the way for bilateral conventions.

And it must be realized that economic peace cannot be
won through any single brave action, it will be a long war
of slow advance and gradual infiltration, and it would
prove a fatal mistake to act upon the belief that hard and
fast rules can be laid down.

For instance, it is generally agreed that economic barriers between countries should be removed as far as possible, and that tariffs should be regulated so as to help
and not hinder trade. But when Mr. Hoover and Mr. Gibson in their book suggest that tariffs "be equal to all nations" they seem to overlook certain established facts. Geographical conditions, historical traditions and practical
needs render necessary wide exceptions to this principle,
which in the realm of pure reason is so right. There exist
regional arrangements which are vital to populations in a
good many areas; they will continue to exist. And any attempt to do away with them would provoke resentment
and prove futile.

In questions of international legislation as in questions
of national legislation it will be experienced that any law
that is found by public conscience to have no reasonable
title and to have no moral justification, any law that is
contrary to the public consensus, will defeat its own purpose as did prohibition in the United States and in a good
many other countries.

Between various groups of countries bordering on each other or having very particular interests in common there exists what might be called good-neighbor relations and preferential customs tariffs, or there may be no customs duties at all. Between the Scandinavian countries, between Switzerland and the surrounding districts of France, there were such arrangements; and we may hope that in an intelligently regulated future there will be such an arrangement between the states belonging to a Danubian Confederacy. Once again it is the story of the walls and the gates.

After all tariffs are not a primary question. High tariffs like other trade barriers put up during the last decades were an outcome of panic, of national, political or economic desperation, and not the logical result of a well-considered line of policy. If we want to win the peace we shall have, when we are planning our commercial policy, to think in terms of the economics of national production and not in terms of tariffs. And when we are thinking of international finance we shall have to consider financing production (as already mentioned when discussing the development of colonies) and not in terms of central banks. Before considering commercial policy we should consider the ways and means of securing full employment of all productive resources. (In this connection a small reform might be agreed upon in the statistical systems: to publish figures of employment and not of unemployment, the hopeful and positive figures instead of the depressing and negative figures. Incidentally, figures of employment are also more reliable and easier to control.)

The primary concern of governments must be to stimulate and not to restrict enterprise. But, on the other hand, there can hardly be any doubt that in a good many fields of activity government control or rather intergovernmental or international control will be needed. And it would be well if industrialists, bankers, business men would learn to understand the difference between public control and public operation of certain groups of industrial, banking and business undertakings. Without entering upon the highly interesting but tremendously involved problem of whether governments before deciding their commercial policies should try to elaborate some far-reaching system for the international dovetailing of production, we may probably agree that for the maintenance of peace public control will be needed in the armament industries. The reduction of armaments mentioned in Articles 8 and 9 of the Covenant of the League of Nations must become a reality and the necessary organs of control be instituted. Any future Disarmament Conference will have to consider not a quantitative reduction of armaments, which has practically no importance, but international control of strategic minerals. Some years ago it was felt that to prevent military war it would be necessary to control coal, iron ore and petroleum; experts now seem to think that control of a group of key minerals, such as tungsten, magnesite, molybdenum, certain phosphates, etc., would prove sufficient.

Of course, this control would be unrelated to economic or commercial requirements. But it seems not unlikely that for some time at least, it will be found necessary to establish some kind of control with certain primary products, such as wheat, sugar, natural rubber, tin—to prevent undue price increases, and regulate supplies. It is not precluded that it may prove necessary to extend such control to important semi-manufactured or easily definable goods, such as steel. But it should always be borne in mind that government interference in itself is not an indication of good economic health, but a medicine administered to cure a disease. It may be necessary to take quite strong doses of it, and over a long period of time, but any overdose may be dangerous and incapacitate the patient indefinitely.

Government interference will be different from the international control needed to keep an eye on monopolies and cartels.

It must not be forgotten that as long as the war lasts, governments are not only the greatest buyers of goods, but in certain industries the only customers and clients. In many cases government buying and government support should naturally stop automatically when the last battle is won. Such an abrupt discontinuance would play havoc with tremendous industrial, economic and social interests. The most intimate and trusting coöperation between governments, industries and labour will be needed to ease the process of the colossal adjustment when the war is over. And this can be done only if governments decide to carry out a positive economic policy.

As an advance action preparing the way to win the peace, it will be desirable to establish some central agency for the discussion of economic and reconstruction questions similar to the Inter-Allied Relief Commission. This agency should deal with economic and financial policy as a whole, industrial development schemes, the transition from war to peace economy and all related problems of production and distribution, transport, etc.

In this connection it is natural to point to Article 7 of the Mutual Aid Agreement between the Governments of the United States and the United Kingdom:

"In the final determination of the benefits to be provided to the United States of America by the Government of the United Kingdom in return for aid furnished under the Act of Congress of the 11th March, 1941, the terms and conditions thereof shall be such as not to burden commerce between the two countries, but to promote mutually advantageous economic relations between them and the betterment of world-wide economic relations. To that end, they shall include provision for agreed action by the United States of America and the United Kingdom, open to participation by all other countries of like mind, directed to the expansion, by appropriate international and domestic measures, of production, employment, and the exchange and consumption of goods, which are the material foundations of the liberty and welfare of all peoples; to the elimination of all forms of discriminatory treatment in international commerce, and to the reduction of tariffs and other trade barriers; and, in general, to the attainment of all the economic objectives set forth in the Joint Declaration, made on the 12th August, 1941, by the President of the United States of America and the Prime Minister of the United Kingdom. At an early convenient date conversations shall be begun between the two Governments with a view to determining, in the light of governing economic conditions, the best means of attaining the above-stated objectives by their own agreed action and of seeking the agreed action of other like-minded Governments."

The program laid out is broad and hopeful. It is essential that it should be acted upon, and that it should be made a multilateral and not only a bilateral plan of action.

The study of all these problems cannot be undertaken by a general peace conference. They must be approached in a different way.

Mr. Hoover and Mr. Gibson in their book suggest that:

". . . the longer-view problems should be assigned to a series of separate international commissions, their conclusions to be brought in after political and economic life has begun to recuperate and destructive emotions given time to cool off."

The suggestion, if not new, is timely and sensible. But an organization is needed to prepare the agenda for such commissions and collect the necessary information. Fortunately we have such an organization.

In his report to the Assembly of the League of Nations in December, 1939, the Secretary General stated:

"Since the depression which began in 1929, there has been rather a state of quasi-permanent emergency than any general operative system [of economic organization in the world]. The problems of economic organization that will have to be faced after the termination of hostilities will therefore prove to be extremely complex and grave.

"During the past ten years, these problems have constantly occupied the attention of Governments and of international bodies sitting at Geneva and elsewhere. Many proposals for their solution have been put forward. All these problems and these proposals put forward failed because of some inherent defect or because the political conditions—that have led to war—rendered their application impossible. Has there not been rather a lack of will to solve than of ability to find solutions? Have any deep-lying economic changes been overlooked? On all these subjects there is a vast mass of material at Geneva, and on them the Secretariat has a unique experience and contacts with persons all over the world whose concern they are. It is of the utmost importance that this experience and these contacts should be preserved; and that the material should be reduced to such a form as to render it of immediate use and value when the time comes.

"But the war itself is daily giving rise to structural changes and structural strains that will produce new problems for ultimate solution. It will be necessary, therefore, for those engaged upon the examination of the issues to which I have just referred to keep themselves constantly informed about current developments. This, with the aid of an active Economic Intelligence Service, they should be able to do."

Fortunately, this active Economic Intelligence Service is at work. At an invitation from Princeton University, the Princeton Institute of Advanced Study, and the Rockefeller Institute of Medical Research, this section of the League of Nations Secretariat since the fall of 1940 has been working at Princeton, N. J. And after the meeting in London in April, 1942, of the Emergency Committee of the Governing body of the International Labour Organization and the meeting of the economic and the financial committee of the League, full coöperation between the staffs in Montreal and in Princeton should be ensured.

It is one of the most important steps as yet taken toward winning the peace.

XXVII: Some Conclusions

In spite of much difference of opinion in principle as well as in detail among those who have made publicly known their ideas about the peace to come there seems to be a striking agreement of opinion on a number of points:

(1) No peace can follow immediately after the cessation of hostilities; there must be what was called to start with a cooling-off period, but what is now considered a necessary period of transition, which may last for a few or a number of years. Mr. Harold Nicolson, Lord Davies, the American Commission to Study the Organization of Peace, Mr. Hoover and Mr. Gibson, Undersecretary Sumner Welles, Secretary Hull all agree. During this period (which has already begun in the midst of war) there will be an organic growth of plans, of organizations and of institutions which will be important for the final post-war settlement.

(2) When fighting is over it will be necessary for some time, maybe for a considerable time, for the United Nations to occupy, or rather to administer the totalitarian countries and to police large sections of the territories that have been involved in the war, until conditions have been stabilized to such an extent that national governments can take over and national constitutions be reinstituted or rewritten.

(3) Before there can be any great conference to settle the final peace terms there must be a number of conferences of experts meeting for specific purposes to discuss

particular problems and try to find a solution of them. The final peace conference will be more in the character of a coördinating and codifying conference than of a policy-making assembly. The policies must have been decided upon and to a large extent carried out before that body can meet.

(4) There is also a consensus among those entitled to have an opinion that there will be no reparations imposed on the totalitarian powers when the war is over.

"There can be no real reparations. . . . The first World War proved that no considerable sums could be collected in any event." (Hoover-Gibson.)

"Nothing is more demonstrable than the fact that we cannot pay for this war either now or when it's over with the money of other men. Nothing is more demonstrable than the fact that the reparations theory of the 1920's merely gave the world another shove toward the present catastrophe." (James B. Reston.)

An entirely different matter is that the totalitarian countries will have to surrender what they have expropriated or stolen in occupied countries, including economic interests in industries and business, in land and in real estate, and make what restitution is possible for wanton destruction of property.

(5) All the United Nations having proclaimed that they do not want more territory or possessions of any kind, there should be no difficulty in reëstablishing national boundaries, although some rectifications may be justified as between Hungary and Roumania, as between Czechoslovakia and Hungary, as between Italy and her Eastern neighbors. (The boundaries given to Italy at Versailles had little justification in geographical, historical or national factual conditions, and the Italian regime has been extremely unkind to national minorities.) There also seems to be a consensus that there ought to be established

some kind of Danube confederacy binding together economically the states along this great Eastern European
waterway. The agreements reached between the Greek
and the Jugoslav Governments on January 15, 1942, and
between the Polish and Czechoslovak Governments on
January 25, 1942, are strong indications of the feasibility
of policies of friendship and federation in Eastern and
South-Central Europe.

The Baltic problem will be one of the most difficult to
solve. The fate of the three Baltic states created in 1918
and the question of Russian interests in the Baltic, of
the Aaland Islands, of Danzig and of Memel will need its
own conference of experts and the most delicate handling.

In the East the problems of Manchuria (Manchukuo)
and Korea will require the most careful study by liberal
minds and the most expert knowledge before final decisions are taken.

(6) The mandated territories abused by Japan, and
other mandated territories should be placed under the
administration of an international mandates commission
as developed above (p. 171). There is also a strong current
of opinion for creating an international colonial office in
collaboration with the International Mandates Commission and establishing colonial policies on a new footing.

(7) A very strong feeling is prevailing that one of the
needed guarantees for winning the peace will be enforced
adjudication of differences and litigations between states.
The international lawyers on the American Commission
to Study the Organization of Peace are in favor of it. So
are most writers not belonging to the class of career diplomats. Lord Davies has been an advocate of compulsory
adjudication for many years. And to supplement the Permanent Court of International Justice he wants the establishment of an Equity Tribunal.

Mr. Hoover and Mr. Gibson have an opinion not far
removed from his:

"Each nation should agree to refer all disputes to arbitration or to refer them to judicial settlement or to establish cooling-off periods with independent investigation."

No dissenting voice has been lifted concerning compulsory adjudications, arbitration, or both.

(8) On another important point there is also a widespread agreement of opinion: that Article 19 of the Covenant of the League of Nations * should be made a live reality but in a stronger form.

Mr. Hoover and Mr. Gibson suggest:

". . . that the application of any nation for revision of treaty provisions, not sooner than ten years after its conclusion, should be implemented by the appointment of a committee of outstanding statesmen not interested in the dispute to report and negotiate a reasonable settlement."

It may not always be easy or without risks for a weaker nation to demand revision of treaty provisions. And there has been a strong feeling that the treaties themselves should provide for an automatic consideration of revision at regular intervals after the lapse of stated periods of years.

The Atlantic Charter mentions that it is essential that the totalitarian nations should be disarmed. But no more definite program has been worked out. The question of an international army, an international police force, or both, has been discussed. But no definite plans have been made; and they can hardly be made before nations have agreed more fully on the kind of world organization to be set up.

Before mentioning the questions which are controversial or not sufficiently discussed, there is some reason to discuss one particular problem included in the program mentioned under point 5.

* "The Assembly may from time to time advise the reconsideration by Members of the League of treaties which have become inapplicable and the consideration of international conditions whose continuance might endanger the peace of the world."

Popular sentiment has advocated the re-creation of all the individual states of Germany as they existed before Hitler or even as they existed before 1870. This is hardly the voice of wisdom. If the Germans, when they are found mature for full national self-government, decide to establish Bavaria, Württemberg, Saxony, Baden and all the rest of principalities once more, they must be entirely free to do so, but if, as is more likely, they decide to have unity of state, they must be equally free to make that decision. But when the boundaries of Germany shall be established, it must be the pre-Hitlerian.

It is one of the marvels of the Nazi propaganda machine that it has succeeded in creating an historical myth about persecuted Germans and a German unity disturbed by evil enemies. This myth is reflected in the book by Mr. Hoover and Mr. Gibson:

"Any survey of the history of Europe will show that, in its periodic defeats, this race has been dismembered into separate states."

How has it been brought about that educated persons in any country can honestly believe extravagant Nazi distortions of history? Politically speaking there was no Germany before 1870. The attempt of Nazi propagandists to identify modern Germany with the defunct Holy Roman Empire of the Habsburgs cannot stand any factual examination. And the territory that is now called Germany was never dismembered. Nothing is more dangerous to historical truth than to paint the picture of bygone centuries in terms of modern ideas and conceptions unknown and uninvented at the time depicted. The history of Europe before the nineteenth century was not the history of national interests and conflicts, but the history of dynastic interests and conflicts. And the history of what is geographically called Germany to a large extent is the history of the rivalries and wars between the Habsburg and the Hohenzollern families. Prussia, the power-center of modern Germany, is a very new state in Europe and not of Teutonic origin. The Prussians were Slavs, as were all the peoples of present-day Northeastern Germany, Slavs that had lived on the land between the Russian steppes and the Baltic before the Sanskrit-speaking peoples came to India, the Greeks to Greece or the Italian peoples to Italy. And, neither the Prussians, nor the Pomeranians, nor any of the Wend peoples spoke a Germanic language. They spoke their dialects, closely related to the old sister languages of Latvia and Lithuania. Any traveler in Prussia will have noted the Slav names of villages and localities. With iron and blood the Germans tried to conquer, to enslave or exterminate the Slav owners of the country. This fight had been going on for five centuries when Emperor Sigismund (in 1415) gave to his staunch supporter Count Friedrich of Hohenzollern the fief of the northern marks and created the electorate of Brandenburg (after the Wendish fortress Brannibor)—even the name was Slav. The Great Elector of Brandenburg, by in turn betraying his allies, the Poles and the Swedes, acquired the duchy of Prussia, and his son in 1701 bought the consent of the Habsburg Emperor to crown himself "King in Prussia." During the following hundred and sixty-five years Prussia was never dismembered but eventually dismembered all her neighbors. The partitions of Poland in 1772, 1793, and 1795 more than doubled the territory of Prussia.

It is necessary to mention these simple facts here to throw some light on a statement made by Mr. Hoover and Mr. Gibson. They write:

". . . in the subjection of large groups of Germans to Poland and Czechoslovakia was laid a powder train to the new explosion."

What are the facts?

One fact is that for generations the Germans have persecuted and oppressed the Poles in their old Slav country. It was one of the sore spots in Europe years before the last war.

In 1907 the great Norwegian poet and writer Björnson published in a number of European newspapers and magazines an article on the persecution of minorities. He states among other things:

"In Prussian Poland Polish children are forbidden to confess God in their own language. Small children are punished for praying to God, and their parents are punished for the sins of the children. A student at a college was expelled because his young sister in the primary school could not pray in German. The Prussians are spitting after children in the streets because they speak Polish. They are ousting the Poles from their farms; in every way they try to kill their living soul."

Such is the background of what the distinguished writers call "subjecting large groups of Germans to Poland." The peace-treaties after World War I tried to make some restitution for the cruel injustice under which the Poles had been suffering. Of course, a number of Germans living on their ill-acquired lands in Poland could no longer lord it over the Poles; they resented it bitterly and won the sympathy of certain groups of people.

Another fact is that Czechoslovakia never had been part of Germany; that Austria never has been part of Germany. For more than a hundred years Austria (to which Czechoslovakia belonged) was at war with Prussia; the last time was in 1866. And there was a deep resentment against the Prussians among the German-speaking people in Austria which did not prevent the persecution and oppression of millions of Slav-speaking people in the Empire, particularly in Hungary.

Björnson wrote in his article:

"The Magyars in their homeland suppress three million Slovaks. They forbid them to use the tongue of their fathers, their souls. They sneer at their love of historic traditions. They close the museums, they confiscate the funds that should be used to make them familiar with the life of their ancestors. They term them "swine" in the Parliament, they kick them down the stairs; they are spitting after them in their newspapers."

There is a Czechoslovak minister to Washington. His name is Hurban. He started his career in his father's newspaper when his father was sent to jail, administratively, for having printed Björnson's article.

Centuries of national persecution might have tempted the new-born state of Czechoslovakia to retaliate. But the Czechs refrained; there were no complaints from the German-speaking minorities. At the time of Munich the *London Times* wrote: "No state has treated its minorities so well as has Czechoslovakia."

Still we hear this talk of "subjecting large groups of Germans to Czechoslovakia." And it is far more dangerous when men like Mr. Hoover and Mr. Gibson seem to accept the Nazi thesis than when Professor Renner puts it on the map. They state:

"There can be no lasting peace in Europe with a dismembered Germany, any more than there could be a lasting peace in North America if other nations tried to separate the states or to put parts of them under Mexico."

It is difficult not to conclude from the manner of presentation that what they have in mind is that Germany should keep Austria and Czechoslovakia and what the Germans claim of Poland. The parallel, in that case, is wholly misleading.

Fortunately, responsible leaders of nations are not led astray. The American position as concerns Czechoslovakia and Poland is perfectly clear. As to Austria, Secretary Hull stated on July 27, 1942:

"This Government has never taken the position that Austria was legally absorbed into the German Reich."

The Leader of the British Labour Party, Lord Privy Seal C. R. Attlee, in his statement "The Peace We are Striving For," declared:

"It is right to affirm that Austrians, Czechs, Poles and Germans are nations with the right to room to live, but it would be premature to consider exact boundaries until principles have been accepted."

Only after years of normal life can it be made clear whether a majority in Austria really will want to join a new Germany.

Along the German-Polish frontiers, possibly in other Slav countries and Roumania, with small pockets of German-speaking inhabitants the question can arise of offering people an option, letting them decide individually whether they want to be citizens of and live in one country or the other, and then organize the necessary transfers. Such an exchange of populations on a modest scale was effected along the Danish-German frontier in Schleswig.

Perhaps the question of "dismembering" Germany is not so controversial as it may seem. Those who really believe that Germany has any legitimate demand on Austria, parts or the whole of Czechoslovakia and sections of Poland, will be few, even if they may seem powerful.

The program of these eight points will mark a long step forward, but it will in no way be sufficient to win the peace.

Attention has been called in previous chapters to the importance of embodying in an international Bill of Rights the excellent and important principles for the protection of religious liberty and human rights underlined both in the Atlantic Charter and in the Washington Declaration of the United Nations. This can most effectively be done by establishing an International Penal Code and creating in a somewhat different way the International Criminal Court so carefully prepared. In this connection it has also been stressed that the problem of education and of reëducating certain nations is of such vital importance for the stability of any peace that an international educational service will have to be instituted, and that large-scale offenses and crimes against religious freedom and human rights planned in textbooks and engineered in the schools shall fall under the jurisdiction of such a court. It has also been suggested that the present system of international courts of justice should be supplemented and extended.

Indications have been given concerning the future world organization to be set up. An attempt has been made to demonstrate the framework which is needed, and to make clear that only by emphasizing personal responsibility in international life can we hope to obtain the results all nations are claiming for, that only by coördinating what is valuable in the League system with essential points in a system of federation can we establish the elastic machinery that will be needed. It is not so much a system to defend democracy as to re-create democracy; it is not so much intended to replace national governments, traditions and sovereignty as to reorganize them and make them collaborate, fully realizing the interdependency of states and the hard political fact that if we want to win the peace and not lose it again we have to recognize in action that in a modern democratic world every single nation has to be his brother's keeper.

Some of the suggestions made may seem startling, some of them appear utopian; but nations have to start thinking along new lines and to get accustomed to new conceptions of international life. The whole problem is one of will-power and of spiritual energy as against mental lethargy. There are no insurmountable obstacles, but a good many barriers in the minds of conventional individuals to be broken down. The entire world should have realized by now the tragic truth in the words De Valera spoke at the League in the summer of 1936:

[If the Great Powers] "would be prepared to make now, in advance, only a tithe of the sacrifice each of them will have to make should the war be begun, the terrible menace which threatens us today could be warded off."

Not only Europe, but Asia and Africa, the tiniest islands in the Pacific, the Arctic Oceans, have been drenched in blood. Tremendous sacrifices have been demanded from America and Australia. And in the hearts of all the fighting men, all the working men, all the suffering men is this hope for the future:

"I'd like me to know that all over the world
A just flag of freedom was flying unfurled."

The land of our vision, of the four freedoms and of a just and durable peace is no empty dream. It is within our grasp. Whole nations are ready to march, slowly and inexorably, prepared to advance as soon as leaders whom they can trust shall give the order:

"Go forth; for it is there."

THE END

Index